Coherence in Writing

Research and Pedagogical Perspectives

Ulla Connor

Ann M. Johns

editors

Teachers of English to Speakers of Other Languages

Staff Editor: Helen Kornblum
Publications Assistant: Rosanna Landis
Copyright © 1990 by

Teachers of English to Speakers of Other Languages, Inc.
Alexandria, Virginia
Printed in the USA

Library of Congress Catalog No. 88-50781
ISBN 0939791-34-X

Table of Contents

Introduction

The authors of the chapters in this book view coherence from a number of theoretical and research perspectives and discuss applications of these perspectives to teaching. Several of the chapters were first presented at a TESOL '86 colloquium titled Coherence: Theory and Practice. Because this and succeeding colloquia on related topics were well received and coherence is a popular topic in the current literature, we were encouraged by the TESOL Publications Committee (1986) to compile the manuscripts for this volume. The co-editors of this volume shared the work equally. The order of the names is merely alphabetical.

Although coherence is of increasing interest to researchers around the world (e.g., de Beaugrande, 1980; Carrell, 1982; Connor, 1984a; Enkvist, 1985; Kintsch & van Dijk, 1978), practical applications of coherence theories have been slow to appear (perhaps because the concept is not well understood and has been variously interpreted). One problem with the definition of coherence is that there are at least two competing orientations: one that emphasizes the reader's interaction with the text and one that focuses on the text itself (Johns, 1986c).

Some researchers describe "coherent text" as text in which the expectations of the reader are fulfilled. Phelps (1985), for example, described coherence as "the experience of meaningfulness correlated with successful integration during reading, which the reader projects back into the text as a quality of wholeness in its meaning." De Beaugrande and Dressler (1981) posited that coherence is based upon "a continuity of sense among the knowledge activated by the expressions of the text" (p. 84). Brown and Yule (1983) also viewed coherence as related to the reader's interpretation of linguistic messages.

Despite this recent focus on the interaction between reader and text, coherence continues to be discussed as a function of the text itself as well. Researchers in both camps agree that a certain number of surface signals in discourse are necessary for ease of processing. Enkvist (1978, p. 126) wrote:

> If a text is to be well formed, it must have semantic coherence as well as sufficient signals of surface cohesion to enable the reader to capture the coherence. . . . The general rule is that every sentence of a well-formed text must have a cross-reference to at least one other sentence of that text, and there has

to be an overall coherence involving the text as a whole (p. 113).

The purpose of this book is twofold: to present important coherence models and to suggest how insights from coherence theory and research can be introduced to the classroom. The contributors, representing a variety of linguistic and cultural orientations, are involved in English as a second language (ESL), English as a foreign language (EFL), and foreign language teaching and research. The book is organized in four sections: Theoretical Overview, Coherence Models, Studies of Student Writing, and Pedagogical Approaches. The reference list at the end of the book contains entries for all works cited.

In the first section, Nils Enkvist's chapter, "Seven Problems in the Study of Coherence and Interpretability," suggests that coherence is very difficult to study and to teach because it embodies a large number of variables. He identifies seven problems related to the study of interpretability of coherence in discourse: (a) the relation between cohesion and coherence; (b) messages and metamessages; (c) inference in interpretation; (d) relevance of situational context; (e) receptor knowledge and degrees of interpretability; (f) text strategies, text categories, and patterns of exposition and argument; and (g) strategy, structure, and process. Encouraging linguistic research that considers the context—or pragmatics—of discourse, Enkvist calls for a process model of coherence that is sensitive to the seven problems he identifies.

In the next chapter, "Coherence in Spoken and Written Discourse," Liisa Lautamatti discusses two types of discourse coherence, *propositional* and *interactional*. Lautamatti shows how these types are related to the mode and level of style in text. The concept of *frame* is also introduced, and techniques are suggested for applying this concept to studies of coherence in everyday conversations, prose texts, and poetry. Lautamatti also suggests ways in which discourse coherence can be viewed in terms of the discourse topic.

In the second section, specific models of coherence are discussed. First, in "Pragmatic Word Order in English Composition," Kathleen Bardovi-Harlig presents an analysis of discourse that is concerned with the organization of *given* and *new* information in sentences. Interested specifically in the placement of *topic* and *focus*, she argues that English sentence structure in extended discourse is sensitive to the pragmatic relations of the elements and thus influences text coherence. She explains six sentence types that are related to pragmatic considerations and can be directly taught: (a) preposed adverbial, (b) *there* insertion, (c) passive, (d) cleft, (e) topicalization, and (f) lexical choice. Her discussion is followed by classroom-tested exercises for ESL composition.

David Harris examines the role of opening sentences in paragraphs in "The Use of 'Organizing Sentences' in the Structure of Paragraphs in Science Textbooks." Replacing the traditional notion of the topic sentence with a new one, the "organizing sentence," Harris studied the particular functions of the opening sentences in a sample of 100 paragraphs taken from college textbooks in the natural sciences. He found that these opening sentences fell into five functional or organizing sentence types. These types and their frequencies in the data are described, and suggestions for applications to teaching and research are made.

The third chapter in the Coherence Models section, "Inductive, Deductive, Quasi-inductive: Expository Writing in Japanese, Korean, Chinese, and Thai," deals with the common assumption on the part of English-speaking readers that a juxtaposition exists between inductive and deductive texts; therefore, readers automatically classify as inductive a text that does not have a deductive organization. After analyzing composition examples written by speakers of each of the identified languages, Hinds concludes that these texts share what he calls a "delayed introduction of purpose" or quasi-inductive style, which "has the undesirable effect of making the essay appear incoherent to the English-speaking reader but is acceptable to the native speaker." Hinds suggests that the purpose of texts of this type is not to convince but to present issues for reader consideration, a viable and extensively employed purpose among speakers in the languages identified.

In the final chapter in the section on coherence models, "Toward Understanding Coherence: A Response Proposition Taxonomy," Peter McCagg suggests a semantically based model of coherence to account for inferences made by readers as they interpret texts. Specifically, McCagg proposes a "response proposition taxonomy" that provides a model for analyzing idea units in summary protocols of a reading passage. In this taxonomy, a distinction is made between text-based and inferential propositions, the latter being divided into two subcategories: schema based and text induced. McCagg includes numerous sample analyses of texts and accompanying recall protocols by ESL students to illustrate the use of his model.

In the first chapter in the section on studies of student writing, "Types of Coherence Breaks in Swedish Student Writing: Misleading Paragraph Division," Eleanor Wikborg reports the results of a study analyzing coherence breaks caused by inappropriate paragraphing in the discourse of 144 essays written by advanced EFL students representing five academic disciplines. Three criteria that determine when a coherence break will occur emerged from this analysis: (a) when two equally brief paragraphs elaborate on the same topic, (b) when a paragraph break separates a topic sentence from one or two specifying sentences, and (c) when a new paragraph marking topic shift is too short to establish itself as independent. She offers specific suggestions for pedagogical applications.

"Building Hierarchy: Learning the Language of the Science Domain, Ages 10–13" by Suzanne Jacobs is unique to this volume because it focuses on the developmental aspects of coherence among children. Positing that coherence in academic discourse is achieved through the recognition and use of hierarchical structures, Jacobs notes that children at the age of 11 vary in their abilities to construct and support these hierarchies with appropriate vocabulary. She makes an argument for using a bilingual approach that places value on the discourse of their first language (oral language) as well as their second (the language of literacy).

In "Pointers to Superstructure in Student Writing," Lars Sigfred Evensen develops a taxonomy of pointers to rhetorical superstructure and applies it to EFL student writing collected in a large-scale Scandinavian writing project. He makes a distinction between these *pointers* and *connectors* based on the notions of global and local coherence. Among the pointers indentified, he includes five categories: metatextual deixis, internal logical structure, topic markers, temporal points, and connectors used as points. Evensen concludes by discussing the implications of his work to teaching.

In the following chapter, "Nonnative Speaker Graduate Engineering Students and Their Introductions: Global Coherence and Local Management," John Swales distinguishes between global and local coherence of texts. Using his model for the four-step introduction, he examines 20 research papers written for his English for Academic Purposes class. Through this analysis, he provides a convincing argument for the importance of global coherence in research introductions. These papers and his discussion demonstrate that expert readers often tolerate local mismanagement of text if it is coherent at the global level. Teaching implications, especially in English for Specific Purposes classes, are essential to his paper.

In "Coherence as a Cultural Phenomenon: Employing Ethnographic Principles in the Academic Milieu," Ann Johns describes an instructional technique, the "journalog," which was developed to assist linguistically diverse students in assessing audiences in an academic environment. Because an important element of coherence depends on reader response, students are encouraged to analyze the rules of usage in their academic classroom by juxtaposing the characteristics of their own approach to discourse to that of the "experts." Johns reports the success of journalogs in a history class, in terms of increasing student knowledge of the discourse domain and their relation to the target reading audience.

In the final chapter, "Improving Coherence by Using Computer-Assisted Instruction," Constance Cerniglia, Karen Medsker, and Ulla Connor introduce a linguistically based method for students to examine coherence in their own texts. First they describe the theory behind topical structure analysis and then show the steps students can employ for performing this analysis. The second part of the chapter deals with the development and use of a computer-assisted exercise to teach topical structure analysis in writing classes.

We hope that this volume, which contains views of coherence from different theoretical and practical perspectives, will be valuable to students, teachers, and researchers in the fields of ESL reading and writing. We wish to thank the authors for their cooperation. We also thank Diane Larsen-Freeman, chair of TESOL Publications Committee (1986), Mary Niebuhr, chair of the TESOL Publications Committee (1987), Helen Kornblum and Julia McNeil, current and former directors of TESOL publications, and two anonymous reviewers for their constructive suggestions in editing this volume.

Ulla Connor
Ann M. Johns

I. Theoretical Overview

Seven Problems in the Study
of Coherence and Interpretability

Nils Erik Enkvist

Åbo Akademi

Åbo, Finland

Seven Problems in the Study
of Coherence and Interpretability

For this volume I was invited to produce a brief introductory list of some of the problems that bedevil the study of discourse. In complying, I will be deliberately flying high to survey a vast expanse of territory, trying not to mind the thinness of the atmosphere. Another cost of my high flying will be a blurring of details. Fortunately, many of these details have been discussed at length in the referenced works, and several more will appear in the chapters of this volume.

In harnessing the magic number *seven* to lead my title, I am culpable of considerable arbitrariness. Of course, more than seven times seven sections would be needed to exhaust the subject. Further, all seven problems are interrelated and overlap in various ways: In a wider perspective, they are all part of the same problem, that is, an analysis of the features of text, discourse, and communication that give a receptor an intuition of coherence and make the text interpretable. Those who find my grouping and conjunction of arguments inopportune are cordially invited to regroup them. Their substance is more important than their labels.

Problem One: Cohesion and Coherence

For better or for worse, most of the world's linguists have cherished their positivist heritage: Their most successful traditions bid them to describe what is manifestly there, in sound waves or on paper, rather than what is not. They are happier with overt, concretely describable entities than they are with more or less metaphorical verbalizations of elusive shades of meaning and hermeneutic experiences aroused by texts. Even the abstract deep structures of classical generative-transformational grammar were supposed to be ontologically justifiable. Some linguists assumed that they reflected psychological realities; to others they were necessary as halfway houses produced by explicit rules of a well-defined generative game. But no linguist would have advocated their use as mere reifications of some kind of vague, fleeting, protean experience beyond the reach and support of evidence.

Against such a background, there is nothing surprising in the fact that text linguists and discourse analysts also began by maintaining well-established linguistic approaches. They tried to base their analyses of what cements sentences into texts on formally describable, and thus tangible, cohesion markers that could be heard or seen on the surface of discourse and text. Such efforts began by extending the methods of sentence grammar, traditional, structural, or transformational, beyond the single sentence. Those who need chapter and verse may look at early treatments of cohesion such as those in Halliday and Hasan (1976) or (should they happen to be proficient in Finnish) in Enkvist (1975).

Thanks to the snowballing interest in discourse linguistics, it soon appeared that the tracing of overt links with traditional syntactic techniques was not enough (e.g., Enkvist, 1978). One could construe texts that seemed odd, despite an impeccable tight intersentential linkage. For example:

> (1) My car is black. Black English was a controversial subject in the seventies. At seventy most people have retired. To re-tire means "to put new tires on a vehicle." Some vehicles such as hovercraft have no wheels. Wheels go round.

Another type of surrealistically weird text whose intersentential links seem all right at first examination is:

> (2) Susie left the howling ice cube in a bitter bicycle and it melted. It soon tinkled merrily in her martini. Into her drink she then also poured the grand piano she had boiled in a textbook of mathematics the night before. She chewed the martini, read the olive and went to bed. But first she took her clothes off. She then took her clothes off.

In (1), the sentences are all right in isolation, but their links fail to connect. We cannot produce a summary of (1) because the sentences do not add up to a consistent world picture. In (2), there is a similar lack of a consistent scenario or text world not because the sentences fail to connect by overt surface signals, but because they make use of the capacity of natural languages to produce contradictions or images of a counterfactual, impossible world. Compare (1) and (2) with:

> (3) The net bulged with the lightning shot. The referee blew his whistle and signaled. Smith had been offside. The two captains both muttered something. The goalkeeper sighed for relief.

No existing grammar, or other description of English, can explain why (3) makes better sense than (1) or (2), yet it does to those who know about soccer. The lack of connectivity in (1) apparently resists simple syntactic description. To explain what makes texts weird, it is not enough to look at (2) and say ad hoc that *ice cubes* are minus animate whereas *to howl* is plus animate and that ice cubes do not howl, except perhaps metaphorically. Nor is it enough to produce a dictionary of collocations to indicate that in nonmetaphoric use *to chew* must have a solid, chewable object˙ and *to read* must have an object naming something that can be read. Instead, we would need an enormous apparatus explaining what is common and feasible and what is not. Granted, statistics have shown that in certain kinds of text, such as newspaper prose, some collocations recur more often than we used to think. However, there is an enormously long way from such observations to full inventories of potentially reasonable collocations. An attempt at listing all the word sequences that describe plausible scenarios would explode all practical limits. To explain in syntactic algorithms why bitter bicycles, the tinkling of melted ice cubes, the boiling of pianos in textbooks of mathematics, and myriads of other absurdities strike us as freakish twists of reality would be a hopeless task. It is a basic fact about natural languages that they can express an infinite number of new metaphors and new impossibilities. Conceivably, we might invent more impossibilities and absurdities than there are plausible states of affairs in the real world.

The difference between (1) and (2), and (3) will emerge more clearly if we turn from syntax to meaning. Clearly, (3) is a text around which a soccer-wise reader can build a consistent world picture—a scenario or text world—in which the text makes sense. We can summarize (3) as a report on a situation in a soccer game, a goal disallowed by the referee, or an offside goal. (1) and (2) will intractably resist such summarizing. In other words, (3) is interpretable in a way in which (1) and (2) are not. The difference is something we feel at once because we know both the language and the world and because the world as built up by the text does not tally with our experience of the real world. In this sense, our intuition of coherence is a hermeneutic phenomenon. We must understand a text, that is, build up a world picture around it, to say that the text is coherent. Conversely, a text strikes us as incoherent if we cannot build up a plausible scenario around it.

Using a word as fuzzy as *plausible* amounts to sweeping a number of awkward questions under the rug. Plausibility can be approached in two ways. If we relate plausibility to truth-functional semantics, we can say that a text is plausible if we can build a scenario around it, that is, a text world describing a state of affairs in which that text might be true. ("Might be true" rather than "is true" to allow for fiction and fantasy.) If we relate plausibility to pragmatics, we might say that a text is plausible if we can assign it to a system of human interaction conforming to maxims such as those explained by Grice (1975) or Leech (1983) or Sperber and Wilson (1986).

Discussing these matters becomes easier if we give labels to the relevant phenomena. In several quarters it has become customary to distinguish between *cohesion* and *coherence*: Cohesion is the term for overt links on the textual surface such as those in (1) and (2), whereas coherence is the quality that makes a text conform to a consistent world picture and is therefore summarizable and interpretable. Thus (1) and (2) have cohesion but not coherence, and (3) has coherence although it lacks overt, grammatically describable cohesion markers such as repetition or anaphora. The coherence in (3) follows from our being able to surround it with a plausible text world.

There is another problem here. If we define cohesion as a quality resulting from overt, grammatically describable links, we should also specify what we mean by *grammatically describable*. This is complicated by the fact that different grammars are capable of different things: Some succeed in describing more than others. Still, I take it there is no grammar, actual or potential, capable of explaining what gave coherence to (3). We have to know that terms such as *net, referee, blew his whistle, offside, captain, goalkeeper* all belong to one semantic field, and we must also know that the events described could plausibly co-occur in an actual soccer game as they co-occur in the text. It is impossible to imagine that any grammar or syntax could ever contain enough encyclopedic information about the world, not only about soccer but about everything in the universe, to reduce all such instances of coherence to matters of syntax.

Problem Two: Messages and Metamessages

Having defined two fundamental concepts, cohesion and coherence, I turn to another fundamental distinction relevant to all studies of message interpretation. In this section, I join those who claim that every message is interpreted at two levels. A message has referential meaning in explaining a text world, and it has symptomatic meaning in that it carries a metamessage telling us something about the state, condition, and intentions of its producer. Let me start with an example.

At an English professors' conference at Aberdeen, the participants, wives included, were taken to a nearby castle, given a tumbler of malt whiskey each, and then shepherded to the front lawn to enjoy a marching concert by the Police Bagpipe Band. One of the wives mistook Professor A from Germany for Professor B from Finland; she promptly addressed him in Finnish, of which he was completely innocent. When he looked increasingly puzzled, Mrs. X first raised her voice in competition with the bagpipes, and when this did not help, introduced herself, Finnish fashion, by pumping his hand vigorously while telling him (all in her loudest Finnish) where (she thought) they had previously met. When Mrs. X's husband appeared, X, who knew A well, said, "I see you have met my wife." "She is your wife, is she?" said A with an unmistakable tone of commiseration.

This true story was cited to remind us that all messages, whether understood or not, are accompanied by metamessages that also carry meaning. Professor A understood nothing of Mrs. X's frantic Finnish; all the same, he had a very definite idea of Mrs. X's behavior and mental condition. With Tannen (1984), we might label such features accompanying discourse in its situational context collectively as the metamessage of the message. Thus the problem is, how are we to study what metamessages contribute to the total meaning of a message? Discourse is, by definition, text seen in its situational setting, and the metamessage, interpreted as a symptom, is a part. Therefore, students of discourse must by definition concern themselves not only with message but also with metamessages.

Discussion of message and metamessage is meaningful only if we can distinguish between the two. Where does message end and metamessage begin? Such questions are akin to those on relations between linguistics, metalinguistics, and, perhaps even more, paralinguistics. The classical approach has been to say that linguistics includes everything we do to describe a corpus of linguistic data, metalinguistics refers to the study of the language we use to describe language, and paralinguistics refers to the study of features accompanying language but not part of the study of the linguistic system proper. Similarly, I have used the term *metatext* to refer to text about the text, for example, when a lecturer begins a lecture by saying "This morning I shall start by speaking about X, and then go on to say something about Y." Such phrases, which are particularly frequent in long, planned monologues such as lectures, describe the composition of the text but do not contribute to the subject matter of the lecture itself. By analogy, a *metamessage* would be a message about the message often expressed through paralinguistic means such as voice color, loudness, speech rate, etc., as well as through interaction such as interrupting others versus delaying one's responses, politeness patterns in speech and behavior, and so forth. *Paralanguage* has been a term for the ragbag disposing of what linguistic theories and models cannot manage. Therefore, what is linguistics proper and what is paralinguistics depends on the scope of a particular linguistic theory. Generally, linguistics has tended to expand to cover more and more of what used to be paralanguage.

Stress was brought into linguistics by Verner's Law; *intonation* came into English syntax in the 1920s and 1930s, thanks to linguists such as Harold Palmer, Daniel Jones, Lilias Armstrong, and Ida Ward; and, most recently, *hesitation, correction,* and *repair* have begun to be subjects of systematic analysis by various ethnomethologists and students of impromptu speech. In other words, features once dismissed as mere *parole* or performance have often turned out be structural essentials of *langue* or competence as our grasp of the nature of language has widened in scope and gained in depth. Similar shifts are likely to take place in the defining of metamessages in relation to messages.

Still, there remains a large zone beyond messages that is obviously a domain of metamessages. A person's nonlinguistic behavior while speaking, which involves the uncontrollable symptoms of his or her physical and mental states, can have a crucial effect on the receptor. Anger, for example, is a state we often detect (or think we detect) even when the verbal message itself remains polite. In such instances, the clues in paralinguistic features belie the verbal smoothness of the text itself.

What corresponds in writing to such metamessages? Perhaps the choice of submedium (handwriting, typing, use of word processor), the format and quality of the paper, the layout, and other physical traits in the choice of forms of letters and types of background. There are, for instance, people who believe that polite, social notes should be written with a fountain pen, not in pencil or even in ballpoint, on high-quality paper and that a letter of thanks should always go beyond one page (which motivates the use of small stationery!). Shaky handwriting reveals ill health, old age, or extreme nervousness; messy typing reveals a lack of typing skill; and so on.

As Tannen (1984, 1986) argued at length, particular tensions can be introduced into the communication when the partners have different metamessage patterns and conventions. New York Jews, she suggested, are quicker and more aggressive in conversation than people from other parts of the United States. In the eyes of these New Yorkers, communication partners who are slow to respond are considered rude and sluggish. *That's Not What I Meant!* (1986) contains Tannen's discussion of conflicts that arise through misunderstood metamessages.

The very concept of metamessage is amorphous. One might go so far as to suggest that literary criticism, or any kind of criticism of anybody's speech or writing, is really an analysis of metamessages—of what the message itself tells us about its producer. Perhaps we should not worry overly about neat demarcation lines between message and metamessage. We should, however, remember that every message is accompanied by a metamessage of some kind and that the metamessage can be just as important as the message proper, and sometimes even more so.

Problem Three: Inference in Interpretation

Messages are not only interpreted in terms of what they overtly contain. Metamessages are one type of information that the receptor deduces or infers from the message proper; part of the business of discourse interpretation consists of adding information not explicitly and overtly present on the textual surface. This kind of adding of information or *inference* plays a crucial role in communication, although it refuses to yield to assays by traditional linguistic methods. All the same, it has begun receiving its due share of attention in many of the recent studies of text and discourse such as de Beaugrande and Dressler (1981), Brown and Yule (1983), and Levinson (1983). Is the following coherent?

> Life with Stephen, who as you know is nine, is just great.
> For Christmas he got a chainsaw from his godmother. I am
> wondering how much the new floor will cost me.

Presumably, the reader infers the connection between the 9-year-old's chainsaw and the need for a new floor: the reader knows that new floors cost money; and the reader infers that *just great* should be given an ironical reading. In such instances, most people, at least those who know what a chainsaw is and what it does, will have no difficulty filling in the missing link by inference and thus make the text cohere by bridging. Of course, the example also brings with it the inevitable metamessage.

One of the embarrassments in discussing inference is its ubiquity. Much, if not all, of mathematics and a great deal of logic are concerned with inference because they start with certain axioms and postulates and go on to show what inferences can be drawn from them. Scientific and scholarly arguments abound in inferencing. In these areas, inference is subject to conscious rules: Training in mathematics, logic, and scientific argumentation involves a study of processes of inferencing.

In the study of the role of inferencing in natural-language comprehension, including that of authentic impromptu speech, we must proceed in the same way as in the study of natural languages in general. All we know about a natural language is ultimately based on the *sprachgefuhl* of some competent individual: the linguist, selected informants, recordings, and texts reflecting the linguistic competence of their producer. Similarly, there is no a priori way in which we can list all the world's possible or potential inferences. Inferencing depends crucially on the knowledge and relation of the text producer and text interpreter, and on the situation, something we might call *Inferenzgefuhl*. General principles of inferencing can be stated only at a high level of abstraction. To understand the concrete details of inferencing in actual situations, we must start out by eliciting data either from ourselves or from others on how a particular instance of inferencing in a particular text has actually worked between specific communication partners in a specific situation.

Inference is based on human laziness, or, in a prettier phrase, on the avoidance of needless effort in communication between people who share certain assumptions about the world. Inferencing is essentially a transitivity relation between propositions: if p then q, if q then z, therefore (and here comes the inference) if p then z. To people who know the transitivity relation between p, q, and z, the middle proposition, q, is unnecessary and can be skipped in the interests of economy. Note that inferencing requires a shared world picture between text producer and interpreter, a world that supplies the missing inferential link between p and z. If the text producer is to manage inference properly, he or she must adapt the message to the knowledge and text-processing capacity of the receptor: The text producer must estimate what the receptor already knows and how good the receptor is at discourse processing under the relevant circumstances. Recovering such a missing link can also be studied as an instance of problem solving. Recall the example of the boy and the chain saw: The text remains incoherent unless we fill in the missing middle propositions, such as boys like to operate machines; when operating machines they may have little respect for property precious to their elders. The discourse producer and receptor must share such views of the world if the inference is to work.

To manage those aspects of textual coherence that build on inference, we must also include retrievable world knowledge in our model. We know about the world partly because of our knowledge of the situational context surrounding the relevant act of communication (including the personalities involved) and partly because of our experience of matters beyond the immediate situational context. When we start interpreting a piece of discourse, we activate and draw on the relevant parts of our knowledge store to fill in gaps in the actual chain of propositions. To stop us from going on inferencing forever, in wider and wider circles, there is a built-in stopping mechanism: When we judge that gaps have been adequately bridged and that further additions would be irrelevant, we desist from further inferences.

Inference is a blanket label covering a large spectrum of phenomena. Linguists and philosophers have worried about distinctions between *pre-suppositions* and *entailment* and between *conventional* and *conversational implicature* (see, e.g., Kempson, 1975; Wilson, 1975; McCawley,

1981). A presupposition is usually defined as an assumption that survives the so-called negative test: Irrespective of whether I say *Susie knew she had failed* or *Susie didn't know she had failed*, I am presupposing that Susie had failed. An entailment, on the contrary, does not survive negation. If we say *Susie has two sons*, this entails that Susie has one son. If we negate the sentence, *Susie hasn't got two sons*, we cannot conclude that Susie has one son; she may have no children or she may have daughters only. *Conventional implicature* relies on semantic content. *Susie has stopped beating her husband* implies that Susie must have beaten her husband. *Conversational implicatures* imply because of the ways in which we use language: *Susie hasn't stopped beating her husband* usually indicates that Susie still beats her husband. This is a conversational custom that can be retracted: *Susie hasn't stopped beating her husband because she never started beating him.* Note that conversational implicatures differ from strict logic. If we say *Susie has two sons*, we normally mean two sons only, although strict logic admits it as true even if Susie has more than two sons. But there might indeed be other situations where we could say *Susie has two sons* even if she had three or four, for example, if we discuss Susie's taxes in a society where two sons entitle a mother to a special type of tax relief.

Problems of presupposition, entailment, and implicature can be both subtle and complex. They have a way of leading to elaborate explorations of semantics, pragmatics, and the difference between formal logic and the logic underlying message building in natural languages. These differences have occupied many linguists to the point where they have had little time left to look at actual inferencing patterns giving coherence to authentic discourse, including improptu speech, under specific situational and contextual constraints. It is worth repeating that we need more empirical attention given to inferencing in authentic communication, perhaps even at the expense of some of the more arcane philosophical niceties. We need more information about what a hearer or reader with a certain store of previous knowledge really does when faced with a text in a specific situation. An example of a study that attempted a concrete, though introspective, approach is Crothers (1979). Literary criticism also contains a wealth of examples of what critics have inferred out of literary texts both in terms of message and metamessage.

Problem Four: The Relevance of Situational Context

In authentic communication, a text does not carry one single, constant, immutable meaning. On the contrary, a text is a trigger releasing a process of interpretation, which depends on the situation and the interpreter. Together these two form the context in which the message is interpreted.

In a lecture room, the lecturer says to her assistant, "Lights please." Does this mean turn on the lights or turn off the lights? The answer depends on whether the lights were off or on when the *lights please* was uttered. Consider the dialogue:

A: Shall we walk to the theater or take the bus?
B: Walking would take us 40 minutes.

Does B actually prefer walking or going by bus? The interpretation depends entirely on the situation. If A and B have an hour to kill, the weather is pleasant, and both like walking, it could mean that B opts for walking. If A and B are in a hurry, the weather is bad, or A knows that B does not enjoy walking for more than 20 minutes, it could mean that B opts for the bus. Thus the text is certainly interpretable, but in what sense will depend on the situation, the speakers, and their views of each other.

In our glance at inferencing, we already saw something of the importance of situational relevance. In interpreting discourse, we always choose the most probable, least surprising, and therefore the least informative alternative (Joos' Law; cf. Joos, 1972). We must judge what I call *situational relevance* in order to evaluate the different information values of available alternative interpretations.

Situational relevance exists at a number of levels. One level is intratextual: It invokes textual context in deciding which of the possible interpretations is relevant in that particular context. For example:

(4) Susie won the set. Her serves had a nasty spin, and her smashes were really great.
(5) Susie won the set. But then she always has such luck with lotteries, and this time she could really use the china.

The second sentence of (4) takes us into the world of tennis, where *set* has one meaning, and (5) into the world of lotteries and china, where *set* has another meaning. The text itself gives clues as what world we should activate in order to interpret the text.

Problem Five: Receptor Knowledge and Degree of Interpretability

I have argued at some length that messages are not interpreted in a contextual vacuum. A message triggers a process of interpretation, and this process is strongly affected by who interprets the message and under what conditions. In addition to the situational context, the interpreter's previous knowledge plays a crucial role determining what he or she gets out of a message, both in referential and in symptomatic meaning and in message and in metamessage.

Thus what controls interpretation is not only receptors' knowledge of the mechanics of syntax but also the extent of their ability to retrieve relevant information out of their schemata, scripts, and other organized deposits of knowledge . Similarly, text producers are dependent on what they can retrieve from their cognitive store and on their estimates of what the receptors can comprehend, which in turn can be defined in terms of the text producers' knowledge of their receptors. The interpretation of metamessages is also a matter of knowledge. A receptor must have systematically and retrievably organized stores of experience before he or she can identify, group, and analyze those various features that together make up the metamessage.

I am assuming that a text is interpretable to all those who can, under prevailing circumstances, build around that text a text world in which that text seems plausible. Such a definition suggests that interpretability is, to begin with, a threshold concept. Under the circumstances, either a receptor can or cannot build a world around the text. If the receptor can, there are many degrees of interpretability depending on the size and extent of detail of the receptor's text world. Obviously, a doctor will get more out of a medical text and a Chomskyan linguist will get more out of a Chomskyan text than will a layman ignorant of medicine or of Chomskyan linguistics. In real life, we might even have to reckon with transient conditions. In an unpropitious hour, in anger, pain, fatigue, or under the influence of drugs, a person's text-processing abilities may well be temporarily under par.

In literary criticism and in the teaching of composition, scholars abstract from individual variations in interpreting abilities when they test and criticize the text itself: They presume that the text is the dependent variable and the judges, interpreters, are the independent variable. In linguistic proficiency testing, however, linguists often use the same process in reverse: They assume that the text is the constant, independent variable and that the language learners are the dependent variables. Instructors make pupils listen to or read a text and then have them answer a set of questions designed to show their degree of success as interpreters and comprehenders of the text. It is assumed that those who know the language well will understand more of the text than those who do not. But, text comprehension is always affected by the individual's previous knowledge of the receptor and of the situational context. Designers of language tests are well aware of such risks, which is why they try to find texts on relatively neutral subjects, that is, on subjects with which all their testees can be presumed to be roughly equally familiar or at least on subjects whose mastery can be seen as part of the curriculum.

It would be tempting to link an individual's capacity for using his or her knowledge stores for inferencing with his or her likes and dislikes of certain types of literary text. Science fiction, for instance, is a genre whose interpretation involves the building of a plausible text world around a counterfactual text with the help of the science fiction writer. The enjoyment of poetry with a syntax different from that of ordinary expository prose sets considerable demands on the scenario builder. The poem may provide a wealth of seemingly disparate cues leading the reader to a set of scenarios which are difficult to combine and to reconcile with each other. A great deal of effort may be involved in the building of such text worlds around a poem. Perhaps such strenuous scenario building involves too much effort for some, who then reject modern poetry as incomprehensible and distasteful. Others find pleasure in such semantic gymnastics and become poetry lovers, and even poets.

Problem Six: Text Strategies, Text Categories, Patterns of Exposition and Argument

"What is wrong with our students," a wise colleague once said to me, "is not that they don't know enough English but that they cannot think." In this sense, *thinking* equals a capacity for logical argumentation: not only producing sentences and linking them with cohesion devices and making the discourse coherent by anchoring it in a plausible world, but also of marching forth one's propositions in justifiable order. We are born, we live, and we die in time; in language, the time dimension of the human condition is linear. We can say only one thing at a time, and the order of presenting views to the receptor can be crucial.

In fact, a study of compositions by advanced students of English as a foreign language (Lindeberg, 1985b) suggests that the difference between essays impressionistically graded as *good* and *poor* does not lie in the number of cohesive ties between sentences, but rather in the ways propositions link into arguments. Thus essays offering a series of unsupported propositions under certain circumstances lead to an undesirable staccato provoking low grades, and essays that back up their claims with supportive arguments, even at several hierarchic levels, strike examiners as better.

Different types of texts—descriptive, argumentative, operational, narrative—have acquired characteristic *macrostructures*, that is, characteristic patterns in which propositions are linearized and hierarchized to lead the receptor to the appropriate text world. In a narrative text, the main frame of the text tells the reader about actions, usually by a hero, heroine, or a limited group of such heroes and heroines. These actions take place in a temporal frame, which is signaled to the receptor, either by telling the story in chronological order or by somehow marking the departure from such chronologies. Another device narrators must worry about is the relation between event time and narrative: Is the narrator going to telescope what happened in 10 years into a 30-second story or expand what happened in 30 seconds into a 1-hour narrative? Or, is event time identical with narrative time, as often in drama? If a narrative contains descriptions, they are usually subordinated to the main frame of the text and inserted where they best support the story. A text strategy is thus the operational program that produces a text through a sequence of operations all the way from major textual macropatterns to the minute syntactic detail. The strategy is the guiding principle in the process of discourse structuring.

Some kinds of text may have multiple strategies that produce structures resulting from a main-frame strategy and hierarchically subordinate strategies, even at several hierarchic levels (on such structures in argumentative texts, see Tirkkonen-Condit, 1985). For example, a tourist guide usually first advises tourists where they ought to place themselves, and then tells them what they are supposed to see, inserting information about historical and other matters under each sight. In a tourist guide, the hierarchy prototypically runs top-down from place to sight, to information about the sight, and this information might in turn consist of description, narrative, and so forth. The locative main-frame strategy comes to embed levels of other strategies. Correspondingly, an operational text usually first identifies the objects to be operated and then tells the receptor what to do. Cookbooks, for instance, begin by listing ingredients and implements and then give the operating instructions.

This sixth problem was originally defined as a conjunction of the problem of patterning exposition and argument, and the problem of strategy and text category. Many kinds of texts have conventional patterns and hence conventional strategies; in them, optimal coherence results from conforming to the optimal strategy. Weather reports are an instance of such conventionally structured texts. Some other kinds of text on the contrary set unconventionality at a premium: A poem or an advertisement may be effective precisely because it refuses to conform to established macrostructural patterns. Contemplation of the problem of strategy and text category will of course lead us to all the complexities of text typology, genre, argument analysis, and the like. Among the many questions practical language teachers often ask is, what about persuasion? Is persuasion a text type, or is persuasion a specific use to which any text type can be put? A parable, for instance, might be characterized as a narrative put to persuasive use. To explain such use we need a hierarchy integrating discourse functions and text types, and perhaps stylistic variants of text types, into a single descriptive system.

Problem Seven: Strategy, Structure, and Process

The discussion of strategies leads into the seventh and final problem in my inventory; namely, the closely related issues of structure and process.

Strategy is a process term, which has often been used loosely and perhaps metaphorically without attempts at definition. If we regard text as linearizations and groupings by conjunction and embedding of underlying predictions in a text base, a strategy may be defined as the sum of principles governing such textualization of underlying text atoms or predictions (Enkvist, 1987a).

To understand what a strategy is, we must refer to *decision theory*. Whenever people have to choose between alternative actions, they must make a decision. Decisions are usually made either consciously and rationally or unconsciously and ratiomorphically, the latter term referring to a process that follows rational principles but is carried out automatically, without apparent conscious reflection. Whether rational or ratiomorphic, a decision is based on weighing various considerations. For example, when writing a metrical poem in rhyme, a poet often has to choose between a good rhyme and normal canonical word order: If a poet wants to place a good rhyming word at the end of a line, he or she has to jettison the normal subject-verb-object English word order. In such instances, there is a conflict between two strategic parameters, two principles of organizing the text, and one or the other must win because it is judged to be the more important. Strategies arise as outcomes of conspiracies between allied text-organizing principles and of conflicts between irreconcilable ones. Victory crowns the strong.

A processual point of view is required to explain what is meant by text strategies as principles of discourse organization. This raises the classic question of whether language is product, rule, or process (cf. Coseriu, 1985).

My answer, like that of Coseriu, is that language is all three, depending on the beholder's point of view. Linguists know what they might gain and what they might lose by adopting one of these three views to the exclusion of the others. The traditional viewpoints are that language is product, structure, and that its structures might be described with rules. But how can such a structure-and-rule- oriented view be reconciled with the fact that we often communicate successfully with "deviant," structurally ill-formed utterances? Such deviance is not only common in impromptu speech but also in poetry (where its more flagrant forms are stigmatized as poetic license), in advertising, and in puns of the more outrageous kind.

Generative grammarians, it is true, have criticized their predecessors for having merely classified a closed set of already existing sentences. They opted for a processualism in terms of strict and syntax-bound rules by defining language as an open set of sentences satisfying certain predetermined conditions of well-formedness. But they set up such conditions in advance and therefore could not manage the variations caused by the speaker, receptor, and situation. They had to describe the processes of sentence production and comprehension in terms of a fixed and static set of rules embodying the sentence producer's so-called competence. This "competence" did not, however, include the ability to understand and produce varying kinds of discourse under the influence of varying situational factors. Despite their processual stance, then, generativists still failed to reckon with the influence of the speaker-writer, receptor, and their environment on message formation and to explain how communication can succeed even when sentences fail to satisfy certain predetermined well-formedness conditions.

A linguist who wants to capture all the complexities of such influences would have to emphasize the producer's options in terms of strategies, including not only the choice of sentence patterns but also larger macro-patterns of discourse, always observing both the assets and the shortcomings of the human mechanism as it works in a specific context and situation. For instance, phenomena such as the use of hedges, pragmatic particles, hesitation, and repair in impromptu speech should not be dismissable as mere *parole*, performance, or as imperfections of the human condition to a process linguist. On the contrary, they should be seen as essential features of communication, contributing among other things to what we experience as fluency. To the extent that hesitation and correction phenomena have become traditional and codified in a specific natural language, they should also be regarded as part of the linguistic code rather than as mere unstructured aberrations.

There are also corollaries for the teacher. Students should be taught how to hesitate politely and elegantly with an impression of fluency in a foreign language. Hesitation patterns are not necessarily biologically conditioned universals but may consist of elements of culturally determined, acquired patterns of communication. If it were impossible to hesitate, to correct what went wrong, and to repair blemishes in one's discourse, processing language in real time would turn into a hazardous undertaking indeed—hence the uses of linguistic machineries for hesitation and correction and the desirability of paying attention to them.

Conclusion

In terms of seven problems, then, I have tried to outline a number of topical questions in the study of textual coherence. I have tried to emphasize that coherence is a concept with a crucial hermeneutic ingredient: We must understand a piece of discourse if it is to strike us as coherent. And, so far at least, no grammar, dictionary, or study of cohesive links between sentences has succeeded in drawing a line between what is interpretable and what is not. One reason for the relativity of interpretability is the dependence on situational context and the knowledge of the world shared by the producer and the receptor of discourse. If we are to model textual coherence, we must build a process model that is sensitive to situation and context including the world knowledge of the communication partners.

For the study and teaching of languages and of communication, such observations are of direct and concrete relevance. The knowledge that language and culture go together is commonplace, which gains in importance once we consider that cultural knowledge is part of the background of discourse comprehension. Linguists have been able to ignore the necessity of cultural scenarios only because they have so often learned and taught languages whose culture is sufficiently akin to their own for them to transfer familiar patterns into a new language without major trouble. But there are instances, ranging all the way from niceties of literary style to elementary politeness patterns in conversational etiquette, in which such transfer might lead at best to negative responses and at worst to umbrage and communicative disaster.

Such discussions lead to the question of tolerance of aberrant behavior, which also varies from one society and social group to the next. If a nonnative speaker is wrestling clumsily with the syntax and phonology of a language, in some groups he or she is forgiven. But once nonnative speakers show, a certain, even modest, proficiency, native speakers are apt to assume the nonnative speakers know precisely what they are doing and give them black marks even for sins of which they are unaware. Quite a few communicative errors reside not merely in faulty syntax and lexis but also in a neglect of accepted patterns and use of discourse, in shortcomings of coherence and fluency, and in misinterpreted metamessages.

Contrastive pragmatics and advice on how to achieve communicative competence in an unfamiliar social setting or in a foreign style, dialect, or language should also focus on discourse management, including coherence. A message may be interpretable even when its sentences fail to follow preconceived norms of well formedness. The goal is to prepare students for communicative success. To cite the gist of an old paper of mine (Enkvist, 1973), as teachers we should strive to measure success rather than to count errors.

Discussion questions

1. Review Enkvist's seven problems in the study of coherence and interpretability. In your own writing experience, what has caused the greatest problems for you? What would be the problems for ESL students? Could you sequence the problems in difficulty for ESL students?
2. Enkvist mentions different text types having varying text structures (p. 1). Describe them. (Others have called these formal schemata (Carrell, 1983, 1987).) Are text structures important in reading comprehension? Give research evidence as well as your own opinion. Will the knowledge of text structures aid in writing achievement in a second language?
3. Enkvist also mentions the importance of world pictures, scenarios, or text worlds in developing or comprehending coherence (others have called these schemata). How important are these? Compare their importance with the knowledge of text structures.
4. Enkvist concludes by asserting that "our advice on how to achieve communicative competence in an unfamiliar social setting or in a foreign language should also focus on discourse management." What does he mean by discourse management? Do you think that this is feasible at the beginning levels in second language learning? Can you mention a textbook that manages the teaching of discourse management successfully with beginning-level students?

Extension Activities:

1. It is fair to say that Enkvist is concerned primarily about the comprehensibility of texts—examining coherence problems from the reader's and hearer's point of view. However, writers need to be aware of their audiences' reaction to certain pragmatic and linguistic features of texts. Psychologically oriented experts in writing research (e.g., Flower & Hayes, 1981) have examined writing processes of individuals—viewing writing from the writer's point of view. Review Flower and Hayes's cognitive process model of writing in light of Enkvist's proposed pro-

cess model of coherence and interpetability. Comment on the place of Enkvist's seven problems in the Flower and Hayes model.

2. Analyze for their cohesive elements the three passages with varying levels of coherence that Enkvist explains in the first section of the chapter. Use Halliday and Hasan's (1976) categories of cohesive elements (see Connor, 1984a and Johns, 1981, for applying the categories to student writing). Compare levels of cohesion with Enkvist's explained levels of coherence in these passages.

3. Enkvist lists inference as one of the seven problems in the study of coherence: "If the text producer is to manage inference properly, he or she must adapt the message to the knowledge and text-processing capacity of the receptor: The text producer must estimate what the receptor already knows and how good the receptor is at discourse processing under the relevant circumstances." In many disciplines, considering the receptor is done through a formal audience analysis. Using the Huckin and Olson text (1983), discuss how audience is analyzed in business and professional writing.

4. Enkvist discusses the importance of metamessages in oral and written speech. Review what Enkvist says about metamessages of writing and analyze the last piece of mail you received for metamessages in it.

Coherence in Spoken and Written Discourse[1]

Liisa Lautamatti

University of Jyväskylä

Jyväskylä, Finland

[1]From "Coherence in Spoken and Written Discourse" by L. Lautamatti, 1982, *Nordic Journal of Linguistics*, 5, pp. 117–127. Copyright 1982 by *Nordic Journal of Linguistics*. Adapted with permission.

Coherence in Spoken and Written Discourse

In this chapter I discuss two facets of discourse coherence. One is the type of coherence that is created by the organization of information in discourse and by the development of the semantic content. This aspect was defined by van Dijk (1977b, p. 93) as "a semantic property of discourses, based on the interpretation of each individual sentence relative to the interpretation of other sentences." As van Dijk showed (1977b), it is possible to follow the development of the semantic content in discourse in terms of its discourse topic, which in turn consists of several subtopics, and also to discover some of the principles that regulate the introduction of new information into the discourse. The type of coherence van Dijk referred to is based on the function of consecutive sentences as information units. On the sentence level, this coherence is reflected as textual cohesion. The cohesive items can be shown to indicate the type of ordering of information that discourse coherence normally requires, for example, from general to more specific concepts, from wholes to parts, and so forth. Similarly, the given-new contract underlying the development of the discourse topic shows in the use of definite versus indefinite noun phrases, pronominalization, and so forth. This type of coherence, which is based on the organization of the propositional content of the discourse, will here be called *propositional coherence*.

However, we often come across instances of verbal interaction in which propositional coherence is either lacking or difficult to establish, and in which, consequently, textual cohesion may be absent. Thus, in contrast to Halliday and Hasan's (1976) definition of cohesion as a necessary but not sufficient condition for a text, Widdowson (1978) pointed out that there are types of discourse that, though they show no overt cohesion, are still coherent since they are based on a meaningful chain of communicative acts. He gave the following example, which will also serve our purposes:

A: That's the telephone.
B: I'm in the bath.
A: O.K.

Just as the symptomatic surface cohesion is lacking here, so is the type of propositional coherence that was previously described. It may be concluded that there exists another side to coherence independent of propositional coherence, which is created by the existence of a sequence of utterances and their illocutionary values, which form a communicative whole. These utterances are perhaps easiest to follow when they form pairs such as greetings, requests and responses, and so forth (see Coulthard, 1977).

It seems natural to assume that any verbal interaction must be based on such sequences of communicative acts, however loose. In the absence of an established term, I will refer to this type of coherence as *interactional coherence*.

Coherence and Type of Discourse

The two views of discourse coherence relate to the type of discourse to be analyzed. Propositional coherence seems to be more prominent in written language, while interactional coherence in its most clear-cut forms can be found in spoken discourse. Because the relation of the type of the mode of discourse is quite complex, I examine those features of the speech event that seem to relate to a particular type of coherence and discuss their relative importance for the two modes.

Some of the essential features of a speech event that relate to the type of discourse coherence produced are examined here in the form of a *cline*. It is then possible to work out the approximate positions on the cline of different types of discourse.

Factors of speech event resulting in interactional coherence	Factors of speech event resulting in propositional coherence

cline

◄─────────────►

- participants share the immediate pragmatic context of communication
- participants have possibility of immediate feedback
- participants may rely on shared knowledge

- little time for advance planning

- corrections, additions, etc., become part of the discourse

- no immediate pragmatic context shared

- no possibility of immediate feedback
- little shared knowledge may be assumed (apart from a general encyclopaedic kind)
- plenty of chance for advance planning
- corrections, additions, etc., can be removed from the discourse

Typically, one end of the cline is represented by speech events such as
family conversations, conversations between friends, or casual encounters
between people who know each other fairly well. At the other end there
are discourse types such as novels or other kinds of extensive texts. These
differences can be illustrated by the following two segments of discourse.
The first is a segment of family conversation with the kind of incoherence
features that make the transcript incomprehensible in places. (This segment, "A Davies Family Breakfast," is an extract familiar to those who
have attended courses in applied linguistics at the University of Edinburgh.)

Anne: Meggie's had a very good sleep has she . . . she was
       fast asleep oh no she wasn't asleep . . .
Alan: come on Meggie do you want porridge
Megan: yes please
Anne: and since we were asleep (and???) with Hester
Hester: yes
Anne: but you weren't
Hester: I know
Anne: were you still reading them
Sara: they were both wideawake when I was when I went
       up . . .
Hester: I was . . . up watching television at 10 o'clock
       (Mum)
Anne: Mm . . . you weren't
Hester: yes I was
       (cough)
Anne: for instance you were very naughty to come down
       again . . . (?) you just get worn out

The utterances are often syntactically elliptical and include different kinds
of fillers. There are sudden topic shifts that also break up the cohesive
pattern (e.g., when the conversation moves from sleeping to reading).
Further, the interlocutors are regulated partly by the need to react to
each other's turns and partly by their own need to communicate something. And finally, there are utterances that are impossible to interpret
outside the original context of conversation, and that may also disturb the
cohesive pattern.

A narrative extract from Innes (1972) shows a different kind of coherence:

He'd better take a look at his map by matchlight. It seemed
inconceivable that the road should be totally devoid of human

> dwellings for more than three or four miles at the most. But
> he'd have a look. He ought to have checked on the point at
> the start. He took the map from his pocket, and felt for his
> matches. He hadn't any.

Cohesive patterns are more obvious here and form a tighter network than in conversation. Propositional coherence is created by successive references such as those realized by the personal pronoun *he*, or by cohesive lexical sequences such as *map—road—miles*, or *take a look— matchlight—have a look—matches*. There are no abrupt topic shifts or utterances that can only be interpreted in terms of the pragmatic context. On the other hand, the sequences could be moved to another place without disturbing the development of the topic. Such sentences are *But he'd have a look* and *He ought to have checked on the point at the start*.

Interestingly, the ends of the cline correspond with Joos's (1967) intimate and formal levels of style. Although I started with a distinction between spoken and written language, the list of features corresponds with this distinction of formality of styles rather than with the distinction of the two modes. It is, after all, possible to find examples of spoken language that represent the formal end of the scale (e.g., formal speeches) or examples of written language from the end of the scale representing intimate style (e.g., notes exchanged by pupils in class). Formality of style also seems to go hand-in-hand with the type of coherence present in discourse. Thus, at the formal end of the cline, propositional coherence is characteristically dominant, while at the intimate end, interactional coherence is more prominent. To conclude, the type of discourse is more obviously related to the formality of the speech event than it is to the mode of language use.

Such complex modes of discourse as texts written to be spoken and heard (speeches, declarations, etc.) or texts spoken to written and read (dictations) fall on the more formal end of the scale. The reason for this seems to be the amount of advance planning present in both types of speech event.

To summarize the relation between the type of speech event and the type of discourse coherence, interactional coherence is typically more prevalent than propositional coherence in discourse in which the participants or producers of the discourse share the immediate pragmatic context of communication, little advance planning is done, and immediate feedback is possible. In this kind of discourse, we characteristically find references that can only be understood in that context and by the participants themselves. Typically, both or all participants take part in the production of discourse. The more interactional the discourse is in character, that is, the more the participants are regulated by each other's successive communicative acts, the more dominant interactional coherence becomes.

If, on the other hand, one of the participants is dominant and takes up more time of the discourse than the other(s), his or her share in the discourse probably shows more propositional coherence in the handling of the topic than those of the other participant(s). To create propositional coherence, the participant requires a fair amount of time during which he or she is not interrupted. This may offer one explanation to the apparent incoherence of speech of people in subordinate positions who have had little opportunity to practice confidently the production of coherent stretches of longer discourse.

On the other hand, propositional coherence is typically prevalent in discourse in which the producer and the receiver do not share the immediate pragmatic context of communication, that is, the universe of discourse had to be made explicit and self-sufficient, and immediate feedback is lacking and therefore requires some advance planning. As described here, the two extremes are represented by casual conversations on the one hand and scientific texts or novels on the other.

Coherence and Frame

One way to explain propositional coherence in discourse is to consider it as a way of developing the discourse topic by the aid of *cognitive frames*. This term, adopted by van Dijk (1977), is used to refer to subsystems of knowledge about different phenomena. We can think of frames as a method by which the human mind stores information relating to different objects, events, etc., in a hierarchical, and thus maximally economical, way. For example, what the reader knows about the *cat*, the "cat frame," gives coherence to a sequence of textual references such as *cat—mouse* or *cat—milk* on the other hand, the reader will probably have to adapt his or her knowledge to fit a new universe of discourse or to work out a new way of combining two familiar frames if the successive references take the form of *cat* and *angel*.

Propositional coherence can be considered a means of linking different parts of a single frame by proceeding most commonly from top to bottom in the structure of hierarchically ordered information, that is, from more general to more particular concepts (van Dijk's "normal ordering" [1976b p. 104]). Second, the discourse referents may combine (or force the reader to combine) separate frames and thus create a specific condition in which the combination of frames is valid. A case in point here is an example given by van Dijk (1972) to illustrate sequences that, he claimed, cannot possibly form a continuous discourse:

> We shall have guests for lunch. Calderon is a great Spanish writer.

In discussing this example, Widdowson (1979) showed a way of linking the utterances by creating an adequate context for them. In other words, coherence is created by juxtaposing two separate frames, one of a special kind of lunch and the other of a list of great writers. For those familiar with both frames—the people supposedly organizing these special lunches—the combination of the two frames presents no difficulty.

The previous example illustrates a typical way of using frames in everyday conversation that explains its apparent lack of propositional coherence. If a common frame or a number of common (shared) frames can be assumed, then the references evoking the frame(s) and the ways of combining the frames may be implicit. It is the lack of knowledge of these frames as a whole or of their essential parts rather than of the specific referents that makes the comprehension of such conversations difficult for an outsider.

Longer pieces of written discourse, on the other hand, typically explain the frames being used and make more explicit the way in which they are linked. Modern lyrical poetry forms an interesting type of literary text if we consider the way in which it uses frames to create a segment of discourse. Its way of referring to the frames used resembles conversational language in its implicitness. Modern lyrical poetry evokes a frame with a single reference and may move on to a completely different one with no explicit linking device. Because the abrupt linking of frames in poetry is not based on the same kind of interaction and shared pragmatic context as in everyday conversations, poetry can be viewed as deviating discourse (cf. Widdowson, 1978). In poetry, flashing out frames for the reader to work out and combining them in unexpected ways create a new, unique whole through which the single references are then reinterpreted.

Coherence and Discourse Topic

In this section, I attempt to analyze the relation of the two types of discourse coherence, in particular their significance to the discourse topic. However little overt propositional coherence casual conversations may have, they usually seem to have some kind of a topic. Intuitively, one might say that the topic of the following conversation is "who is going to answer the phone."

A: That's the telephone.
B: I'm in the bath.
A: O.K.

If this is considered the topic, then, obviously, the interaction itself is felt to be part of the topic. Similar types of topics would be quarrels, disputes, makings of agreements, and so forth. In each, the manner of interaction is as important for the discourse topic as the actual propositional content of discourse. If the conversation lacks the topic altogether, for example, if the interaction consists merely of greetings or introductions, these interaction types might, in intuitive analysis, be considered the topic of discourse.

Thus, in discourse in which there is little apparent propositional coherence, the propositional content and its treatment in the interaction are intertwined, and the treatment of the discourse topic becomes part of the topic itself. Expressed opinions, agreements, questions, and answers form the organizing framework for the actual content. Because the participants share not only the immediate pragmatic context but also a considerable amount of background information, the development of the discourse topic may consist of numerous references that can only be understood by the participants themselves and information that in other circumstances would be offered as new may be marked as if given. This makes it difficult for anybody outside the speech event to analyze the propositional coherence or to follow the development of the discourse topic. For the participants themselves, of course, it is the use of frames, however implicit, that creates an adequate amount of propositional coherence. One way to establish the existence and nature of this implicit propositional coherence might be to find ways of retrieving the links underlying the discourse referents by, e.g., going through the conversations with both or all of the participants.

However, propositional coherence increases with longer stretches of discourse produced by one of the participants. The fact that the speaker is not interrupted makes it both possible and necessary for him or her to create a different type of coherence, that is, an organization of information in terms of successive subtopics. The treatment of the given and new information may still remain in the form characteristic of the intimate style, that is, relying on presupposed or implicit shared knowledge, but the overall development of the discourse (sub)topics becomes easier to follow.

Relation of the Two Types of Coherence

In cases typified by casual conversations, propositional coherence intertwines with interactional coherence and may even be overtly more or less lacking. Is this also the case with interactional coherence at the end of the cline typical of formal written discourse? Will it be more difficult to detect as propositional coherence increases? Again, I begin by considering cohesion as an underlying propositional coherence and find that there are cases where the pattern of lexical cohesion and, to some extent, pronominal cohesion of a written text may break down completely. English for Special Purposes (ESP) teachers are probably familiar with situations in which the student who is able to follow the argument in a foreign language about a topic relating to his or her own field of study fails to comprehend an illustrative example or analogy considerately provided by the producer of the text (usually a native speaker). This occurs because the example—an attempt to make the matter at hand more concrete or to bring it closer to everyday experience—entails ideas, terms, and expressions that are outside the learner's restricted knowledge of the foreign language.

I have a personal recollection of this kind of incident. A foreign lecturer at a Finnish university, who was giving a talk on American drama to an audience which included first-year students, had worked out an introduction to his talk that was meant to be sufficiently concrete for everyone to follow. It contained a simile in which the development of American drama was compared to making vegetable soup. Although it was concrete, this comparison, with its unexpected list of unfamiliar names of vegetables, had a completely opposite effect on some of the listeners.

In such cases, there is no propositional coherence between the example and the argument proper, which would be reflected as actual lexical cohesion. The discourse is coherent because it consists of a sequence of communicative acts such as illustration and its explication or presentation of illustrative material and a general statement. In the last resort, then, we have to explain some sequences on the basis of interactional coherence alone.

Studies of scientific texts have in fact shown that interactional coherence may be as essential in written discourse as propositional coherence. Interestingly, the existence of interactional coherence was first established in texts representing scientific disciplines that have strict, almost formulaic requirements for the organization and presentation of information. Although the interactional coherence of descriptive and narrative texts may be difficult to analyze because the communicative acts following each other offer few or no structural cues and because their functional value usually exists only in relation to each other, scientific and many other types of informative texts necessitate a sequence of definite acts, such as the presentation of facts, hypotheses, conditions, solutions, conclusions, and so forth. Furthermore, the presentation of these acts has to be carefully ordered. It is not surprising that the presence of interactional coherence in written discourse has been easier to establish in texts based on a formulaic succession of a number of distinctly different communicative acts than in texts with a sequence of descriptive statements (e.g., narrative or descriptive texts). Furthermore, the presence of organizing phrases (e.g., *for example, we may assume, certainly, in addition,* etc.) in scientific texts makes it easier to establish the nature of successive acts.

This is not to say, of course, that narrative or descriptive texts do not have interactional coherence. However, the sequence of statements may be less tight or less strictly determined, even to the extent of being interchangeable (cf. Gutwinski, 1976). Their succession may be less rule governed than in scientific texts, and we need to know more about the nature of these rules.

Final Remarks

In discourse of the type in which both propositional coherence and interactional coherence are manifest, their relation presents an interesting problem. The same principles of normal ordering seem to exist in both types. Thus, the normal order of propositional development would be that of whole-to-part; the order of statements in scientific texts has been observed to follow the principle of general-to-particular. The order of information presentation is reflected as textual cohesion in the relation of lexical items such as synonyms and hyponyms, general terms and specific concepts, whole-to-part descriptive terms, and so forth. The succession of communicative acts, on the other hand, may offer few structural clues, and the functional values of the successive sentences can only be established by careful examination of their mutual relations. These observations of the close relation between the two types of coherence suggest that underlying principles of discourse development relating to the function of discourse as interaction in which the participants typically strive for increased shared knowledge may exist. Both of the two facets of discourse coherence examined in this chapter may be seen as an overt expression of this *strife.*

Discussion Questions

1. Review Lautamatti's definitions of *propositional* and *interactional coherence.* List explicit linguistic ways in which these are achieved in texts, both oral and written.
2. Lautamatti states that *scientific texts* have both interactional and propositional coherence. Discuss general characteristics of scientific texts. Using the cline on page 32, discuss which factors of speech events

resulting in interactional coherence apply to most scientific texts. Discuss which factors of speech events result in propositional coherence in most scientific texts.

3. *Cognitive frame* is used by Lautamatti as a technique for developing discourse. Discuss the ways in which *frames* help text coherence. Are frames related to the content of texts, the structures of texts, or both? Compare frames with schemata (see e.g., Tannen's work (1979) in the first language research framework and Carrell's (1983) work in the second language context).

4. Explain the role of cognitive frame in the two samples used in extension activities 1 and 2. Compare the explicitness of frames in the samples.

Extension Activities

1. Select a short article in a newspaper (300–500 words) to examine propositional and interactive coherence in a text. Analyze its coherence features using Lautamatti's definitions and techniques. Note sections of noncoherence and speculate on reasons for them.

2. Examine coherence features in conversation. Tape record a conversation between people who know each other well. (A breakfast table conversation between family members or people who live together will work well.) Select 5 minutes from the conversation and transcribe it (use Lautamatti's manner of transcribing, which is not overly concerned about phonetic transcription and sophisticated transcription models). Analyze both coherence patterns. Compare patterns of coherence with the patterns in the newspaper article. Explain the differences, if any.

3. Create a lesson to teach the concept of frame for either a spoken language or writing class for ESL learners. Specify the level of the class.

II. Coherence Models

Pragmatic Word Order in English Composition

Kathleen Bardovi-Harlig

Indiana University

Pragmatic Word Order in English Composition

A well-formed coherent text is more than a series of grammatical sentences lined up one after another like so many blocks in a row. The sentences in well-formed writing are more like pieces in a jigsaw puzzle; the sentences interlock, each sentence building on the preceding ones while at the same time advancing discourse. Coherent writing, then, is dependent on how sentences fit together to form a whole. The fit is achieved by the way the elements are arranged within the sentences and the choice among the sentence patterns themselves. This chapter outlines the theory behind this view of discourse, describes the pragmatic functions of certain constructions in writing, and concludes with pedagogical suggestions appropriate for a variety of levels of composition instruction.

Overview of Discourse Pragmatics

The analysis presented in this chapter is concerned with the organization of elements within the sentence (see Firbas, 1979, 1982). Although I will primarily address the notion of coherence in written discourse, this is only one area of interest for theories of discourse. For other aspects, approaches, and a historical perspective, see Enkvist (1987a).

Topic and Focus

A sentence has three levels: the syntactic, the semantic, and the pragmatic. A sentence in isolation, such as an example in a textbook or a linguistics article, has syntax and meaning, but no context. A sentence that occurs in context has a pragmatic value as well. Just as subject and predicate are units of syntax, there are also units of pragmatics. To see how the pragmatic units are organized in an English sentence, let us consider the exchange in (1) and the diagram of B's response in (2), based on a diagram in Dahl (1974).

(1) A: What does John drive?
    B: John drives a Chevy.

(2) topic _____ comment

    John _____ drives   a Chevy

    background   focus

A sentence may be said to be composed of a *topic* and a *comment*. The topic is what the rest of the sentence is about. In (1) the question is about *John*, thus establishing the topic of B's response. The comment is what the speaker says about the topic; in this case, the speaker brings up a topic, *John*, and says that he drives a Chevy. A sentence can also be divided into *background* and *focus*. The background includes whatever is known from the preceding context. Because speaker A knows that John drives something, *John drives* forms the background of B's response in (1). What speaker A does not know, however, is what type of vehicle John drives. *A Chevy* is the new information and thus is the focus of the sentence. The difference between comment and focus is that the comment contains known, as well as new, information; the focus consists of entirely new information.

In my experience, students (and teachers) can most easily identify the relatively smaller units of topic and focus. Therefore, this discussion will concentrate on these two poles of pragmatic organization.[1]

Topic.   As an entity of discourse, topic has been described in various ways. First, and perhaps most intuitively appealing, is the description of topic as what the rest of the sentence is about. Reinhart (1981) called this "pragmatic aboutness." Because topic is an aspect of connected discourse, we find that topics are generally *discourse anaphoric* (Kuno, 1972). Just as a pronoun may be anaphoric, that is, it refers back to a full noun phrase introduced earlier (e.g., *John . . . The*), a topic is anaphoric, that is, it refers back to a section of discourse previously introduced. Thus, an entity is frequently introduced into the text prior to becoming a topic. For this reason, topics are often described as given or known information. It is not surprising to find that pronouns often serve as topics.[2] *Mary*, introduced in the first sentence of (3), becomes the topic *she* in the second sentence. Similarly, in sentences (5) and (6) the topics, labeled with the subscripts i and j, have been previously introduced in (4).

(3) I saw Mary yesterday. She's feeling much better.

(4) When Augustus came out on the porch *the blue pigs*$_i$ were eating *a rattlesnake*$_j$—not a very big one.

(5) *It*$_i$ had probably just been crawling around looking for shade when it ran into the pigs.

(6) *They*$_j$ were having a fine tug-of-war with it, and *its*$_i$ rattling days were over. (McMurtry, 1985, p. 13)

In addition to being explicitly introduced in the discourse, entities that will later become topics may also be implicitly introduced, as pointed out in Price (1981). She identified discourse elements that are implicitly introduced as belonging to the class of inferable entities. Given a particular setting, the existence of an entity may be predicted. *The clerk*, in (7), is an example. Here *the clerk* is context-dependent in the sense that the hearer/reader can infer its identity through plausible reasoning: Given the setting of a post office, the presence of postal clerks can be predicted.

(7) I went to the post office yesterday and *the stupid clerk* couldn't find a stamp. (Prince, 1981, p. 237)

Similarly, once *children* is introduced in example (8), the entities *the boy* and *the girl* can be identified as given information.

(8) Near a large forest lived a poor woodcutter with his wife and two children. *The boy*'s name was Hansel and *the girl*'s name was Gretel. (Thompson, 1974, p. 55)

Given entities are generally definite due to the fact that they have been introduced in the preceding text. Demonstratives and pronouns, whether used as determiners or noun phrases, and proper names and definite articles are all definite and may all function to mark the topic as can be seen in example (9).

(9) My mother has written a new book.

It's
The book's
Her book's   about gardening.
This one's
Rosy Roses is

Focus. At the opposite end of the pragmatic scale from topic is focus. In contrast to topic, which relates a sentence to the preceding discourse, the focus advances communication by contributing unknown information. The focus is generally independent of the context, that is, it cannot be identified from preceding discourse because it is new information. If new information were obscured in a sentence, for example, if noise interfered with a telephone message or a coffee spill on written work obscured the focus, the information would be lost. In other words, the focus cannot be predicted as topics can be. If the topic were lost in (9), it could be reconstructed, but *sports car*, the new information in (10), could not be reconstructed.

(10) Do you know what Jack's done?
He's bought himself a sports car!

If the focus is a noun, it is generally indefinite, as in *a sports car* (example [10]).[3]

Every sentence must have a focus (Firbas, 1982). There are complete sentences that are focus-only, but topic-only utterances are generally incomplete. Focus-only sentences occur most frequently in spoken English. They include direct and indirect commands such as *Fire!* and *Run!* as well as short answers to information questions. Although native English speakers may answer a question with a complete sentence, they often do not do so; therefore, the question in (1) may have alternate answers as suggested in (11).

> (11) What does John drive?
> John drives a Chevy.
> A Chevy.

The second answer, *a Chevy*, is a sentence composed of a focus only. Focus-only sentences may occur more frequently in spoken than in written English.

In summary, pragmatic units have several characteristics. In general, the topic is the foundation of the sentence. The topic is what the rest of the sentence is about; it is context dependent; it may be given information; and, it is probably definite. The focus is the part of the sentence that advances communication most. It is context independent; it is new information; and it may be indefinite.

Basic Distribution of Pragmatic Elements

Firbas (1979, 1982) indicates that the basic order of information-bearing elements (i.e., content words) moves from given information at the beginning of the sentence to new information at the end of the sentence or from topic to focus. There are exceptions, however, as seen by comparing (12) and (13).

> (12) What did John eat?
> John ate the beans.
> (13) Who ate the beans?
> John ate them.

Beans, the focus of (12), occurs at the end of the sentence while *John*, the focus of (13), occurs at the beginning of the sentence. Because the location of the pragmatic elements within the sentence may vary, Firbas stipulated that topic and focus must be defined independently of word order; in other words, topic and focus are not word order concepts.[4] Thus, Firbas's term *basic distribution* indicates a preferred, but not inviolable, arrangement of the pragmatic elements of a sentence. Similarly, whereas topic frequently coincides with subject in English, the subject is not necessarily the topic as example (13) shows. Explicit topic markers such as *as for (topic)*, *speaking of (topic)*, *getting back to (topic)* may also be used to front a topic that would otherwise occur late in the sentence as in *Speaking of Mary, John sure has been seeing a lot of her lately.*

Notice that regardless of word order, a focus is consistently marked by primary sentence stress in spoken English (Bardovi-Harlig, 1986). Stress is occasionally represented in written English as in (14).

(14) The puzzle suddenly became clear. *Marsha* had stolen the documents.

Because marking the focus by indicating stress is not a technique that is available to writers on a regular basis, written text frequently is restricted to the basic distribution of topic and focus.

Grammatical word order. Because it maintains a constant word order governed by syntax and not pragmatics, English has been called a *fixed* or *rigid word order* language. More recently, this syntactic control in English has been called *grammatical word order* to distinguish it from languages that exhibit *pragmatic word order* (Rutherford, 1983). In contrast to languages such as Czech and Chinese that fill the first position of the sentence with a topic, which is pragmatically determined, English fills the first position with a subject, which is syntactically determined.

Although English does not arrange information-bearing elements within sentences principally according to pragmatics, the language is not insensitive to pragmatic influence. Thus, though English writers must employ the grammatically based subject-verb-object word order, they can make pragmatic decisions within this constraint. The choice of one sentence pattern over another allows the speaker/writer to create a sentence that reflects the basic distribution of pragmatic elements in a conventional, that is grammaticalized, manner. Notice that in (15) and (16) the writer can make a choice between active and the passive to organize the known and unknown elements in a grammaticalized, that is, syntactically conventional, way.

(15) Do you know what happened to John?
?A car hit him.

(16) Do you know what happened to John?
He was hit by a car.

In view of the fact that the choice of one sentence over another encodes a pragmatic relation, we come to understand why equally grammatical sentences are not interchangeable in either spoken or written discourse as examples (15) and (16) illustrate.

Pragmatic Word Order in English

This section of the chapter describes the function of five sentence types that are useful to writers and also briefly explores the way in which the choice of lexical items allows the basic distribution of pragmatic elements to be met. The (a) examples in (17)–(22) list the constructions that will be considered in this section; the (b) examples are the corresponding unmarked forms.

(17) Preposed Adverbials
 a. Just inside the door are the display cases and shelves for breads and pastries.
 b. The display cases and shelves for breads and pastries are just inside the door.
(18) *There*-insertion
 a. There is a mouse in the cupboard.
 b. A mouse is in the cupboard.
(19) Passives
 a. The victim was shot by an unknown assailant.
 b. An unknown assailant shot the victim.
(20) Clefts
 a. What John lost was his keys.
 b. John lost his keys.
(21) Topicalizations
 a. Speaking of Mary, she's been absent a lot lately.
 b. Mary has been absent a lot lately.
(22) Lexical Choice
 a. John bought a book from Bill for five dollars.
 b. Bill sold a book to John for five dollars.

The (a) and (b) pairs are what Prince (1981) called *cognitively synonymous*, that is, (a) is true only if (b) is true. The pairs have the same information content. In spite of this equivalence, these sentences are not interchangeable in most contexts. Because they organize the information in different ways, the members of these pairs have different pragmatic shapes, therefore fitting into the discourse puzzle at different places.

Preposed adverbials. In general, preposed adverbials allow known information to occur early in the sentence and new information to follow it. Consider the discourse fragment in (23)–(25) in which the preposed adverbial in (24), *because of his misadventures*, summarizes known information. Following the text in (23), the preposed adverbial is preferred to the sentence in (25). The question mark indicates lack of pragmatic fit, not lack of grammaticality.

(23) Everything went wrong for Jack this morning. His alarm clock didn't ring, he burned his breakfast, his car wouldn't start, and he missed the bus.

(24) Because of his misadventures, he was late to work.

(25) ?He was late to work because of his misadventures.

One subset of sentences with preposed adverbials consists of sentences with preposed prepositional phrases. These sentences typically serve to introduce new information or set a scene. Given this function, it is not surprising to find this sentence pattern at the beginning of a text. The preposed adverbial is best known in, but certainly not limited to, the fairy tale as in example (26).

(26) Once upon a time, in a far, far away land, lived a king. Now, this king had two daughters.

Descriptions typically feature preposed prepositional phrases as well.

(27) By the window is a black bronze rhinoceros, a James L. Clark piece for which Edith demonstrated her dislike by impaling telephone messages onto the tiny "tick" birds in the rhino's back and hanging her summer hat from its horns. (Johnson, 1986, p. 101)

In the case of preposed prepositional phrases, subject–verb inversion may also occur, thus permitting complete compliance with the basic distribution of pragmatic elements. Preposed adverbials allow the new information, that which will become the topic in the following sentence, to occur near the end of the sentence. In the first sentence in (26) *a king* is the focus; *a black bronzed rhinoceros* is the initial focus of (27). In both cases, the focus becomes the topic in the following clause. Notice also the shift from indefinite focus to definite topic.

There-insertion. Functionally related to the preposed adverbials are *there*-insertion sentences. Sentences with existential *there* also typically introduce the existence of an element. Although their introductory function frequently places sentences with existential *there* at the beginning of a text as in (28) and (29), they are by no means restricted to that environment. Any introduction may employ this construction. Example

(29a) begins an advertisement for New Brunswick, Canada; examples
(29b) and (c) begin successive paragraphs in the advertisement's text.

(28) There was once a fisherman who went fishing everyday.
(Thompson, 1974, p. 14)

(29) a. There's a place you can go where you can enjoy all the
buried treasures and secret hideaways of a maritime
holiday.
b. There's a grand luxe resort where the flag is lowered
each evening to the skirl of the pipes. . . .
c. And there's more. (Johnson, 1986, p. 77)

Given their similar discourse function of introducing a new discourse
entity, it is not surprising to find both preposed prepositional phrases and
there-insertion in the same sentence. Examples (30)–(32) exhibit both the
constructions. This combination is found in a full range of writing, from
fiction to expository prose.

(30) Long ago, in ancient times, there was a king who. . . .

(31) In most people there coexists, along with a powerful procedural representation of the grammar of their native
language, a weaker declarative representation of it. The
two. . . . (Hofstadter, 1980, p. 363)

(32) In between the declarative and procedural extremes,
there are all possible shades. (Hofstadter, 1980, p. 363)

Unlike the preposed adverbial construction that allows the somewhat
unusual subject–verb inversion, the preposed adverbial/*there*-insertion
combination maintains the typical English SV order by supplying the
grammatical dummy *there* to fill the subject position.

Passive. The choice of a passive over an active sentence (or vice
versa) may also allow the information-bearing elements to follow the basic
distribution of pragmatic elements. Passive sentences typically allow the
topic to occur at the beginning of the sentence. If the agent *by*-phrase is
present, the passive construction also allows the focus to occur toward
the end of the sentence. Compare the choice of (34), which originally
occurred in the text, to (34').

(33) Some reflection on the frequency of J's words is in order
here.

(34) Each of her innovations [new words] was accompanied by
a high frequency peak at some period, often at the outset.[5]

(34′) ?A high frequency peak at some period, often at the outset, accompanied each of her innovations.

Because no agent is expressed in (36), the primary function of the passives is to allow the fronting of the topic. Compare the original text in (36) with an active alternative (36′). (35) provides a background for both of these examples.

(35) The Gardners reared an infant chimpanzee named Washoe in the company of human signers. Her upbringing was similar to that of a human child, except that she slept in a trailer in the backyard of the Gardners' home.

(36) She was given constant attention and her human companions continuously communicated with her and with each other. She was coaxed to produce signs and given food and social rewards for doing so. . . . (de Villiers & de Villiers, 1978)

(36′) The Gardners gave her constant attention and her human companions continuously communicated with her and with each other. They coaxed her to produce signs and gave her food and social rewards for doing so.

The choice of the passive in (36) over the active clauses in (36′) illustrates the relation between topic and syntactic pattern. The topics in (36) and (36′) are different. In (36) the topic is Washoe, represented in the pronominalized form *she* in both sentences. The comment describes how she was treated. In (36′), on the other hand, the topic is the Gardners. The comment describes how they treated Washoe.

WH-Clefts. The WH-cleft construction explicitly divides the given information in the sentence from the new information.[6] The WH-clause that functions as the subject contains the topic, whereas the predicate contains the focus. The familiar saying *What this country needs is a good 5-cent cigar*, for example, is most appropriately used in a discussion concerning the needs of the country. The topic *this country needs something* is expressed in the WH-clause. Similarly, the response in (37) reiterates given information in the WH-clause. Imagine that one neighbor has disturbed another in the middle of the night and the exchange in (37) ensues.

(37) What do you want at this hour?
What I want is for you to turn down your stereo!

As Prince (1978) pointed out, there can be situational as well as linguistic contexts for WH-clefts. Students who make appointments to see their instructors would generally like to discuss something in particular. Thus it would be appropriate to begin by saying (38).

> (38) Well, what I wanted to talk to you about was. . . . (Prince, 1978, p. 889)

Similarly, an instructor beginning a class might say something like (39).

> (39) What we're going to look at today (this term) is. . . . (Prince, 1978, p. 889)

The speaker can begin a lecture with this cleft because we expect a lecturer to have an agenda. Naturally, WH-clefts occur in connected discourse as well.

> (40) Nikki Caine, 19, doesn't want to be a movie star. What she hopes to do is be a star on the horse-show circuit. (Prince, 1978, p. 887)

Prince observed that materials inside the subject WH-clause represent material that the cooperative speaker can assume appropriately to be in the hearer's consciousness at the time of hearing the utterance. This characterization includes both linguistic and nonlinguistic contexts.

Topicalizations.   Not frequently found in English writing are unmarked (or bare) topicalizations in which the topic is simply fronted as in (41) because this type of topicalization requires a special stress and intonation contour.

> (41)   A: I wonder where I can get fleas for my biology experiment.
>   B: Fleas my dog has. (Dooley, 1982)

Writers do, however, employ topicalizations in which the topic is explicitly labeled by a phrase such as *as for*. Explicit topic markers include such phrases as *speaking of, as for, concerning, about, regarding, as far as "X" is concerned, which we're on the subject of "X", turning to, now (for), returning to, getting back to,* (Bardovi-Harlig, 1983), and probably many others. Although they seem to have individual functions such as reiterating the topic of *speaking of* does or of indicating a change of topic as *as for* does, explicit topic markers share the function of signaling the topic.[7] Explicit topic markers occur in both spoken discourse as in (42) reported by Svartvik and Quirk (1980, pp. 327–28) and in written discourse as in (43) and (44). In (44), the use of explicit topic markers not only labels the topic but also fronts a topic that would otherwise occur late in the sentence.

(42) Conversation describes grandmothers and continues. And he will remember Granny with fond affection right the way through, *Now Granny*, yes, I can remember her. She was five foot four. . . .

(43) Our blinds were half drawn and Holmes lay curled upon the sofa, reading and re-reading a letter which he had received by morning post. *For myself*, my term of service in India had trained me to stand heat better than cold, and a thermometer at 90 was no hardship. (Doyle, 1917, p. 63)

(44) *In regard to the basic distribution of CD*, it is Czech that comes closest to *its* implementation. (Firbas, 1979, p. 51)

Lexical choice.   Although not a choice between syntactic patterns per se, the choice between certain lexical items, usually predicates, allows a choice between different argument patterns. This, in turn, allows the speaker/writer to organize the information-bearing elements according to their pragmatic value. The verbs *buy, sell, pay*, and *cost*, for example, describe a commercial event (Fillmore, 1977); the difference between them lies in how they arrange the information. The verb *buy* takes the buyer as the subject and the item purchased as the direct object; the seller and the price are encoded in prepositional phrases. *Sell*, on the other hand, takes the seller as the subject and the item purchased as the direct object; the buyer and the price are encoded in prepositional phrases.

(45) John bought a book (from Bill) (for ten dollars).

(46) Bill sold a book (to John) (for ten dollars).

Verbs pairs such as *buy* and *sell* are known as converse predicates. Other converse predicates include *lend/borrow, give/receive, charge/pay*, and *precede/follow*. Similar pairs include phrasal verbs such as *rent from/rent to* and *benefit/benefit from* (Quirk, Greenbaum, Leech, & Svartvik, 1972) as well as prepositional predicates (that is, *be* plus a preposition or verb plus preposition such as *stand behind/stand in front of*). Reciprocal verbs (Quirk et al., 1972) such as *marry, (be) married to, (be) opposite, (be) similar to, (be) far from, (be) different from* also arrange sentence elements by pragmatic value. Thus, in a conversation about John, (47) is appropriate while (48) is not; on the other hand, (48) is appropriate in a conversation about Jane while (47) is not.

(47) John has been married to Jane for fourteen years.
(48) Jane has been married to John for fourteen years.

Summary

I have tried to show in the preceding survey of syntactic structures and their discourse functions that English sentence structure is in fact sensitive to pragmatic organization. Because English word order is determined by grammatical principles (although allowing for some freedom in, the case of reciprocal verbs where the arguments can appear either as subject or object according to their discourse function), pragmatic sensitivity is manifested by the selection of particular syntactic patterns. These patterns allow the distribution of elements from given to new in a conventional or highly grammaticalized manner.

Application

Returning to the original analogy, if a composition is a puzzle then it is not sufficient to give students only the puzzle pieces (the syntactic constructions); they must also develop a sense of the pragmatic value of these constructions. There are a variety of ways in which one can introduce and develop the concepts of topic and focus in composition classes. This section offers sample lessons concerning pragmatic organization.

The lesson types outlined in this section can be adapted to illustrate the pragmatic function of any syntactic pattern and may also be used at a variety of competency levels. The level may be adjusted by selecting texts for the students of appropriate sophistication in subject matter, vocabulary, and syntactic structures targeted. Similarly, the lessons may draw on the learners' developing implicit knowledge of pragmatic fit or may cultivate explicit knowledge as well if appropriate to the level of the students, their academic preparation, and the instructional goals. A lesson drawing on implicit knowledge alone might ask the student to choose a pragmatically appropriate sentence from a set of synonymous sentences or to identify sentences in a text that do not fit pragmatically and to write alternative sentences that do fit. A lesson that incorporates explicit knowledge as well might then ask the students to discuss the arrangement of given and new information within a sentence or paragraph, to identify topicalization types, or to trace topic progression within a text. The sample lessons suggested here are arranged in increasing order by the amount of production required on the part of the student.

Topic-Focus Dominoes

Topic-focus dominoes visually exploit the composition-as-puzzle metaphor. This activity allows learners to build a text and possibly to rearrange it as they progress. Working alone or in pairs, students match sentences to the previous sentences. Because moving dominoes is less permanent than writing, students may feel freer to experiment with possible combinations.

Like traditional dominoes, discourse dominoes have two halves. On each half is one sentence, a member of a cognitively synonymous pair, that is, both halves contain the same information, but have different pragmatic organization as shown in Figure 1.

> The big red
> car hit John.
>
> John was hit by
> the big red car

Figure 1. Topic-focus dominoes contain synonymous pairs of sentences.

A completed set of dominoes is schematically represented in Figure 2 (the topic and focus are represented by letters).

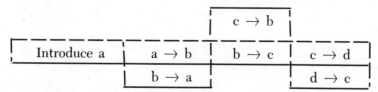

Figure 2. Completed "domino text" is read across the aligned row from "introduce a" to "c → d."

Many texts can be easily converted into dominoes with synonymous sentences. This exercise may employ any of the syntactic constructions previously discussed and is appropriate for any level. I have used the text shown here with low-intermediate students (students who are in their second 200 hours of intensive English training in a multiskill program). The following text adapted from Kenan (1979) provides practice with *there*-insertion sentences, passives, and lexical choice. (Students do not see the text before they construct their own.)

> There are millions of left-handed people in the world. A number of them got together in 1975 and formed an organization called Lefthanders International. This organization fights dis-

crimination and educates the public. Prejudice has led people to believe that left-handers are "strange." Left-handers are not strange but may actually be more creative and more athletic than right-handers.

The corresponding dominoes each have two sentences, one from the original text and one not from the original text, arranged arbitrarily on either the top or the bottom:

(1)a. There are millions of left-handed people in the world.
  b. Millions of left-handed people live in the world.
(2)a. A number of them got together in 1975 and formed an organization called Lefthanders International.
  b. An organization called Lefthanders International was formed in 1975 by a number of them.
(3)a. Fighting discrimination and educating the public are the goals of this group.
  b. This organization fights discrimination and educates the public.
(4)a. People believe that left-handed people are strange because of prejudice.
  b. Prejudice has led people to believe that left-handed people are "strange."
(5)a. Left-handers are not strange but may actually be more creative and more athletic than right-handers.
  b. Right-handers may be less creative and less athletic than left-handers.

After the students have constructed a text, they may enjoy comparing their composition with the original.

Identification of Pragmatic Mismatches

An activity that can be done at any level is to identify sentences that do not fit well into the text. This sample lesson may be used by beginners and highlights the difference in pragmatic fit between active and passive sentences. In the following text, the pragmatic mismatches are identified by the crosshatch (#), which does not appear in the students' version.

Last Saturday Bill and Jane helped their parents clean out the garage. The garage was such a mess that there was no room for the car!

Bill and Jane collected their bicycles, balls and skateboards and returned them to their places. (#)Next, the leaves were swept out. They also bundled up the old newspapers for recycling and put them in the trunk of the car. Their mother orga-

nized and cleaned the garden tools while (#)the electric tools
were put away by their dad.
    Finally, the garage was finished. Bill and Jane could find
their toys and their parents could find their tools. Best of all,
there was even room for the car!

After the students identify the pragmatic mismatches they may rewrite
the sentences for a better fit. Possible revisions of the ill-fitting sentences
might include, *Next, they swept the leaves out* and . . . *while their dad
put away his electric tools.*

Alternatives in Context

In this type of exercise, students are presented with a text in which
one or more sentences are missing. They then choose from two or more
grammatical alternatives a pragmatically appropriate sentence to fill the
blank. This exercise differs from discourse dominoes in that both preceding and following text is given, whereas with dominoes the students build
the text piece by piece.
    The subject matter of this passage suggests its use with more advanced,
academically oriented students. The pragmatics of preposed prepositional
phrases and lexical choice (*determines* vs. *depends on*) are highlighted in
this lesson. The following is adapted from Hall (1969).

(1) Scientists have a basic need for a classification system.
_____(2)_____. (3) The hypothesis behind the proxemic classification system is this: It is the nature of animals, including
man, to exhibit behavior which we call territoriality. (4) In so
doing, they use the senses to distinguish between one space or
distance and the other._____(5)_____.

(2)a. Behind every classification system lies a theory or hypothesis about the nature of the data and their basic
patterns of organization.
   b. A theory or hypothesis about the nature of the data and
their basic patterns of organization lies behind every
classification system.
(5)a. The transaction, the relationship of the interacting individuals, how they feel about each other and what they
are doing determines the specific distance chosen.
   b. The specific distance chosen depends on the transaction,
the relationship of the interacting individuals, how they
feel about each other and what they are doing.

Construction in Context

A natural follow-up to selecting alternative sentences given a context is to have the students construct their own sentences in context. The content of the missing sentence may be provided or not depending on the subject matter and how obvious the information in the missing sentence is.

Guided Production

Production may be guided at two levels, the sentence level and the discourse level. In other ways similar to the traditional guided composition, guided production that aims to increase pragmatic awareness provides students with directions for pragmatic organization.

At the sentence level.   A very basic lesson on sentence-level pragmatic arrangement employs converse predicates. Students are given a set of facts and a prompt and are asked to construct pragmatically appropriate sentences. For example, the following fact set coupled with the prompt *write a sentence about Bill* should yield something like *Bill bought a motorcycle* (because the directions specify *Bill* as the topic); the directions *write a sentence about the motorcycle* should yield *The motorcycle (it) cost $3,000.*

The item: Motorcycle	The buyer: Bill Bradford
The price: $3,000.00	The seller: Mr. Royal, owner
	of Royal Motors

These single-sentence directions could also be sequences to form a text.

At the discourse level.   Unlike sentence-level guided composition that focuses on the arrangement of elements within the sentence, discourse-level guided composition emphasizes the pragmatic function of syntactic constructions through instructions such as *introduce, reiterate,* and *reintroduce.* As in the preceding lesson, students are given a set of facts, this time about the library users, as follows:

Two kinds of library users:
a. quiet, studious, serious
b. noisy, social, not serious

The fact are again accompanied by directions. Because students construct their own texts, a range of constructions may be employed and students will, of course, have different compositions. A *there*-insertion sentence is a likely candidate for the introduction (direction 1), while explicit topic markers may introduce a topic (direction 3). Notice that an approximate length is specified in instruction (2) to ensure that the amount of text between (1) and (3) is sufficient to warrant the use of an explicit topic marker later.

1. Introduce two kinds of library users.
2. Describe one type of user. Give details. Include an example of someone you know of this type (at least 4–5 sentences).
3. Reintroduce the second type of library user and describe that type.

The following is an example of a text excerpted from an essay produced by an intermediate ESL student, which was written after visiting the library, that combines a description of the university library and a classification of its users. (Portions not relevant to the following student's development of the discourse have been omitted.)

> While I was walking in the library I saw two kinds of users: serious users and not so serious—social users.
> The serious students are the most number in the library. They always seem busy. They spend their time on reading and writing. . . . Also, the serious students study on weekends.
> The other kinds of students are social students. They seem the opposite of the first kind of students. Also you can recognize the social students when you see them in the library because. . . .

When the writer first mentions the two types of library users (*I saw two kinds of users*), it is new information and occurs at the end of the sentence. Once introduced, the entities *serious users* and *social users* are both eligible to become topics. *The serious students* is the topic of the following sentence (as well as the topic of the paragraph). The development and description of the first type of library user separates any subsequent mention of the second type of user, the social user, from its original introduction. The distance between introduction and second mention requires reintroduction of the entity, which the writer accomplishes nicely in the sentence *The other kind of students are social students.* The writer places *social students* at the end of the sentence and the active topic *kind of students* at the beginning.

Compare this text with the text in (8), repeated here for convenience.

(8) Near a large forest lived a poor woodcutter with his wife
and two children. *The boy's* name was Hansel and *the girl's*
name was Gretel. (Thompson, 1974, p. 55)

In (8), *two children* introduces *the boy* and *the girl*. These entities can
serve as topics of their respective clauses without reintroduction because
no other material intervenes. Such is the case with *serious users*.

Composition. The best practice in assembling the pragmatic puzzle
is, naturally, writing a composition. The exercises and activities that I
have suggested aid learners in becoming aware of pragmatic organization
in English, but cannot replace actual text construction. They are intended
to complement, but not necessarily precede, student composition.

In fact, student-generated texts can easily be integrated into lessons
on topic-focus organization. Anonymous student compositions may serve
as the text for pragmatic mismatches, topic-focus dominoes, alternatives
in context, or construction in context exercises. (I believe that whenever
student work is used, good topic-focus development should also be identified. In this way, an exercise in identifying and repairing pragmatic
mismatches expands to allow students to note pragmatic matches as well.)

In the revision stage of the composing process students may also identify topic development in their own compositions. As authors, the students have the advantage of being able to compare their intended topic
(I wanted to talk about Bill and say that he bought a motorcycle) with
the expressed topic (*Bill* [topic] *bought a motorcycle from Mr. Royal*
compared to *Mr. Royal* [topic] *sold a motorcycle to Bill*). Connor and
Farmer (in press) have found the identification of topic-focus organization
by student writers in their own work to be part of a promising revision
strategy.

Conclusion

Current theories of discourse have much to offer classroom teachers.
As I have shown, studies of the pragmatic organization of the sentence
and of how sentences fit together in text can be translated into easily
adoptable practice. As teachers become familiar with current work in
discourse, they will undoubtedly identify and develop additional means
for utilizing this valuable tool.

Author's Notes

A preliminary version of this paper was presented at Midwest TESOL
in Ann Arbor, Michigan, November 7, 1986.

I would like to thank Richard Bier, Jeff Harlig, and the editors of this volume for their helpful comments on earlier versions of this paper. Special thanks are due to Cheryl Engber and Ann Burke of the Center for English Language Training at Indiana University and to their students who tested the guided composition exercises.

Notes

[1]Topic and focus correspond to the Prague School concepts of *theme* and *rheme*. In the work of Firbas (1961, 1979, 1982) *transition* replaces Dahl's (1974) comment and background as shown in example (i).

    i. John drives a Chevy
       theme—transition—rheme

Topic and *focus* are used here because they are familiar, nontechnical meanings that can be exploited for classroom use without the introduction of additional vocabulary.

[2]These concepts are similar but not completely interchangeable. For more detailed discussion of discourse anaphora, see Kuno (1972); for context dependent, see Firbas (1979); and for given and new, see Prince (1981).

[3]According to Firbas (1961), it is very likely in English that the focus will be a noun (or nominal). This may account for the preferences of so-called empty verbs such as *do* and *make* with nouns in native and nonnative students' compositions as in (i), over content verbs as in (ii).

    (i) John made a complaint.

    (ii) John complained.

[4]This is not the case in another functional approach that I will not examine in detail here. Halliday (1967) and Quirk et al. (1972) defined the theme (=topic) of a sentence on the basis of word order. Quirk et al. explained:

"The expected or unmarked 'theme' of a main clause is the

(1) subject in a statement: *he* bought a new house.

(2) operator in a Y/N Q: *Did* he buy a new house?

(3) WH-element in a WH Q: *Which* house did he buy?

(4) main verb in a command: *Buy* a new house."

(1972, p. 945)

Following this analysis we would be forced to conclude that John is the topic in the responses in both (12) and (13). This is undesirable because the concept of topic loses all pragmatic unity. That is to say, the sentence-initial occurrences of *John* have different pragmatic functions. In (12) (*John ate the beans*, in response to *What did John eat?*), *John* is a topic in that it is given and predictable information. However, in (13) (*John ate the beans,* in response to *Who ate the beans?*), *John* is new and context-independent, making it the focus of the utterance. A word-order definition of topic as the subject of a statement fails to capture the different pragmatic functions that a subject may have.

[5]This example comes from a source that I can no longer identify.

[6]WH-clefts, also known as pseudo-clefts, contrast with *it*-clefts (or clefts) such as *It is John who stole the cookies.* See Prince (1978) for a discussion of the differences between the two cleft constructions.

[7]See Keenan and Schieffelin (1976, p. 381) for discussion of the discourse function of *as for* and *concerning.*

[8]Connor and Farmer's (in press) study suggests that explicit knowledge of topic-focus organization may prove to be very useful at the revision stage of writing. They taught ESL students in intermediate- and advanced-level writing courses to do topical structure analysis so that the students could trace and modify topic progression as part of their revisions.

Discussion Questions

1. Bardovi-Harlig speaks of semantic, syntactic, and pragmatic levels of a sentence. Most of our classroom composition teaching focuses on the syntactic level; however, Bardovi-Harlig explains how we might teach pragmatic elements. How would you introduce these elements to the classroom?

2. What features of pragmatics, other than those mentioned in this chapter, should be considered by teachers and students in writing classes?

3. Compare the techniques for topic development and maintenance suggested in this chapter with Lautamatti's, as discussed in the Cerniglia, Medsker, and Connor chapter in this volume. For what purpose would each of these models be used in the classroom?

4. Look at the examples of the five sentence types that are useful for writers discussed under the heading *Pragmatic Word Order in English.* At what proficiency level(s) are these items generally taught, if at all? Considering their value to coherence, should textbook writers introduce these sentence types at earlier proficiency levels?

5. Bardovi-Harlig notes that *stress* is important to listener identification of topic in spoken language. What can writers do to assist readers in identifying topic in written discourse?

Extension Activities

1. Bardovi-Harlig speaks of coherent writing as "a question of how sentences fit together to form a whole." What have you learned so far about the various features in English sentences that contribute to a coherent,

whole text? Select a short coherent passage and identify all of these features within the sentences.

2. Early in the chapter, Bardovi-Harlig explains four concepts, *topic*, *comment*, *background*, and *focus*. Working with a small group, analyze a short coherent passage, identifying the parts of the sentences pertaining to *topic* and those that can be classified as *comment*. Then analyze the same sentences for *background* and *focus*. What are the differences between *topic* and *background* and *comment* and *focus*? Given your experience with these concepts, which would you teach to students?

3. Analyze what you consider an incoherent paper written by a less than proficient student for *topic* and *comment* categories. Do you find analysis of this paper difficult? Why or why not?

4. Attempt to teach one or two of the sentence types suggested by Bardovi-Harlig to a group of students for purposes of improving coherence in their writing. Which is easiest and which most difficult to teach? Which do the students find as most valuable to their understanding of coherent prose? Which might you avoid teaching, at least until the students are at advanced levels?

The Use of "Organizing Sentences" in the Structure of Paragraphs in Science Textbooks

David P. Harris

Georgetown University

The Use of "Organizing Sentences" in the Structure of Paragraphs in Science Textbooks

For over a score of years, a variety of rhetorical and discourse studies have challenged the traditional view of the English expository paragraph as a self-contained, logical unit usually beginning with a topic sentence. Thus in the mid-1960s, Rodgers (1965, 1966) traced the conventional definition of the paragraph to the purely theoretical formulations of the 19th-century Scottish logician Alexander Bain and showed how later rhetoricians perpetuated, refined, and elaborated on the Bainian model without bothering to test their theories through the empirical analysis of actual paragraphs. This seems to have been left to recent investigators such as Braddock (1974), who, through the study of a sample of paragraphs from essays appearing in periodicals, found that a relatively small percentage of paragraphs began with topic sentences and a very sizeable proportion had no single topic sentence at all. As Stern (1976) observed, paragraphing practices, far from being governed by immutable logic, reflect a considerable variety of forces, including individual writers' personalities and even publishers' notions of the kinds of format that will attract their readerships. Further, there is considerable support today for the view that the basic unit of expository writing is not the physical paragraph (one or more sentences set off by indentation) but the *conceptual paragraph* (Lackstrom, Selinker, & Trimble, 1973) or the *paragraph bloc* (Irmscher, 1979). Such a unit of discourse may be conterminous with a physical paragraph but will often comprise two or more physical paragraphs and may begin or end within the body of a physical paragraph. If this analysis is valid, it would surely help to explain Braddock's findings regarding the paucity of paragraph-opening topic sentences.

Yet writers of expository prose clearly have their reasons—strategies—for beginning physical paragraphs where and how they do, and when native speakers are given nonparagraphed chunks of prose to segment, they will show a large measure of agreement as to places where new paragraphs might begin, although no two subjects may propose precisely the same overall pattern of segmentation.[1]

The present study began as an attempt to see what particular functions the opening sentences of physical paragraphs serve in college textbooks in the natural sciences. Science textbooks were selected because of the investigator's suspicion that scientific writing might tend to adhere to conventionalized organizational patterns. Because of the problem of defining topic sentence, as well as the evidence that paragraph-opening topic sentences, however defined, do not seem to be the norm, it was decided instead simply to see what *organizing functions* are served by the opening sentences of paragraphs in science texts. That is, what specific roles do opening sentences play in setting the direction of a writer's discoursal progress? No assumptions were made as to whether these openers would or would not be attempts to encapsulate the main idea of a paragraph.

The initial efforts at analyzing the opening sentences in a corpus proved sufficiently productive that it was decided to add a second objective to the study: to determine whether there were common tendencies in the use of additional organizing sentences within the paragraphs. That is, once writers have indicated the general direction of their argument in the opening sentence, are they likely to change direction within the paragraph, and if so, where and how?

Method

For sampling purposes, it was decided to focus on writing in four of the natural sciences: biology, chemistry, geology, and physics. Five representative textbooks in each of these areas were chosen from the shelves of a university library, the criteria being that (a) the books were appropriate for first-year university students rather than being highly technical works designed for other specialists, which possibly would be written in quite a different style; (b) the authors were American, and the books were published in the United States (to avoid the problem of possible British–American stylistic differences); and (c) the books were relatively recent, having been published within 25 years of the time the sample was collected.

Five paragraphs were taken from each of the 20 textbooks, two at the beginning of sections and three from the interior of sections. This was done because of the possibility that section-opening and section-internal paragraphs might be organized differently. Because the central concern of the study was with organizational patterns, only paragraphs at least three sentences long were included in the sample. (The mean paragraph length for the 100 paragraphs was subsequently found to be 5.91 sentences.) Finally, paragraphs consisting entirely of arrays of data were not used in the sample.

As should be clear from the foregoing, no claims can be made that the selection of paragraphs was random in the statistical sense, for the above-mentioned criteria of position and length had to be met. The investigator did, however, make every effort to avoid a careful reading of the paragraphs as he selected them so as not to favor those paragraphs he found easy to read, perhaps because of particular organizational patterns. We shall say, therefore, that the selection was made on a relatively arbitrary, rather than strictly random, basis. A list of the 20 textbooks, organized by discipline, is found in the Appendix.[2]

Findings

Analysis of the Opening Sentences

Analysis of the 100 opening sentences in the corpus disclosed that these sentences fell into five functional or organizing sentence (OS) types, of which two were by far the most frequent.[3] Following are brief descriptions of the five OS types, each followed by two or three examples giving both the OS and a small portion of the subsequent material in the paragraph. The percentage of OSs conforming to each pattern is indicated in parentheses.

Type I. Type I (30%) announces or identifies the topic. In a few cases this is done by posing a question or setting up a hypothetical situation. Little or no new information is provided by Type I OSs other than, in some instances, the introduction of a new term. The experienced reader will assume that new information will be provided in succeeding sentences.

> In order to understand more fully how food is processed for conversion to energy, we shall turn our attention to higher organisms, and primarily to man. Like many invertebrates, man possesses the means to grind his food—namely teeth. . . . (Biology, 6)
>
> How can the sequence of amino acids of a peptide be determined? Basically the procedure involved the following steps. . . . (Chemistry, 41)
>
> Suppose we have a very large flat horizontal plane. At the center of this plane, in a position we shall take to be the origin of an inertial polar coordinate system (see Sec. 6.1), there sits a single observer. . . . (Physics, 93)

Type II. Type II (42%) states a scientific fact, describes a natural phenomenon, or offers a brief definition of an object or process. The tense is usually the "universal present." The experienced reader will assume that the remainder of the paragraph will provide details.[4]

> Single-celled organisms live in environments in which food is abundant and usually continuously available to be taken into the cell. Thus, they are faced only with the problems of effecting the necessary chemical changes to convert food into energy. . . . (Biology, 8)
>
> The ability to hear is the ability to detect mechanical vibrations which we call sound. Under most circumstances, these vibrations reach us through the air. . . . (Biology, 12)
>
> Baja California and the Imperial Valley and Coast Ranges of California are part of the circum-Pacific belt of earthquake activity and display the greatest seismicity in North America. Movements on the San Andreas fault, or on its several branches and related subparallel faults, can generally be defined as the cause of the shocks. . . . (Geology, 51)

Type III. Type III (8%) indicates the number of parts or categories into which something is divided or states that there are important similarities or differences between two things. The experienced reader will assume that the following sentences will describe these categories, similarities, or differences.

> Isotopes are classified into two groups, *radioactive isotopes* and *stable isotopes.* Radioactive isotopes are those whose nuclei undergo disintegration or "decay." (Biology, 20)
>
> There are several differences to be noted between the chemical and the biological reactions. In the chemical reaction molecular hydrogen, H_2, is produced, whereas in the biological reaction the H atoms become associated with the enzyme. . . . (Chemistry, 45)

Type IV. Type IV (13%) identifies an important natural event or scientific investigation or finding in the past. The experienced reader will assume that the following sentences will provide more details or recount the steps in the process.

> Charleston, South Carolina, was the site of another bad earthquake in 1886. A few minor vibrations preceded the major shock, which lasted for 70 sec. . . . (Geology, 55)
>
> That food is translocated out of the leaf during the night was first demonstrated late in the last century by the German

botanist Julius Sachs. He found that the dry weight of leaves diminishes during the night. . . . (Biology, 13)

Type V. Type V (7%) points out a false assumption, the lack of clear evidence or understanding of a phenomenon. Experienced readers will assume that the following sentences will set things straight or provide needed information.

It is sometimes thought that this experiment proves that chlorophyll is necessary for photosynthesis. It really does not prove this because starch may be formed in any cell of the plant. . . . (Biology, 15)

Turbidity currents are elusive. Ordinarily the best evidence of their existence that can be offered is that a turbid mass of water disappears under the head of a lake and that, after a reasonable interval, what is assumed to be the same turbid mass boils up at the outlet. . . . (Geology, 62)

The data in Table 1 summarize the distribution of paragraph-opening OSs by type and field. The five OS types occurred in fairly similar proportions in the 40 paragraphs that opened sections in the textbooks and in the 60 paragraphs that occurred later in textbook sections. The proportional difference did not reach the 10% level for any of the OS types.

Table 1. Distribution of Opening Sentences by Field and Type (percent)

Field	Sentence Type				
	I	II	III	IV	V
Biology	32	44	8	8	8
Chemistry	20	40	24	8	8
Geology	16	48	0	28	8
Physics	52	36	0	8	4
TOTAL	30	42	8	13	7

Analysis of the Number and Placement of OSs in the Paragraphs

Paragraphs in which the opening sentence is the sole true organizing sentence constitute the most frequent pattern in the sample accounting for 53% according to the investigator's analysis. As will be demonstrated later, there will be some differences of opinion among experienced readers performing this kind of analysis. Two examples from physics materials, each with a brief analysis, follow.

> The effect of pressure on the boiling point of water is well illustrated in the action of geysers. If it is 100 ft. down from the surface of a narrow column of water to a cavity surrounded by hot rocks, the pressure at these rocks is about 4 atm, three of the four being due to the column of water. At this pressure water boils between 140 and 150 C. Once water in the cavity begins to boil, bubbles rush up the column carrying quantities of water with them, thus reducing the pressure at the cavity and encouraging more rapid boiling until the temperature of the water in the cavity is lowered to the point at which boiling ceases. (Physics, 89)

Analysis: The paragraph opens with a Type I OS announcing the topic to be treated. The remaining three sentences describe the process announced in the OS, with no change of direction by the writer.

> One hundred years later, in 1798, Lord Cavendish succeeded in measuring the gravitational interaction of laboratory-sized objects. The apparatus he used is diagrammed in Fig 21–17. Two small spheres were mounted on opposite ends of a light rod 2 meters long. This rod hung horizontally with its center below a fine vertical wire from which it was suspended. At the ends of the rod and on the side of the case which contained the apparatus, Cavendish mounted ivory rulers with which to measure the position of the rod. When Cavendish placed two large masses near the small spheres at the ends of the rod, the small spheres were attracted toward the big masses and the wire suspension twisted. (Physics, 83)

Analysis: The paragraph opens with a Type IV OS, reporting an important experiment in the history of physics. The five sentences that follow provide details of the experiment: the apparatus, procedure, and results.

Most of the remaining paragraphs in the sample, amounting to 41%, contain two OSs, the second occurring with approximately equal frequency (a) immediately following the opening OS, (b) around the middle of the paragraph, or (c) in paragraph-final position. An example of each of these three patterns, with a brief analysis, follows.

> Plant growth studies were stimulated by observations of plant movements in response to external stimuli such as light (phototropism). Charles Darwin and his son Francis performed some of the first studies on plant movements in the 1870s and thus provided the groundwork and stimulation for further study in this field. Their studies on the coleoptile of grass seedlings, a sheath-like structure of only a few cells in thickness which covers the emerging shoot of grass, showed that when a coleoptile is exposed to light from one side, it will bend toward the light. This bending was prevented either by covering the tip or removing it (Figure 8-8). Since the actual bending occurred along the stem just below the tip, Darwin, in his book *The Power of Movement in Plants* (1881), suggested that the stimulus for growth passed from the tip to the stem. (Biology, 4)

Analysis: The opening OS is a variety of Type IV, reporting a general historical fact about early plant-growth studies. The second sentence is also a Type IV OS; it focuses on the pioneer studies of the Darwins. Thus the movement of the OSs is from the general to the specific. This is generally the case when the first two sentences of a paragraph are OSs.[5]

> Although the collision theory is intuitively appealing and does not involve complicated mathematics, it does suffer from some serious drawbacks. Since it is based on the kinetic theory of gases, it takes a "hard-sphere" approach and totally ignores the structures of molecules. For this reason, it cannot satisfactorily account for the probability factor at the molecular level. Furthermore, without quantum mechanics, it cannot calculate the activation energy. A different approach, called the *absolute rate theory*, which was mainly developed by Eyring and others in the 1930s, provides us with a greater insight into the details of mechanism on the molecular scale. It also enables us to calculate the rate constant with considerable accuracy. (Chemistry, 32)

Analysis: The opening sentence is a variation of Type III, stating that there are a number of drawbacks to an acceptance of the collision theory. These are then identified in the following three sentences. The fifth sentence, beginning "A different approach," is a Type II OS that shifts the focus to a competing theory. The advantages of this theory over the previous one are identified at the end of the fifth sentence and in the concluding sentence of the paragraph.

> Changes in the estimated distance to the Andromeda galaxy are instructive. In 1929 this distance to it was determined by the Cepheid method to be about 900,000 light-years. In 1944 this calculated distance was reduced to approximately 750,000 light-years by a correction for a dimming of its light caused by obscuring gas and dust in our own galaxy. In 1952 this revised figure was doubled to about 1-1/2 million light-years. Since 1952 the distance has been revised again by some astronomers to be approximately 2.2 million light-years. The actual luminosities of the Cepheids in this and other galaxies are still uncertain and not known precisely. (Geology, 70)

Analysis: The material preceding this paragraph explained how the Cepheid method of calculating distances was corrected in 1952 and subsequently. This paragraph opens with a Type I OS, announcing that the topic will be an example of the effects of such changes in methodology. The example is then presented chronologically in the following four sentences. The last sentence is a Type V OS, stating that the luminosities of the Cepheids are not precisely known. This point is pursued in the next paragraph, which begins, "Thus these distances are mere estimates, the best that can be made with the information at hand. . . ."[6]

Finally, our analysis of OS patterns in the sample of 100 paragraphs left us with a residue of a half-dozen paragraphs that appeared to have three OSs. Some of these could be characterized as *catalog paragraphs*, that is, paragraphs that simply list events, types of materials, and the like, or, as in the following case, identify topics of chapters to come.

> In this section we shall set up an "experiment in principle" for observing the motion of objects in two dimensions which will satisfy the operational principle even for objects which move with speeds approaching that of light. The goal of this analysis will be simply the description of the motion of these objects by a single observer. The description of this motion by two or more observers will be considered in Chapter 12. The equations of motion for these objects will be considered in Chapter 13. (Physics, 92)

Analysis: The first, third, and fourth sentences in this paragraph are all Type I OSs, introducing the material to follow. Only the second sentence is not an OS; it provides a rationale for the plan described in the opening sentence.

Verification Experiments

Unfortunately, analyses of the type conducted in this study are subjective to a considerable extent by their very nature. Therefore, it is imperative to determine whether other investigators would analyze the data in essentially the same way. Further, when one is basing one's observations on as limited a sample as we have here, the question of its representativeness must certainly be considered. And finally, in this study certain assumptions have been made about the way experienced readers would respond to OS cues, and such assumptions, too, need to be confirmed. Consequently, four small verification studies were conducted as a follow-up to the original data analysis.

Experiment 1. To try to establish whether or not the distribution of OS types appearing as opening sentences was peculiar to our sample, we collected and analyzed another sample of 100 paragraphs from another 20 science textbooks, using exactly the same procedures as previously used. The results of the analysis are summarized in Table 2. The proportions of OS types for the total sample are quite similar to those obtained for the original sample and summarized in Table 1. The greatest difference was only 8%—for the frequency of Type II OSs in the two samples. However, certain between-field contrasts in OS patterns that appeared in the first sample (e.g., the much greater use made of Type III OSs in the chemistry texts as compared with the other texts) tend to disappear, while the second sample shows another strong contrast (very little use of Type I OSs in the biology texts) that did not appear in the first sample. From the foregoing we may conclude that, while figures for the individual sciences are not reliable because of the smallness of the samples, the across-field totals seem to be fairly stable.

Experiment 2. At the beginning of this chapter, the speculation was that more technical materials in the natural sciences might be written in a different style than are college textbooks in the same fields. As a limited investigation of this point, we selected 100 paragraphs from U.S.-produced specialized journals in the four natural-science fields and analyzed the paragraph-opening OSs in this sample.[7] A summary of the distribution of OS types, compared with the distribution for the college textbooks, appears as Table 3. What is most striking is that the technical journals tend to make substantially more use of Type II OSs than do college textbooks. Such a difference—if further sampling bears it out— might be attributable to differences in subject matter or in audience. That is, journal articles often report specific experiments rather than survey of

Table 2.   Second Sample of 100 Opening Sentences by Field and
           Type (percent)

Field	Sentence Type				
	I	II	III	IV	V
Biology	4	56	12	20	8
Chemistry	40	48	4	4	4
Geology	16	44	4	24	12
Physics	32	52	4	8	4
Total	23	50	6	14	7

Table 3.   Distribution of Opening Sentences by Type in Professional
           Science Journals and College Textbooks (percent)

	Sentence Type				
	I	II	III	IV	V
Journal Articles	25.0	62.0	2.0	10.0	1.0
College Textbooks[a]	26.5	46.0	7.0	13.5	7.0

[a]Percentages are an average of the figures for the two samples.

a general area, and the authors of the journal articles are addressing their
peers rather than writing to first-year college students. In any event, it
appears that the writers for the journals begin more of their paragraphs
by presenting detailed new information than do the textbook writers,
who may, in consideration of their readership, feel some inclination to
present scientific information more gradually.

Experiment 3. As an estimate of the degree to which other analysts
would agree with the identification of organizing sentences presented
here, the investigator submitted 18 of the 100 textbook paragraphs to
seven colleagues, all of them experienced teachers of applied linguistics
or English as a second language. Paragraphs were selected to represent

a broad range of OS patterns, some being chosen because they had caused particular analytical problems for the investigator. The seven analysts were provided with a brief explanation of the organizing-sentence concept and were asked to mark all the OSs they found in the paragraphs.

The task proved to be a difficult one, no doubt for a variety of reasons: the analysts were often working with quite unfamiliar subject matter, they lacked the normal reader's access to the material in the preceding paragraphs, and some had difficulty remembering the precise purpose of the task, that is, to identify those sentences that signaled the direction or change of direction of the writer's exposition, and instead marked sentences that simply presented striking new information. Further, there were indications in some analysts' oral and written comments that they had found the investigator's brief description of the analytical system rather unclear. As a consequence of all these factors, individual responses varied considerably. Despite the various problems, for 13 of the 18 paragraphs (72%) between five and all eight of the analysts (including, in each case, the investigator) did agree on the precise number and position of the OSs. For four other paragraphs (22%), the analysts were equally divided between two interpretations: either the opening sentence was the sole OS or a sentence around the middle of the paragraph functioned as a second OS (6%). Thus there was only one paragraph in 18 on whose interpretation there was no substantial agreement. Subsequent study of this paragraph suggested that it contained so much new information that the analysts found it extremely difficult to decide which sentence or sentences actually change the writer's direction.

This experiment demonstrates that identifying OSs inevitably involves a measure of subjective judgment, although results seem to indicate that the investigator's analysis of the paragraphs was, all things considered, fairly reliable. Clearly, however, the numerical data presented in the Findings section need to be treated as approximations only.

Experiment 4. In the presentation of the five types of OSs, certain assumptions were made about how experienced readers could use the opening sentences of paragraphs to predict what would follow. For example, a reader who learned from an opening sentence that "Isotopes are classified into two groups" was expected to anticipate that the rest of the paragraph would describe the two groups. This faith in the experienced reader's hypothesis-making skill needed to be tested experimentally.

Subjects were 30 graduate students enrolled in approximately equal numbers in two courses in methods of teaching writing. All but 4 of the 30 were native speakers of English, and those 4 were, according to a variety of criteria, very advanced users of English. It seemed a reasonable assumption that such students belonged in the experienced-reader category.

During one of the regular class meetings of each of the two courses, the investigator gave the subjects a total of 19 opening sentences from the corpus: 10 sentences for one course, 9 different sentences for the other. Subjects were asked to read each opening sentence and write what they thought would follow in the remainder of the paragraph. They were also asked to indicate whether they had done (1) very little, (2) a moderate amount of, or (3) a good deal of reading in each of the four natural science fields represented in the corpus.

In subsequent analysis of the responses, fairly rigorous standards were applied in the assessment of the accuracy of the predictions. The mean for the percentage of subjects correctly guessing the general content of the 19 paragraphs was 80.4%. On average, four out of five subjects had been successful in predicting the general subject matter of a paragraph on the basis of clues in the opening sentence. That these subjects were not accustomed to reading in the natural sciences was indicated by their mean overall score of 1.2 on the 3-point reading-familiarity scale previously described.

Summary and Implications

An analysis of certain structural features of paragraphs in natural science textbooks for college undergraduates yielded four principal findings that may be summarized in the following four points.

First, the opening sentence is critical to the organizational structure of the paragraph, very often providing the experienced reader with a key to the nature of the discussion to follow. Two major functional categories, accounting for about 85% of the opening sentences in both our primary and secondary samples, were identified: (1) The sentence simply announces the topic without actually providing much new information (designated Type I in the study); and (2) the sentence provides vital new information either by stating a scientific fact, describing a natural phenomenon, offering a brief definition of an object or process (Type II), or describing an important natural event, scientific investigation, or finding in the past (Type IV).[8]

In addition to the foregoing, two less frequent categories of opening sentences were also represented in the samples: (3) The sentence indicates the number, parts, or categories into which something is divided or states that there are important similarities or differences between two things (Type III); and (4) the sentence points out a common false assumption or the scientific community's lack of clear evidence or understanding of a phenomenon (Type V).

Second, very frequently the first sentence serves as the sole organizing sentence in the paragraph; that is, the focus established at the outset is maintained throughout the paragraph. At least half the paragraphs in the primary sample appeared to have just one organizing sentence; Type V never appeared as the sole organizer in these data. It is likely that the opening sentence in such paragraphs would be treated as the topic sentence in traditional analysis.

Third, in many paragraphs (about 40% of the primary sample), two sentences function as organizing sentences. It is assumed in this analysis that the opening sentence is always one of these. The second organizing sentence may immediately follow the first, may fall somewhere around the middle of the paragraph, or may be the concluding sentence. Apparently all types of organizing sentences can occur in noninitial position.

When the two organizing sentences occur together in the first and second positions in the paragraph, it is usually the case that the expository movement is from the general to the more specific. When the second organizing sentence occurs in the middle or at the very end of the paragraph, the two frequently present different kinds of new information: two theories, causes, events, results, etc. (Types II and IV). Sometimes the concluding organizing sentence serves to announce the topic of the following paragraph.

And fourth, instances of three organizing sentences seem to be comparatively rare, though they do occur. There were apparently just six in the primary sample of 100 paragraphs.

As indicated by the third verification experiment, some variation must be expected in the way language specialists will analyze such paragraphs, though the evidence does seem to provide *general* support for the analysis. We suggest, therefore, that use of the organizing-sentence approach allows us to analyze certain basic features of paragraph structure, giving us a clearer picture of the precise functions that paragraph openers perform without resort to the vague topic-sentence concept. It must again be emphasized, however, that the investigation was limited to materials in the natural sciences, and it remains to be seen whether the technique, and the organizing-sentence categories, will be equally useful in the analysis of texts in other disciplines—the social sciences and humanities, for example. For the present, three possible uses for the technique and findings are offered.

First, to improve the reading comprehension skills of students in the natural sciences, we might develop exercises along the lines described in the fourth verification experiment, in which subjects were given the opening sentences of textbook paragraphs and asked to predict the nature of the material to follow. As shown by that experiment, experienced native-speaker readers show considerable ability in making such predictions, even for very unfamiliar kinds of material. It may be that such prediction-making skill can be developed in less proficient readers and could conceivably increase their overall facility in reading scientific texts.

Second, we would at the same time do well to caution students that the first sentence in natural-science paragraphs is not necessarily the topic (or main-idea) sentence; this study shows a fairly high incidence·of paragraphs containing two organizing sentences, the second of which marks a change of direction *within* the paragraph. Exercises that teach students to be alert for a second, contrasting, organizing sentence might prove helpful in developing good reading comprehension habits.

And third, to move from pedagogy to research, the procedure outlined in this chapter might make at least a modest contribution to the stock of prose-analysis techniques. For example, the second verification experiment reported suggests that the procedure might identify differences in the organizational styles of scientific texts designed for different audiences—differences of which the writers themselves may have no conscious awareness. We have further suggested that a comparative study of the use of organizing sentences in the natural and the social sciences, and in the sciences and the humanities, might reveal interesting stylistic differences between disciplines. And finally, it seems possible that further analysis of paragraphs by the OS technique might reveal whether such factors as the type, number, and placement of OSs in paragraphs affect the reading-difficulty level of expository texts.

Notes

[1]For the past several years the investigator has been giving his graduate seminar on writing an exercise in which a 21-sentence passage from a well-known history of the English language is presented to students without paragraphing, their task being to indicate where they would begin new paragraphs. Of the more than 50 students who have attempted this task, not one has paragraphed the passage the way that the author did. Yet there has been considerable agreement among the students on places where paragraphs might logically begin, and most students' paragraphs have in at least two or three places matched the author's paragraphs. Similar experiments are reported by Stern (1976) and Bond and Hayes (1984), the latter finding much closer agreement among subjects.

[2]The identification numbers assigned to the five paragraphs in each book are given in parentheses at the end of the entry. For example, the notation (1–5) after the biology textbook by Ford and Monroe means that paragraphs numbered 1 and 2 occurred at the beginning of sections within this text, and paragraphs 3, 4, and 5 were taken from the interior of sections. Whenever examples from the corpus are given in this chapter,

the source will be indicated both by the scientific specialty and the corpus identification number, e.g., Biology, 4.

[3]Paragraphs were analyzed without reference to the surrounding context.

[4]Admittedly, it is not always easy to distinguish Type II from Type I OSs, because the decision rests on whether or not one sees a sentence as containing new subject-matter information or as just announcing a topic. Undoubtedly analysts would in some cases reach different conclusions. It may perhaps be useful to note that three fourths of the sentences classified as Type I are marked by the following kinds of topic-announcing phrases, which are absent from Type II sentences: "Let us look at," "We now consider," "In this section we will examine," "A review is instructive," "The table gives some values," "Here is a crucial question."

[5]The following are other characteristic examples of two paragraph-initial OSs that show a general-to-specific movement:

All of the nutrients from agricultural, industrial, and household sources enter waste treatment disposal systems, and a brief consideration here of those systems can provide us with an important lesson in the effects of the availability of limiting nutrients. Consider the impact on a waterway of dumped, untreated sewage. (Biology, 9)

The periodic nature of an electromagnetic light wave constitutes a kind of *clock*. Consider two observers, one in a strong gravitational field near the Sun and the other in a weak field in a space laboratory. (Physics, 80)

There are ways to spread out far thinner layers of matter. Here is one which you can do in your school laboratory. (Physics, 84)

[6]The following are additional examples of paragraph-final OSs that serve as a transition to the following paragraph or section:

Perhaps the following discussion on auxins will clarify hormonal control (Biology, 1)

How did the match initiate the reaction, and why did the reaction not go initially? (Chemistry, 42)

It may be profitable to review the evidence. (Geology, 61)

[7]Five paragraphs were drawn from each of 2 recent issues of 10 journals: *Biological Bulletin, Biophysical Journal, Chemical Reviews, Geological Society of America Bulletin, Geophysics, Journal of Applied Physics, Journal of Biological Chemistry, Journal of Cell Biology, Journal of the American Chemical Society,* and *Physical Review B: Condensed Matter.*

[8]Combining the original organizing-sentence Types II and IV in this summary seemed justified because they share the feature of being loaded with essentially the same kinds of new information, the principal distinguishing feature being that of time (tense).

Appendix A
Data Sources

Biology

Ford, J. M., & Monroe, J. E. (1971). *Living Systems: Principles and relationships.* San Francisco: Canfield Press. (1–5).

Kelly, M. G., & McGrath, J. C. (1975). *Biology: Evolution and adaptation to the environment.* Boston: Houghton Mifflin (6–10).

Kimball, J. W. (1965). *Biology.* Palo Alto, CA: Addison-Wesley. (11–15).

Nason, A. (1965). *Textbook of modern biology.* New York: John Wiley & Sons. (16–20).

Noland, G. B. (1979). *General biology* (10th ed.) St. Louis, MO: C. V. Mosby. (21–25).

Chemistry

Adamson, A. W. (1976). *Physical chemistry of surfaces* (3rd ed.). New York: John Wiley & Sons. (26–30).

Chang, R. (1981). *Physical chemistry with applications to biological systems* (2nd ed.). New York: Macmillan. (31–35).

Freifelder, D. (1982). *Physical chemistry for students of biology and chemistry.* Boston: Science Books International. (36–40).

Neal, A. L. (1971). *Chemistry and biochemistry: A comprehensive introduction.* New York: McGraw-Hill. (41–45).

Paul, M. A., King, E. J., & Farinholt, L. H. (1967). *General chemistry.* New York: Harcourt, Brace and World. (46–50).

Geology

Eardley, A. J. (1965). *General college geology.* New York: Harper & Row. (51–55).

Longwell, C. R., & Flint, R. F. (1962). *Introduction to physical geology* (2nd ed.). New York: John Wiley & Sons. (56–60).

Menard, H. W. (1964). *Marine geology in the Pacific.* New York: McGraw-Hill. (61–65).

Ordway, R. J. (1966). *Earth science.* Princeton, NJ: Van Nostrand. (66–70).

Seyfert, C. K., & Sirkin, L. A. (1973). *Earth history and plate tectonics: An introduction to historical geology.* New York: Harper & Row. (71–75).

Physics

Marion, J. B. (1971). *Physics and the physical universe*. New York: John Wiley & Sons (76–80).

Physical Science Study Committee (1965). *Physics* (2nd ed.). Boston: D. C. Heath. (81–85).

Smith, A. W., & Cooper, J. N. (1972). *Elements of physics* (8th ed.). New York: McGraw-Hill. (86–90).

Taylor, E. F. (1963). *Introductory mechanics*. New York: John Wiley & Sons. (91–95).

Young, H. D. (1974). *Fundamentals of mechanics and heat* (2nd ed.). New York: McGraw-Hill. (96–100).

Discussion Questions

1. Harris notes that there is a problem in defining *topic sentence*, yet we frequently use the term when teaching composition. How do you define this term when teaching students? Do you think that your definition is adequate? Do your students?
2. How should we teach the concept of the topic sentence? How should we counteract previous teaching of this concept? Should we teach it at all, because no more than 60% of the paragraphs in native-speaker expository prose contain topic sentences (Braddock 1974)?
3. Note that Harris distinguishes between the organization and content (i.e., main idea) functions of opening sentences. How does this juxtaposition compare with formal and content schemata and reader-based concepts discussed by Carrell (1983)? What is the difference between formal and content schemata and the traditional concepts of unity and coherence still discussed in composition textbooks?
4. Do you agree with Harris's typology, or would you like to modify it? For example, his Type II "states a scientific fact, describes a natural phenomenon, or offers a brief description of an object or process." Should all of these categories be subsumed under one type? Why or why not? Harris suggests that Type I and II overlap; can this be avoided?
5. Note Harris's methods for minimizing subjectivity in coding the samples. Do ESL, applied linguistics, and rhetoric require these safeguards in research? What types of journals require this rigor—or more? What journals publish studies that have other requirements for acceptance?

Extension Exercises

1. Read the classic Lackstrom, Selinker and Trimble article cited by Harris, that describes the conceptual paragraph. Examine textbooks or articles in various disciplines for conceptual paragraphs. After finding some, answer these questions: What are the functions of the paragraphs subsumed under the core generalization? Why did the authors indent these subsumed paragraphs?
2. Harris employs first-year textbooks from university classes for his experiment. Using his methodology, compare selected segments from textbooks in the same discipline, such as biology, at two other academic levels, for example, from high school or elementary texts.
3. Harris suggests that textbooks from first-year university classes may differ from journal articles for a number of reasons. Examine five textbooks and five articles from one content area in the social sciences or humanities, and, with a friend, replicate the first part of the Harris study. What conclusions can you draw?
4. Follow the pedagogical suggestions for predictive reading that Harris makes at the end of his article. Do you find differences in predictive accuracy between native and nonnative speakers in your classes? Are students with prior knowledge of content more accurate? Do some students agree on the predictions? If so, what kinds of background knowledge or writing experience do they have in common?

Inductive, Deductive, Quasi-inductive: Expository Writing in Japanese, Korean, Chinese, and Thai

John Hinds

Thammasat University

Bangkok, Thailand

Inductive, Deductive, Quasi-inductive: Expository Writing in Japanese, Korean, Chinese, and Thai

A dichotomy is often drawn between writing that is organized in an inductive manner and writing that is organized deductively. Inductive writing is characterized as having the thesis statement in the final position whereas deductive writing has the thesis statement in the initial position. It is arguably the case that any society with a literary tradition is capable of producing expository texts that contain either inductive or deductive reasoning or some combination of the two. English, for example, allows either type of development, although the model that expository writers apparently aim for and that students are consistently taught tends to be deductive rather than inductive (see, among others, Harris, this volume). Frequent assertions contend that deductive writing contributes directly to the overall coherence of the composition. Thus Hardison (1966) stated:

> Coherence is increased when the materials in the paragraph are arranged according to a definite method. The methods available are the same as those for the essay as a whole. . . . They include the inherent orders of time, space, and process; and the logical orders such as general to specific, least to most important, cause and effect and climax. (p. 46)

In direct contrast to this are languages such as Japanese, which are more commonly claimed to exhibit an inductive style, although the deductive style is also possible (see, among others, Kobayashi, 1984).

In this chapter I survey samples of writing from several Asian languages with the purpose of determining what might be called a regional preference for the logical organization of information in expository writing.[1] The examples I present are all illustrative of what *appears* to be inductive style, although I demonstrate that it is not. These examples have been selected to illustrate this point and should not suggest that they represent the only style of writing permitted in these languages.

I draw two major conclusions, both of which are predicated on the fact that the compositions under consideration obey constraints that are specific to the given languages. The first conclusion is that the writings are well organized and easily comprehensible (despite the appearance of disorganization in the English translations).

The second conclusion is somewhat more pertinent. Each of the examples has a superficial rhetorical structure that approximates the general inductive style familiar to composition teachers and students in the West. This is a fallacious familiarity. I maintain that when English-speaking readers recognize that a composition is not organized deductively, they categorize the composition as inductive, thus preventing them from understanding the true differences between competent English writing and competent writing in other languages. I claim that the dichotomy between inductive and deductive writing is not a valid parameter for evaluating texts across languages.

Japanese

Japanese writing has been characterized by Kobayashi (1984) as progressing from specific to general in contrast to English, which she characterized as progressing from general to specific. For English-speaking readers, the consequences of this reversed arrangement of ideas in direct translations from Japanese texts is a frequent feeling that the composition is disorganized, unfocused, or ineffective. This feeling is certainly not shared by the Japanese readers who read the original texts (see, for instance, Hinds, 1983, 1984; Kaplan, 1987), because whatever the rhetorical style in the original, it is designed to appeal to Japanese audiences.

Professional Japanese–English translators are well aware of this problem, realizing that it may be necessary to reorganize the flow of information from the original. Yutani (1977) discussed some of the difficulties involved in translating newspaper articles from Japanese to English. In the following example the first paragraph is Yutani's literal translation of the news item, and the second is his translation for an English-speaking audience.[2]
Literal translation:

> The results of the 11th General Election for the House of Councillors which had been fought focusing on the success of reversal in power in the Diet were almost confirmed by the official counting of votes tabulated by the evening of June 11 (Sun). The results show that the Liberal Democratic Party (LDP), which was reported to be fighting poorly, did much better than expected, and though the number of the LDP members alone including those not reelected in the House of Councillors was slightly below the majority, that exceeds the number of representatives of nongovernment parties if nonaffiliated councillors who are sympathetic with the LDP and

those belonging to minor parties are added. And Prime Minister Fukuda regained his confidence for the future management of state affairs.

Translation for English newspapers:

> Prime Minister Takeo Fukuda's Liberal Democratic Party (LDP) was assured of its continued rule as the LDP retained its majority in the 252-seat House of Councillors in the Sunday election. The general trend of the ballot became clear with the counting of the votes up to the night of June 11 and the strength of the LDP became evident so as to marginally surpass the Opposition after considering post-election admissions of successful independent candidates of other various factions.

The translation for English readers has a clear statement of purpose as its initial sentence, and the following sentences develop or expand on this statement of purpose. In the Japanese original, the information that the LDP was assured of continued rule is buried in the second sentence (see literal translation). In fact, it is not until the final sentence of the literal translation, which speaks of Prime Minister Fukuda's regaining confidence, that the English-speaking reader is positive that the LDP has been assured continued rule.

The two articles titled "Fee for Asking the Way" and "Who Are the War Dead?," presented respectively as Appendixes A and B, further illustrate this phenomenon on a larger scale. In each case the purpose of the article is not seen by the English-speaking reader until the final paragraph. On the surface at least, this is an indication of an inductive style of writing.

In fact, for us[3] it appears that the purpose of the article is something entirely different than what it actually is until the final paragraph.

Fee for Asking the Way

A brief paragraph-by-paragraph summary of "Fee for Asking the Way" is presented here to facilitate discussion.

1. A statement that there is a fee for asking the way in a tourist area with a justification by the proprietor.
2. A statement of support for the proprietor's position.
3. Illustrations supporting the author's position.
4. Generalization that not only asking the way but unnecessary asking of questions in general is increasing.

5. Statement that one question, although insignificant, becomes significant when it is multiplied by many people.
6. Continued justification for the lack of consideration that motivates unnecessary questioning.
7. Parallel drawn with throwing away cigarettes on subway platform—one is not significant, but when many do the same thing it becomes significant.
8. Statement that the unnecessary disposal of useful items can lead to increase in railway fares and taxes.

The reader is initially led to believe that the article is concerned with a lack of consideration for others (paragraphs 1 through 6). In paragraph 7 the reader is led from that point to a more general point: in a heavily populated area anything done to excess causes difficulties for others. Finally, the reader is shown in the last paragraph that this lack of consideration can lead to increased railway fares (to pay for cleaning the station) and taxes (to pay for additional garbage collection). This is the purpose of the article.

In retrospect, it is possible to see how an article that begins by discussing a fee for asking the way can lead to a discussion of rising railway fares and taxes. However, it is difficult, if not impossible, for the English-speaking reader to predict where the article is going at any point before the final paragraph. Japanese readers do not have this problem because of their cultural expectations (a point that will be discussed later).

Who Are the War Dead?

To facilitate discussion, a brief summary of "Who Are the War Dead?" follows.

1. There were many air raids in cities of Japan 39 years ago.
2. A poem describes the bombing of Toyama City, and the results of that bombing are presented.
3. *War Dead* include more than military personnel; civilians must also be included.
4. This point is reiterated, with a call for self-reflection.
5. This point is applied to the consequences of a nuclear war, especially that the number of civilian dead will be great.
6. PM and Cabinet ministers are pleaded to attend memorial services for civilian war dead.
7. A statement is made against official visits by Cabinet members to Yasukuni Shrine, where those responsible for the war are enshrined.

This article follows a similar development to that in the previous article. The writer progresses from a general account of the effects of war on civilians (paragraphs 1 through 5) to a plea (paragraph 6) for officials to attend memorial services for civilian war dead. The true purpose of the article is revealed in the final paragraph, which asserts that official visits by Cabinet members to the Yasukuni Shrine should not be permitted because that is where those responsible for the war are enshrined. In retrospect, it is possible to see how the author reached the final paragraph, although it is not possible for the reader to see where the article is going from the outset.

As part of the conclusion for this section, I make two points that also apply to the compositions of other languages presented in subsequent sections. The articles examined employ rhetorical conventions shared by English as well as conventions not used in English. The purpose is not to evaluate these essays in terms of their effectiveness as English compositions (they obviously fail in that respect); rather, it is to demonstrate a style of writing that is respected and processed effectively by native speakers of each language.

Further, we must recognize the role that cultural expectations play in these articles. Issues such as increasing taxes, railway fares, and official visits to Yasukuni Shrine are contemporary to the Japanese. Thus English-speaking readers' inability to predict where the essays are going stems from both cultural and temporal distance from the author's intention. Japanese readers are closer in both respects and therefore more able to contextualize the essays than are English-speaking readers.

Korean

Korean shares many syntactic and rhetorical properties with Japanese.[4] One of these properties is the tendency to organize information in essays in the specific-to-general pattern. Eggington (1987) discussed an article published in English by a Korean scholar whose familiarity with Western writing conventions was minimal. Eggington pointed out that there is "no statement of purpose; . . . there appears to be no thesis development, but rather a list of points revolving loosely around an unstated central theme" (p. 158). He further noted that the brief conclusion that accompanies the article is given in the final paragraph and that this "is the first time the reader is informed of the purpose of the paper" (p. 158). Similarly, Koons (1986) found that delayed introductions of thesis statement in expository writing are frequent.

Examining the untitled Korean essay in Appendix C, we see a similar pattern to that illustrated by the Japanese examples.[5] In the first paragraphs (1 through 4) various perspectives on laughter are discussed. In the final paragraph these perspectives are applied to the Philippines. But, in fact, there is more to this article than just this application. For Korean readers this article is actually commenting on the political situation in Korea.

Untitled Korean Essay

1. Laughing is a human activity that "lubricates."
2. There are many types of laughter, but it is difficult for society to implant a truly cheerful laugh.
3. A genuine laugh grows only in healthy, intelligent societies. Relation between laughter and longevity; physiological relations.
4. Laughter aids health.
5. The Philippines has become a laughing stock as a result of the election battle between Marcos and Aquino.

The purpose of this article is not inferred before the final paragraph. It is possible, of course, to trace the trail that leads to the statement of purpose. In retrospect, comments such as "a genuine laugh can only grow in healthy, intelligent societies" (paragraph 3) suggest that this article will do more than discuss laughter from a variety of perspectives; however, it is not possible for English-speaking readers to predict the direction the article will take at that point. Thus we see again that the true purpose of the article is not revealed until the final paragraph, and even then it is revealed through the thinly veiled parallel between the Philippine elections and the Korean political situation.

It should not surprise us that Korean readers understand the rhetorical technique applied here whereas English-speaking readers have difficulty knowing what is actually being referred to. We have only to contemplate the difficulty that most readers have in appreciating the depth of political comment in *Gulliver's Travels* to further emphasize this. With *Gulliver's Travels* we (Westerners) share some cultural affinity; with the essay examined here we are separated from the situation, being unfamiliar with the cultural expectation that criticisms of the government are frequently disguised in metaphor.

Chinese

Kaplan (1966, 1972) suggested that compositions by Chinese (and Korean) writers who write in English may seem out of focus or incoherent. Much of that incoherence arises, Kaplan (1966) asserted because "the foreign student is employing a rhetoric and a sequence of thought which violate the expectations of the native reader" (p. 4).

Most of the literature on Chinese expository writing focuses on the *chi-cheng-juan-he* [起承転結] sequence (see also Cheng, 1985; for a contradictory point of view, see Mohan & Lo, 1985).[6]

1. chi [起] First, begin one's argument.
2. cheng [承] Next, develop that.
3. juan [転] At the point where this development is finished, turn the idea to a subtheme where there is a connection, but not a directly associated connected association (to the major theme).
4. he [結] Last, bring all of this together and reach a conclusion. (Takemata, 1976, p. 26)

Tsao (1983) stated clearly that "the *chi* section in Chinese cannot be equated with the topic sentence in English. The *chi* part has to be related to the general theme in some way or other, but it is not necessarily a theme statement" (p. 111). We may take this statement as an indication that the typical deductive style favored in the West, in which topic is made clear at the beginning, is not favored in Chinese writing.

Examining the sample Chinese text in Appendix D, we see a different pattern than in the Japanese and Korean samples. This pattern is summarized here by paragraph, although many paragraphs contain more than one "topic."

Trial Marriage

1. Definition of *trial marriage*
2. Rhetorical question: What are the merits of trial marriage? Parallel drawn with smoking.
3. Unhappily married people are happier than bachelors.
4. Trial marriage embraces philosophy of "getting drunk when there is wine." Disadvantages of trial marriage.
5. Conclusion against trial marriage.

From Tsao (1983) the reader is led to expect that the initial paragraph will not contain a statement of the purpose of the article. In fact, an introductory paragraph of this type is not uncommon in English expository writing either. The beginning of paragraph 2, however, contains the rhetorical question, *What are the merits of trial marriage?* From an English speaker's perspective, the subsequent statements must constitute an answer to that question. In general, one of two types of responses to a rhetorical question of this type is expected. The first is a listing of the merits. The second is a statement of the type, "There are none," with a subsequent listing of the demerits.

Rhetorical questions and their expected responses may be illustrated by taking a representative number of such questions as they appear in academic writing. Let us examine first two instances of rhetorical questions that are answered affirmatively. The first is from Schachter (1985):

> What, for example, can be said about the ways in which, and the limits within which, parts-of-speech inventories may differ from one another? Which parts-of-speech distinctions are universal and which language-specific? What are the ways in which languages that lack a particular part of speech express the semantic equivalent? And what relations are there between the parts-of-speech system of a language and the language's other typological characteristics? It is the aim of this chapter to provide some answers to such questions. (p. 3)

The second is from Eggington (1987):

> In other words, do Koreans regard the linear structure of the type shown in example 4 as being unclear as English speakers would regard the non-linear structure shown in examples 1, 2, and 3? (p. 161)

Eggington's answer is an extended *yes* as we would predict. Contrast these with the rhetorical question asked in the abstract of a paper by Coppieters (1987) in which a negative answer is given. Had this negative answer not been present, the reader would be led to expect a positive response on the part of the author.

> Do native and native-like (i.e., near-native) speakers develop essentially identical underlying grammars of the same language? Results of extensive interviews indicate that native and near-native speakers of French have strikingly different intuitions on French sentences. (p. 544)

Returning to the Chinese text under consideration, we see that, by turning without signals to a discussion of heavy smokers, the author leads English-speaking readers to believe that the author will argue for trial marriage, because the author has not specifically argued against it. The English-speaking reader therefore has had a reasonable expectation established. We can now ask the rhetorical question, do the subsequent paragraphs support this expectation? The answer is *no*, although it is not until we reach the end of the article that this answer is made absolutely clear.

The third paragraph contains the author's belief that characters who marry after a trial marriage will end by parting. Yet the whole paragraph seems to focus on unhappy marriages in general rather than on the unhappy marriages of those who entered marriage through trial marriage. This paragraph therefore does not directly answer the rhetorical question in the negative.

The fourth paragraph begins with a congratulatory salutation for those whose trial marriages have succeeded. The rest of the paragraph, however, speaks of the subsequent drawbacks of a failed trial marriage. Because the listing of these drawbacks is initiated by the conditional statement, "If it fails (there is always potential for failure)," the English-speaking reader is still able to maintain the belief that the author will argue for the benefits of trial marriage.

In the final paragraph, in which the reader is informed that a trial marriage has "one millionth of a chance to succeed"—a hyperbolic technique not tolerated in good English expository writing—the reader realizes that the author has been opposed to trial marriages from the outset. The author has used a rhetorical technique infrequently employed by English-speaking writers to establish a framework within which to make a point.

The expectations are very different for the Chinese-speaking reader than for the English-speaking reader. The English-speaking reader is accustomed to having issues such as trial marriages debated in print and is able to find advocates for and against such practices. There is much more of a national consensus in Taiwan, however, that trial marriages are undesirable. Therefore, the cultural expectation of the Chinese-speaking reader is that the article will condemn trial marriages, regardless of the form of the rhetorical questions.

Thai

There is little written on Thai expository writing styles (see Ounvichit, 1988). Thai writing, in general, appears to conform more closely to the canons of English expository writing, although repetition is more frequent. This feature is shared with spoken Thai discourse, which has been categorized by Grimes (1972) as an overlay pattern. The first Thai composition in Appendix E illustrates this. This composition will not be discussed further.

There is another common pattern in Thai exposition, which is exemplified by the composition in Appendix F. This composition, although written by a native speaker of Thai, appeared originally in English; therefore, any claims about Thai native writing based on this example must be considered as suggestive rather than conclusive (see, in particular, Hinds, 1983).

The article appears to be a typical movie review and in the first 10 paragraphs is just that.[7] However, in paragraph 11, there is an abrupt change. A comment about the poor editing of a similar type of movie, "Platoon," sets the reviewer off on general criticisms of policies toward editing by censors in Thailand. This leads to a complaint about why movie edits are made (to fit in five screenings a day [paragraph 15]), which leads to the major purpose of the article: to complain about the state of cinemas in Bangkok. Again we see that the purpose of the article is not made at the beginning but at the end of the article.

Discussion

In each of the writings in the four languages, there is a common style. For the present I call this style "delayed introduction of purpose." This delayed introduction of purpose has the undesirable effect of making the essay appear incoherent to the English-speaking reader, although the style does not have this effect on the native reader. There is something in each of the writings that is foreign to the English-speaking reader but that is natural to the native reader. Ebbitt and Ebbitt (1982) reflected Hardison's (1966) definition that appears at the beginning of this chapter:

> Coherence—the traditional name for relationship, connection, consecutiveness—is essential in expository writing. It's essential because you can't count on the minds of others working the same way your mind works. You must guide your readers from one idea, from one sentence, to another. To make a coherent presentation you have to arrange your ideas so that others can understand them. (p. 393)

There is an organizing principle in the writings presented here that allows native speakers to understand the ideas but that is lost on English-speaking readers. Moreover, the Western notion "you can't count on the minds of others working the same way your mind works" may not be relevant to the cultural climate of other countries. In the cultures examined here the author *does* expect that the minds of readers work in a very similar way to his or her own.

Returning to a part of Hardison's (1966) definition, that the organizing principles "include inherent orders of time, space, and process; and the logical orders such as *general to specific* (italics added), least to most important, cause and effect and climax" (p. 46), we are able to account for some of the confusion for English-speaking readers.

English-speaking readers typically expect that an essay will be organized according to a deductive style. If they find that it is not, they naturally assume that the essay is arranged in the inductive style. English-speaking readers know that an inductive style must have certain characteristics and is used in certain circumstances: The author expects a hostile audience and feels that the audience must be led step-by-step to a legitimate conclusion based on evidence presented.

> If you think your readers will have no quarrel with your conclusion, you will probably proceed deductively, stating your conclusions at the outset. If you think your readers will be hostile to your conclusion, you give your reasons first, hoping they will agree with them one by one until they have to reach the conclusion that you did. (Ross & Doty, 1985, p. 127)

The difficulty with the compositions in each of the languages discussed here is that the conclusions do not seem to follow from the reasons that lead up to them. One specific reason the compositions are judged to be flawed is that the English-speaking reader has had a number of expectations disaffirmed. First, the English-speaking reader expects that the composition will be organized deductively. In the course of reading each composition, it becomes increasingly clear that none has employed a deductive style. Second, recognizing that a deductive style is not used, the reader expects the inductive style to be used. In this case the reader expects that each point the author makes will constitute a reason, the sum of which will argue persuasively for the conclusion the author reaches in the final paragraph. However, in each article examined, the concluding paragraph does not constitute a conclusion in the English sense of the term.

The reasons for this are many, but they may be grouped together under a single heading, expectation. If English-speaking readers expect that an article is meant to convince or persuade, they expect that all arguments will contribute directly to that cause. If, on the other hand, they expect that the purpose of an article is to introduce a set of observations related loosely to a general topic, and that the task of the reader is to sort and evaluate these observations, they have a clearer idea of the purpose of writing in some other cultures. Readers in each of the cultures examined here have this expectation when they read.

Seen in this light, we must recognize that the traditional distinction that English-speaking readers make between deductive and inductive writing styles is inappropriate to the writing of some nonnative authors. We may more appropriately characterize this writing as quasi-inductive, recognizing that this technique has as its purpose the task of getting readers to think for themselves, to consider the observations made, and to draw their own conclusions. The task of the writer, then, is not necessarily to convince, although it is clear that such authors have their own opinions. Rather, the task is to stimulate the reader into contemplating an issue or issues that might not have been previously considered.

Notes

[1] All of the examples presented in this chapter, with the exception of the Thai article, which originally appeared in English, share the characteristic of being well structured and easily understood essays in the original languages. Whatever flaws they possess as English essays arise as a result of different rhetorical conventions and different cultural expectations.

[2] Readers wishing to see the original text of this example or of the examples that appear in the Appendixes are encouraged to write to the author.

[3] Here and elsewhere the use of *we* and *us* refers to English-speaking readers.

[4] Although the conclusion to this article that Eggington (1987) discussed in many ways parallels a typical conclusion for a Japanese essay (see Takemata, 1976, pp. 26–27), "A conclusion need not be decisive. All it needs to do is indicate a doubt or ask a question."), Koons (1986) found that decisive conclusions are common in Korean essays.

[5] Koons (1986) further pointed out that the title frequently plays a major organizing role in Korean essays. She stated, "No matter how loosely paragraphs or sentences are connected to each other, Korean readers may try to connect each paragraph or sentence to the main idea which is stated in the beginning as a title" (p. 9). The article under discussion here, ironically, does not have a title.

[6] In Japanese this combination of characters is pronounced ko-shoo-ten-ketsu (see Hinds, 1980, 1983, 1984). In Korean, it is pronounced ki-sung-chon-kyul (see Eggington, 1987). Both Japanese and Korean have borrowed the writing style from Chinese, as well as the descriptor 起承転結. The Thai writing system is based on Sanskrit rather than Chinese, and so it does not seem to be influenced by Chinese expository techniques as much as Japanese and Korean are. This is not to say, however, that a 起承転結 cannot be found in languages other than Japanese, Korean, and Chinese. In fact, Mo (1982) has suggested that this pattern appears in many English paragraphs. Perhaps this observation by Mo will help us to realize that the interpretation of rhetorical patterns may be imposed by the analyst more than by the author.

[7] Longacre (1979), among others, distinguished between a *meaning paragraph* and a *formal paragraph*. The meaning paragraph has internal structure in the form of a unified theme and is determined irrespective of orthographic conventions. The formal paragraph, on the other hand, refers to the convention of indenting a composition. Formal paragraphs may coincide with meaning paragraphs, but more frequently they

are determined by editorial fiat. The reference to "paragraphs" in this composition, then, refers exclusively to formal paragraphs, or indentations, since most of the "paragraphs" consist of only one sentence.

Appendix A
Fee for Asking the Way
(From Tensei Jingo, translated by the staff of the Asahi Shimbun)

It is said that it is written at the entrance to a store in a tourist area somewhere, "Fee for asking the way, one time, 100 yen." This is a story which appeared in the column "Koe" of this newspaper. It's a fact that the world has become a difficult place to live, but I think that the reason that the storekeeper gives is, "It's become so much of a pain that I've acted this way."

While the experience of asking is only one on a particular day from the perspective of the one who asks, the number of times being asked, from the perspective of the one who is asked, might be 20 times, or it might be 50 times.

Among these, there are probably people who leave without saying thank you, and those who ask the road from the inside of their cars. In the midst of his being busy there are probably people who ask the way in a rude manner. He probably even feels like saying just leave me alone.

It's not only talk of asking the way, recently the habit of asking questions easily is spreading. Looking it up in the dictionary. Searching for a number in a telephone book. Looking at a map. Don't we ask too often without doing those things what we should do?

Since even I go around asking people questions too often, I can't say very much, but in an overpopulated country like Japan, especially when you are asking questions, isn't it necessary to understand that your question is one of a 1,000 or one of 10,000?

There may be cases where the one who is asked, facing 1,000 or 10,000 people, is forced to provide 1,000 or 10,000 times the service. It worries me that people might not have a strong sense of consideration.

There are other examples of lack of consideration too. One person throws away a cigarette butt on the station platform. The one who throws this away may think that it is not very important, but if 1,000 or 10,000 people throw them away, the platform will be filled with cigarette butts.

On garbage collection day, when someone throws away something that is still good, it can easily mean that it will swell to 1,000 or 10,000 times that. Swelling expenses to cover the costs of cleaning up cigarette butts and trash may lead to increases in railway fares and taxes.

Appendix B
Who Are the War Dead?
(From Tensei Jingo, translated by the staff of the Asahi Shimbun)

Around this time 39 years ago, there were air raids in Japan almost daily. In April Tokyo saw B29 bombings once every two days—on April 1, 2, 4, 7, 12, 13, 15, and so forth. Tokyo, Osaka, Kobe and Nagoya were bombed and burned.

"In the flow of bombed out river/A praying old woman turns into white wax and sinks." This is a poem by Sakae Fukyama of Toyama City. The big bombing of Toyama City occurred before dawn on Aug. 2, 1945, only a few days before the end of the war. The city was razed, and about 3,000 citizens were burned to death.

Who are the "war dead"? Are the war dead only officers, soldiers and civilian employees of the military who died fighting? It can't be so. In an all-out war, the home front turns into the battlefront and citizens are subjected to such fierce attacks that 100,000 people are robbed of their lives in one night.

There is no mistaking the fact that people killed in bombings, civilians killed in the Okinawa battle and people killed while being repatriated to

Japan are all war dead. To engage in severe self-reflection concerning the fact that the lives of 800,000 civilians were sacrificed is the way to console the souls of the war dead.

That there were so many civilians killed by indiscriminate mass bombings hints at the outcome of a future nuclear war. As pointed out by Shinjiro Tanaka, who says, "In a nuclear way, the people will definitely be abandoned," the number of civilians killed will be far greater than the number of officers and soldiers killed. Beyond that, there is the danger that they will be exterminated. The basic tragedy contained in modern war is the drastic increase in the number of civilians who will be killed.

If, for instance, the prime minister and all Cabinet members officially attended memorial services for the civilian war dead in Tokyo, Osaka, Okinawa, Hiroshima, and Nagasaki, we would welcome the move. We also feel that this is how it will be possible to deeply consider the meaning of war.

Why is the Liberal-Democratic Party now desperately trying to make official visits by Cabinet members to the Yasukuni Shrine in Tokyo constitutional? Why is the party trying to review the government policy to the effect that such visits may be unconstitutional? Those responsible for carrying out the war are also enshrined at Yasukuni Shrine.

Appendix C
Untitled Essay
(From Horizon, translated by Kathy Koons)

Laughing is certainly the lubricating oil of human life. One good laugh in an irritated mood can change the whole thing. Thus the French writer LeVole in the Age of the Renaissance said, "Laughing is a special privilege that only humans can enjoy."

There is a variety of names for laughing depending on the shape of the mouth and the expression of one's feelings. There are so many kinds of laughter; for instance the smile that only uses the eyeballs and the edges of the lips a little bit, the cold smile that uses eyes but not the edges of the lips, the bursting laugh that makes one squeeze the belly, the loud laugh that opens the mouth wide, and the lost smile that only shows the teeth but makes one's face empty looking when he or she is shocked or extremely disgusted. Even though there are so many kinds of laughter, yet it is very difficult for a society to implant a truly cheerful laugh.

Therefore Bergsong said, "A genuine laugh can only grow in healthy, intelligent societies." People have been searching for the reason why they laugh. Recently American scientists have come up with evidence that there is a deep relationship between laughing and living long. They argue that when we laugh, the muscles of the shoulders, the chest, and the abdomen constrict and at the same time, the heart beat increases, therefore raising the blood pressure only temporarily, then suddenly the muscles and the heart begin to relax, releasing the stress.

Dr. Frei at Stanford University seems to be an extreme admirer of laughing. According to him, the effect of laughing is the same as the effect of jogging in that if we laugh 15 times a day, we don't need to go to the hospital. The old oriental saying that the more we laugh, the younger we become; the more get upset, the older we become is an empirical lesson for health.

We shouldn't make ourselves become objects to be laughed at, although it is said that laughing is the secret weapon for a long life. The Philippines is still in the middle of chaos even four days after the presidential election. I'm afraid there might be two presidents—Marcos and Corazon. All our eyes are on the outcome of the Philippine election which looks ridiculous before the world.

Appendix D
Trial Marriage
(Translated by Anne Chou)

Trial marriage to most people is a new type of game; however, its content is not necessarily new. Years ago, the term "cohabitation" was invented to meet social needs. The difference between the two is merely that the former seems to be more fancy. Frankly speaking, it is only a matter of old wine in new bottles. Except for that sheet of marriage contract, trial marriage is exactly the same as legal marriage, both implying a relationship between men and women living together.

What are the merits of trial marriage? Just look at those heavy smokers. In spite of the fact that smoking may result in cancer, still numerous people are very happy to become nicotine addicts, like a school of silver carp moving down a stream. You understand that the merits and faults of anything as bad as smoking are indisputable. So let them talk!

If men and women have to enter the marriage relationship through trial marriage, I believe most of the characters in marriage stories will end by parting. An unharmonious state, naturally, is not uncommon in married life. But the point is that people can adapt themselves to each other gradually. What's the harm in looking at those unhappily married men, who are, at any rate, happier than perpetual bachelors. From these people, you may learn other implications of an unhappy marriage.

If trial marriage succeeds, truly, congratulations! If it fails (there is always potential for failure), both parties may look for another partner. How do they feel then? So isn't trial marriage merely an excuse for practicing the philosophy of "get drunk whenever you have wine"? People who are seeking a trial marriage because of financial reasons may lose their drive to move upward. People who are practicing trial marriage with a flirtatious attitude will inevitably conclude their marriage like a game. People who have been in trial marriages will be seen unavoidably as a "different class" in our society after the trial marriage. Things are even getting more complicated if, unfortunately, they had a baby during that trial period.

As compared with many tasks, trial marriage is an undertaking which demands one hundred-percent success. Then why do we insist on being engaged in such a risky adventure which has millions of chances to fail, and one millionth of a chance to succeed?

Appendix E
Untitled Essay
(Translated by Sukanya Tanewong)

If someone asks, "Where is the Thai identity?" or "What is the Thai identity?" I think many people would have to think about it for a while before they could answer.

This is not because there is no Thai identity, but rather, because Thailand is a country in which there are a lot of what we call "identities."

The words "never mind" may be considered one of the Thai identities. I don't think there is any country in the world where people use the words "never mind" in every situation like Thai people do. "Have you eaten yet?" We answer, "Never mind." "Do you have enough money?" . . . "Never mind." "I have to go home now." . . . "Never mind." "You look pale. Are you okay?" . . . "Never mind." "Sorry about your father's death." . . . "Never mind." "Here is the bathroom. Are you looking for the toilet?" . . . "Never mind."

These are only some examples. Our Thai "never mind" does not only mean "don't mention it" as used by people in other countries, but it also has various other meanings. However, this is not the only identity we have; we also have many other identities.

Thailand is not only one hundred or two hundred years old, but it has been a country a long time. Besides, it is one of the countries which is independent and has a distinct identity which includes, for example, language, culture, art, habits, and even beliefs in holy things. One of these beliefs that we have had since ancient times concerns the construction of "spirit houses." It is believed that each piece of land has a guardian spirit, who must be honored if the human occupants want to enjoy peace and prosperity. A spirit house is usually erected somewhere in the compound, often in the garden but sometimes on the roof in the case of large commercial properties like modern condominiums.

At present almost every Thai household has a spirit house of "Saan Phra Phum," which is a small house-like shrine dedicated to the spirits of the home. The shrine practically faces north and lies outside the shadow of the main house. Simple "Saan Phra Phum" may be in the form of a very small Thai-style house, made of wood, while more elaborate ones may resemble small temples. In either case, these are kept supplied with regular offerings of fresh flowers, incense sticks, and sometimes food to insure the continued protection of the spirit. Such offerings are also made at major road intersections where car accidents have often occurred, in hotel gardens, and anywhere else the people perceive there is the dwelling of a guardian spirit.

Both the words "never mind" and the belief in the "spirit house" I have mentioned above are just some different examples of Thai identities. Yet, as I have said before, these are not the only identities we have, we also have many others.

Appendix F
"Hamburger Hill" Revisits the Valley of Death
Film Review by Cimi Suchontan, (Bangkok Press)
(Appeared originally in English)

Perhaps the bloodiest engagement in the Vietnam War, Hamburger Hill was taken only after enormous US casualties. But director John Irvin's movie version misses the whole point of the tragedy.

Caught up with depicting just brave soldiers, Irvin fails to mention the saddest part of the victory, which was that the troops were withdrawn almost immediately *after* securing the hill.

It seemed the high command decided (after 11 bloody assaults) that it wasn't as strategic as they thought after all.

Walter Cronkite, the war correspondent, was shocked at the outcome. The American public were outraged. The movie, sadly, forgets about it.

In a small way, however, "Hamburger Hill" pays tribute to one of the most illustrious divisions in the US Army—the 101st Airborne.

If you remember Cornelius Ryan's "A Bridge Too Far," the 101st paid a heavy price to take the bridge, using rifle butts as paddles to reach it when assault crafts failed to arrive.

In "Longest Day," the same division was the first to parachute into Normandy by night.

At Hamburger Hill, the 101st once again, like the proud 600 Light Brigade lancers, charges into another valley of death.

The significance of their horrific 10-day attack on the hill ignites some sympathy through the film. Played mostly by new faces, "Hamburger Hill" is still worth viewing. The acting is subtle, often powerful and thoughtful.

For dramatic value, however, "Platoon" proves more interesting.

Meanwhile some readers have informed this reviewer that "Platoon," showing last month at the OA cinemas, was "poorly edited," and many say it was "butchered."

Viewing the original edition on video, I found their comments valid. The crude cuts prove once again how our censors and cinema owners are afflicted with vast silliness.

To start with, the cut scenes (about seven minutes) contained neither sex (nudity—male or female) nor violence. Neither did they contain communist propaganda.

They were simply a few scenes of soldiers smoking strange substances and holding conversations.

So why the cuts? Probably to fit five screenings in. Any movie over two hours long would pose inconvenience to the movie houses.

This only shows the days when you could trust the cinemas are gone.

I recall better times in 1975, when "Godfather II" was screened in its full length (nearly 3 hours) as was the original black and white "Gone With The Wind." No fear of silly cuts or vaseline jobs then.

Gone also are the days when Bangkok cinemas were among the best in Asia; even better than those of Hong Kong and Singapore. Now, they're among the worst. Now you learn to expect horrible things to happen every time you go there.

Clearly the Eighties signals the end of our cinemas. Often providing dumpy services, they couldn't care less if you showed up or not.

The worst editing job came three years ago when they showed "Blues Brothers" *minus* the entire James Brown church singing sequence, the most important scene in the film that explained the plot.

The absurdity confirmed my worst fears that illiterate maniacs were running our cinemas. You can forget about good service. Expect exploitation, as greed rules over better senses.

To think I was, at one time, calling for people to support local cinemas. Indeed, it has become increasingly difficult to defend their existence and except for a handful of good cinemas like Hollywood, the majority of them are worthless.

At this point, if another cinema goes out of business I'd feel pretty good about it. Enough, good audiences, is enough.

Discussion Questions

1. Do you agree with Hinds that English-speaking teachers think of written texts as either inductive or deductive?
2. Although all of the languages examined in this chapter are from the Sino-Tibetan group, Thai is less closely related than the other three. In terms of contrastive rhetoric and generalizations about languages, should Thai be included in this study of regional preferences for discourse styles? Can we speak of regional preferences? If so, what, other than language family, influences the discourse of this region?
3. Hinds provides no direct suggestions for teaching in his discussion, although he alludes to conventional ESL/EFL teaching practices.

What are the teaching implications of Hinds' observations? How would you teach speakers of these languages to juxtapose their own English texts to models written by native speakers?

4. In your opinion, why do speakers of Korean, Japanese, Chinese and Thai employ the quasi-inductive style? Do you agree with Hinds that issues of "cultural'and temporal distance come into play"?

5. Most English teachers tell students that their paragraphs should focus on only one topic and, if possible, should begin with a topic sentence. Is this what we should be teaching as a rule of thumb? If so, why? If not, why not?

Extension Activities

1. Select a text produced by a student whose writing you consider incoherent. Analyze it by summarizing each paragraph, as Hinds does, ignoring sentence-level error. What do you discover about the development of ideas in this discourse? Is it quasi-inductive, or are there other features in the discourse which inhibit expert reader comprehension?

2. Read the famous 1966 article by Robert Kaplan or the more recent 1983 article by Tsao on Chinese discourse, both cited by Hinds. Compare their discussions with those of Hinds. What do they have in common? How do they differ? What can you conclude from these articles about how Chinese write in their first language?

3. Read the Pearson (1983) article titled "The Challenge of Mai Chung: Teaching Technical Writing to the Foreign-born Professional in Industry." What are the implications of the Hinds article for the requirements of business and industry in an English-speaking country? How does the quasi-inductive style influence writing in a business or industrial context?

4. Select one of the articles in the appendixes of this chapter (e.g., "Who Are the War Dead?") and subject it to a test of coherence found in another chapter in this volume (e.g., by Harris or Wikborg). What do you discover about the coherence of the discourse analyzed?

5. Read the article on business letter writing written by Jenkins and Hinds (1987). What is the relationship, if any, between style in the articles discussed by Hinds in this volume and the rules for letter writing discussed in the 1987 article?

Toward Understanding Coherence:
A Response Proposition Taxonomy

Peter McCagg

International Christian University

Toward Understanding Coherence:
A Response Proposition Taxonomy

Coherence refers to a semantic property of textuality. It is an aspect of comprehension that is established in the mind of the reader as a result of a perception of relatedness among a text's propositions and between the text and the knowledge that the reader possesses of the world.

Any relatedness that is perceived by the reader may or may not be signaled by the explicit presence of discourse markers or other cohesive devices in the text. Frederiksen (1979) stated, "While surface discourse features such as anaphora, conjunction and lexical cohesion . . . may require or invite particular discourse inferences, the inferential relations they signal are at a semantic level and should in many instances be valid in the absence of surface linguistic cues" (p. 166). By *valid,* Frederiksen presumably meant that the relations exist.

To the assumption of existence, deBeaugrande and Dressler (1981) added the notion of the accessibility of those relations in their definition of coherence as "mutually accessible concepts and relations that underlie the surface of a text" (p. 4). These concepts and relations are accessed by readers inferentially. Widdowson (1986) suggested that "written text is essentially a set of directions which indicates to readers where they are to look for significance in their own knowledge of the world" (p. v). From this perspective, then, it may be assumed that the process of text comprehension, while involving complex interactions among a number of cognitive skills, is largely, if not entirely, interpretive. According to Schank (1975), inferences serve two primary functions. The first is to fill in gaps in the structure. The second is to connect elementary events or propositions with other elementary events in order to form a higher level of organization. Thorndyke (1976) wrote, "A major function of inferences in discourse is to provide an integrating context for the interpretation of incoming information in order to establish coherence and continuity in the text" (p. 437).

The purpose of this chapter is to suggest a means for extending or supplementing the propositional analysis technique used in many prose comprehension studies so that coherence-building inferences may be investigated more satisfactorily.

Proposition Analysis

Over the past decade and a half, proposition analyses have become widely used in the study of discourse production and comprehension. Because detailed descriptions of the various proposition analysis variations exist elsewhere (Kintsch, 1974; Meyer, 1975; Bovair & Kieras, 1981; Connor, 1984b; McCagg, 1984), I refer readers to these sources.

In reading research using propositional analysis techniques, the general paradigm has been to analyze a text or texts, have people read and respond in some way to the text(s)—usually in the form of a summary, paraphrase, or attempt at total recall—and then to analyze the responses to see which propositions are common to both. This research paradigm is particularly suited to empirical studies of inferencing because one can begin to discover what implicit connections are perceived by readers through analysis of the similarities and discrepancies between stimulus passages and response protocols.

The evaluation of response protocols to date, however, has focused primarily on the number, order, and type of propositions common to both the test passage and to the response. In other words, research has focused on how much information was recalled, whether information from the text was reordered in the response, and whether information contained in the response was recalled from the text's macrostructure (i.e., higher level or important ideas) or the text's microstructure (i.e., lower level or less important ideas). See Meyer (1975) and Connor and McCagg (1984) for two examples.

The problem with scoring response protocols solely on the basis of the number of propositions common to both the response and the reading passage is that much of the information found in the response—information that often demonstrates a deeper or more complete level of comprehension—may not correspond directly to the test passage propositions. Evaluating discourse comprehension by using one of the standard propositional analyses tends to place too much emphasis on the amount of text-based information (information reflected in the explicit or surface structure of the text) that is reproduced, while neglecting the other essential source of information in the comprehension scheme: readers' prior knowledge of the topic of discourse and their powers of reasoning.

Kintsch and van Dijk (1978) claimed that response propositions often result from reader processes of deletion, generalization, and construction. These non-text-based propositions—response propositions that are not explicitly expressed in the comprehension passage—have to date attracted little attention in published research. At least part of the reason for this lack of attention must stem from the absence of a formal way of accounting for propositions occurring in response protocols that are not directly or explicitly expressed in the reading passage itself. The rest of this chapter, through presentation of a specific example of a reading passage and a variety of response protocols, attempts first to demonstrate the need for a response proposition taxonomy and second to outline what such a taxonomy might look like.

A Sample Text

The passage used here is an excerpt from the beginning of a magazine article that appeared in October, 1981.[1] All of the response protocols included were produced by college-age Japanese English as a Foreign Language (EFL) students as part of the data collection procedures for a doctoral dissertation (McCagg, 1984).

The Tylenol Tragedy

The Tylenol tragedy has touched off a wave of renewed concern this October about pint-size Smurfs, E.T.'s, and Wonder Women accepting candy from strangers. As the 31st approaches, city officials in dozens of towns across the country have banned trick-or-treating altogether, or restricted it to daylight hours.

Although this text is not structurally unique, or even particularly unusual, the writer of the passage has observed one of the maxims of Grice's (1975) Cooperative Principle, that is, be only as informative as is necessary. This maxim dictates that message producers anticipate the extent of their audience's prior knowledge of the topic as well as the audience's likely processing capabilities and leave unsaid those aspects of the message that the audience presumably already knows or can work out for itself on the basis of what it knows. Whereas this constraint applies to the message producer, it also has consequences for the message receiver because it leads to gaps in the structure of the message, gaps that must be closed inferentially by the comprehender if coherence is to be established. The writer of "The Tylenol Tragedy" has apparently assumed that the anticipated audience will be able to access information from their store of prior knowledge about the Tylenol poisoning incidents and about Halloween that will enable them to make sense of these two sentences as a coherent text.

To comprehend the central message of this text, the reader must integrate information from both sentences because neither alone expresses the main idea of the text. Careful examination of the text, however, reveals that there are no rhetorical cohesive links that tie the two sentences together. Other than the fact that they are juxtaposed, there are but three semantic links between them. The first is the specification of an approaching date, *the 31st*, that is cohesive with the mention of a month, *October*, in the first sentence (S1). There are at least two levels at which the reader might understand this connection, depending on whether the fact that October 31 is Halloween is part of the reader's background knowledge or not. The second is that *city officials* in the second sentence (S2) fills an argument slot set up by, but left unspecified in, S1. That slot is for an experiencer role for the predicate *concern*. The third link is that the activity mentioned in S1, *accepting candy from strangers* is labeled *trick-or-treating* in S2. Making this connection requires culture-specific background knowledge about customs revolving around Halloween.

The causal relation that makes these two sentences cohere, that enables one to understand them as text, is clear not because of any explicit marker(s) of rhetorical function, but because of the prior knowledge that the reader must have about the Tylenol poisoning incident and its proximity in time to Halloween, and about the nature of Halloween and trick-or-treating. The reader must have the ability to generate coherence-building inferences based on this prior knowledge.

The macrostructure of this sample text is represented in Figure 1. At the highest level of text structure, "The Tylenol Tragedy" is a *covariance structure*. There are several different ways in which text information may covary, including conditionally, concurrently, and causally. In this text, the covariance is between a cause and a result, and the causal relationship is implicit. This is indicated in the macrostructure diagram by placing the rhetorical predicate *cause* in parentheses. The antecedent in the implicit causal relation is itself a covariance structure in which the noun phrase, the *Tylenol tragedy*, serves as the antecedent touching off *concern*, which is the consequence. The second sentence is also a covariance structure, one

Covariance

Antecedent   (CAUSE)   Consequent

Covariance   Covariance

TOUCH OFF   AS

Antecedent   Consequent   Antecedent   Consequent
TYLENOL   CONCERN   OCTOBER 31   BAN TRICK-
TRAGEDY   APPROACHES   OR-TREATING

Figure 1.   Macrostructure Diagram of the Tylenol Tragedy.

of the concurrent type. Here the antecedent is the approach of October 31 and the consequence is the banning or restricting of trick-or-treating.

For readers who may not be familiar with propositional analysis and who do not have time to explore the references listed below, Table 1 provides information about the rhetorical predicates that occur in "The Tylenol Tragedy."

The proposition template presented in Table 2 is a more detailed representation of the text. In the template, each proposition is listed on a separate line and numbered consecutively. After the reference number, the rhetorical function of the proposition is indicated. Where the first letter of the rhetorical function indicator is capitalized (e.g., Proposition 1 [P1], Proposition 2 [P2]), the proposition is part of the text macrostructure; when represented by all lowercase letters, the proposition functions at the level of the text microstructure, (e.g., P3, P5). Words represented entirely in uppercase letters are lexical items found explicitly in the text surface structure.

Aside from the macrostructure-microstructure distinction, there are two basic types of proposition: rhetorical and lexical. (See Meyer, 1975, for a complete description.) In the template presented in Table 2, P1 is an example of a rhetorical proposition. Proposition 1 indicates simply that P2 and S2 covary here causally, but there is no explicit rhetorical device or marker in the text to indicate this relation. This also explains the absence of any lexical items from the text in the proposition. For rhetorical propositions, the rhetorical function indicator (e.g., antecedent, consequent) acts as the predicate of the proposition. Note that at the highest level of its structure, this text is held together by an implicit tie.

Lexical propositions are realized explicitly in the text. They also carry a rhetorical function. In Table 2, P2 is an example of a lexical proposition. Here the fact that the Tylenol tragedy caused something is lexically represented in the text. The fact that this clause serves rhetorically as the antecedent for S2 is indicated by the rhetorical function indicator. When the rhetorical function of a proposition is simply that of a case role of a higher predicate, there is no rhetorical function indicator in the proposition line. Rather, the relation of the proposition to others in the text is indicated in the template by fitting the proposition into an argument slot marked in a higher proposition line. Proposition 8 in the template fills the object slot of P4, that is, it is the object of concern.

A Response Proposition Taxonomy

As previously stated, the reason for developing the taxonomy presented here is to try to provide a systematic way of accounting for propositions

Table 1   Rhetorical Predicates Found in "The Tylenol Tragedy" and the Sample Summaries

Relation	Common Lexical Realizations	Comments
1. Macrolevel		
Covariance	because, if . . . , then, as	Requires logical antecedent and consequence
Antecedent	if, as	The logically former of a covariance complex
Consequence	then, so	The logically following of a covariance pair
Cause	because	One of the covariance relations
Purpose	in order to, so	Another covariance relation
Alternative	or	
Additive	and	The weakest of the relations between macro propositions
2. Microlevel		Correspond largely to case grammar's clause level roles
Temporal	at, in, before, after	May occur as macrolevel relation, especially in narratives
Locative	in, on, at, into, in front of	May occur as macrolevel relation
Modal	can, might, must	Handled as higher-level predication in case grammar models
Manner	quietly, in such a way that . . .	
Modification	old, blue	A garbage category of sorts
Quantity	one, a gallon of	
Label	Sanibel	Commonly proper names
List	A, B, and C.	A time saver

Table 2 **Proposition Template for the Tylenol Tragedy**

S1

	P1	Covariance: (P2), (S2)
	P2	Antecedent: TOUCH OFF, TRAGEDY, (P4)
	P3	label: TRAGEDY, TYLENOL
	P4	Consequent: BE CONCERNED ABOUT, s*, (P8)
	P5	quantity: (P4), WAVE
	P6	modification: (P4), RENEWED
	P7	temporal: (P4), THIS OCTOBER
	P8	ACCEPT, (P9), STRANGERS, CANDY
	P9	list: SMURFS, E.T.'S, AND WONDER WOMEN
	P10	modification: (P9), PINT-SIZE
S2		
	P11	Covariance: AS, (P12), (P13)
	P12	Antecedent: APPROACH, THE 31ST
	P13	Alternative: OR, (P14), (P20)
	P14	Consequent: BAN, OFFICIALS, TRICK-OR-TREATING
	P15	modification: OFFICIALS, CITY
	P16	modification: (P14), ALTOGETHER
	P17	locative: BE IN, OFFICIALS, TOWNS
	P18	number of: TOWNS, DOZENS
	P19	locative: ACROSS, TOWNS, THE COUNTRY
	P20	Consequent: RESTRICT TO, OFFICIALS, TRICK-OR-TREATING, DAYLIGHT HOURS

Note: * represents a syntactically deleted case role. Here the experiencer role has been deleted.

occurring in response protocols that are not directly or explicitly stated in the stimulus reading passage. This response proposition taxonomy is an attempt to account for generalized, constructed, and inferential response propositions: propositions that are the products of readers' attempts to form coherent mental representations of texts.

The following examples demonstrate the need for such an extension to the propositional analysis technique. These samples were produced in response to the instructions "Write a one-sentence summary of the main idea expressed in the passage." All summaries used as examples here were originally written in Japanese and translated into English for analysis by the author.

Summary 1
A Text-Based Response

As October 31st approaches, officials in dozens of towns across America are prohibiting or restricting to daylight hours trick-or-treating.

Summary 2
A Linking Inferential Response

People are worried because someone could put poison in candy at Halloween.

Summary 3
A Generalizing Inferential Response

Just once, if someone does something evil, after that people must continue to live in the fear that the evil could happen again.

These three summaries cover a wide range of response types from almost completely text dependent and noninterpretive (Summary 1) to highly generalized and evaluative (Summary 3). Summary 2 seems to fit somewhere between these two extremes. Summaries 2 and 3 also appear to show evidence of greater or more satisfactory comprehension of the main idea expressed in the text than does Summary 1. The portion of text copied in Summary 1 does not—could not in fact—mention the key causal relation between the sentences.

Summary 1 presents few problems for the standard way of tabulating response propositions because, with two minor exceptions, the propositions produced in this summary match those found in the template for the comprehension passage. Summary 1 would also receive a higher recall score in the standard procedure than either Summary 2 or 3 because it reproduces more text propositions than do the latter two. This is ironic in light of the apparent qualitative superiority of Summaries 2 and 3. It is hoped that the taxonomy presented in Table 3 and discussed later will facilitate the investigation of inferencing phenomena such as those illustrated in these summaries.

Reflecting the two principal sources of information available to the reader, the text and the reader's prior knowledge of the subject matter, there are two major types of response propositions represented in the taxonomy. First, propositions may simply be copied or recalled verbatim from the text itself. This type of proposition is defined as being text based and includes passivised propositions and propositions in which synonymous expressions have been substituted. Comparing the proposi-

Table 3   Response Proposition Types

I. **Noninferential propositions**
   Text-based propositions (TBP)
II. **Inferential propositions**
   A.   Schema-based inferences
      1.   Background knowledge propositions (BKP)
      2.   Perspective propositions (PERSP)
      3.   Evaluative propositions (EVAL)
   B.   Text-induced inferences
      1.   Appropriate macro inferences (++INF)
         a. Linking
         b. Generalizing
      2.   Appropriate microinferences (+INF)
      3.   Inappropriate macroinferences (××INF)
      4.   Inappropriate microinferences (×INF)

tion template of Summary 1 (see Table 4) with that of "The Tylenol Tragedy" reveals that, in this summary, all but two propositions (P3 and P9) are text based. As previously stated, it seems clear that this author has essentially copied a portion of the text that he or she felt expressed the main idea of the text.

If a summary proposition is not text based, it is considered to be inferential. Whereas all response propositions are induced by reader interaction with a text, some inferential propositions are more directly called for by the text in the sense that, without the inference, it would be impossible for the reader to establish a coherent representation of the text that approximates the ideas the writer hoped to convey. Other inferential response propositions are less essential, if no less pervasive, and may best be thought of as additions or elaborations. These propositions may result from a reader's prior knowledge about the topic of discourse, from the reader's perceptions of what constitutes the pragmatic constraints of a summary or other response task, or from rather idiosyncratic reactions to information perceived in a text.

Schema-Based Propositions

The additive or elaborative inferential response propositions are categorized here as schema-based or schema-motivated propositions and are subcategorized into three types in the taxonomy.

Table 4   Proposition Template for Summary 1

P1 Covariance: AS, (P2), (P4)	TBP
P2 Antecedent: APPROACH, 31ST	TBP
P3 modification: 31ST, OCTOBER	+INF
P4 Alternative: OR, (P5), (P6)	TBP
P5 Consequent: PROHIBIT, OFFICIALS, TRICK-OR- TREATING	TBP
P6 Consequent: RESTRICT, OFFICIALS, T-OR-T, DAYLIGHT	TBP
P7 locative: BE IN, OFFICIALS, TOWNS	TBP
P8 number of: TOWNS, DOZENS	TBP
P9 locative: ACROSS, TOWNS, AMERICA	+INF

The first type of schema-based inference reflects the reader's store of prior knowledge about the topic of discourse. Although certainly triggered by information in the comprehension passage, these background knowledge response propositions (BKP) ultimately result from readers supplying extra or supplemental information from their relevant schemata. Summary 4 contains an example of a background knowledge response proposition.

Summary 4
A Background Knowledge-Based Inference

> This year children may get poison candy as they go from house
> to house collecting goodies.

Nothing from the comprehension passage itself suggests that children go from house to house at Halloween. The writer of Summary 4 has supplied this information from his or her store of prior knowledge about the Halloween custom referred to in the comprehension passage.

The second type of schema-based response proposition is labeled *perspective* (PERSP) and may be most easily defined by example. "This paragraph is about . . . ," "It says . . . ," and "The author says . . ." are all perspective propositions. These propositions relate the response to the comprehension passage and reflect an attempt to place the response-writing task into an appropriate pragmatic context.

The third type of schema-based inference is labeled *evaluative* (EVAL) and involves the insertion or addition of personal opinion or evaluation, often through the use of modals, words of emphasis such as *very*, and *especially*, or charged words such as *unfortunately*, and *luckily*.

The first type of inferential proposition mentioned, inferences that are called for by the text, are categorized as text-induced inferences. Two subtypes are distinguished: macro- (across sentences or clauses) and micro- (within sentences or clauses). Macroinferences are inferences made about the macrostructure of a text. These are inferences that enable the reader to perceive implicit relations among sentences or groups of sentences. There are two major types of macroinference, linking and generalizing. Linking macroinferences are generated by readers to close gaps in the explicit text structure, while generalizing macroinferences combine or collapse a number of text propositions into a single generalized response proposition. Before turning to specific examples of the various text-induced inference types, one further distinction is necessary, the distinction between appropriate inferences (those that are authorized by the text) and inappropriate inferences (those that are not authorized by the text).

The following sample summaries are provided to illustrate the taxonomy previously outlined. Summary 2 contains an appropriate macroinference of the linking type, as is indicated in Table 5.

The lexical predicate in P1 of this template, *because*, relates or links two lower level propositions, *someone could put poison in candy* and *people are worried*. As mentioned, understanding the implicit causal link between these two propositions is the key to understanding "The Tylenol Tragedy" as a coherent text.

Summary 3 is a good example of the second type of appropriate macroinference, the generalizing inference (see Table 6). Here the reader has abstracted from the example of the Tylenol incident's impact on a Halloween custom, a general principle of human behavior.

There are examples of appropriate microinferences (+INF) in all of the summaries included in this chapter. In Summary 1, the nonspecific

Table 5　Proposition Template for Summary 2

P1 Covariance: BECAUSE, (P4), (P2)	++INF LINK
P2 Antecedent: PUT IN, SOMEONE, POISON, CANDY	+INF
P3 modal: COULD, (P2)	+INF
P4 Consequent: BE WORRIED, PEOPLE	+INF
P5 temporal: AT, (P2), HALLOWEEN	TBP

Table 6   Proposition Template for Summary 3

P1	Covariance: IF, (P2), THEN (P6)	++INF GEN
P2	Antecedent: DO, SOMEONE, SOMETHING	+INF
P3	modification: SOMETHING, EVIL	EVAL
P4	frequency: (P2), JUST ONCE	+INF
P5	temporal: AFTER, THAT (=P2), (P6)	++INF LINK
P6	Consequent: LIVE, PEOPLE	+INF
P7	manner: LIVE, IN FEAR	EVAL
P8	modification: LIVE, CONTINUE	+INF
P9	modal: LIVE, MUST	EVAL
P10	modification: FEAR, THAT (P11)	+INF
P11	HAPPEN AGAIN, EVIL	+INF
P12	modal: COULD, (P11)	EVAL

location *across the country* was specified as being *across America*. In Summary 2, the phrase, *people are worried* provides an experiencer for the concern that is explicitly expressed. Whether it is a supplied case role or a generalization of *city officials*, it is in either case a micro-level inference, that is, it is generated on the basis of information contained within a single clause.

If readers never misinterpreted or misunderstood a writer's intended meaning, then the categories illustrated to this point would suffice to begin to approach inferencing phenomena in prose comprehension systematically. However, readers often misinterpret or understand only incompletely what they read, especially when they are reading in a second language. Summary 5 demonstrates this point rather clearly.

Summary 5
Inappropriate Inferences

> Halloween is a festival founded on the Tylenol tragedy. It was started as a reminder to prevent children from quietly eating Tylenol poison.

There are three macrolevel inferences made in Summary 5 (see Table 7), none of which is called for by the text. The reader who wrote Summary 5 may or may not have been satisfied with this rendition of the text, but it seems clear from this example (and many other cases similar to it) that even with limited linguistic skills or insufficient or inaccurate prior knowledge about the topic of discourse, readers engage in speculation about probable causes and reasons for information perceived in texts as they attempt to formulate a plausible coherent interpretation. In the area of second language reading research, these inappropriate or misguided inferences may provide the most interesting insights into the nature of reading processes in the nonfluent reader.

I would like to suggest that the taxonomy of response propositions outlined and illustrated here provides a basis for beginning to investigate questions such as: Given the presumed interdependence of components, of the reading process, what are the consequences of limited proficiency in one or more of those components for a reader's ability to generate coherence building inferences? Does familiarity with the subject matter of a text enable readers to compensate for syntactic limitations and thereby facilitate the generation of appropriate inferences? Do readers from different linguistic and cultural backgrounds make the same sorts of inferences when reading in a second language? Do they make the same sorts of inferences when reading in their native languages? And what features of text structure facilitate or hinder inferencing processes for different types of readers?

The taxonomy presented here is based on a limited number of texts and it undoubtedly will require expansion or revision before it can be applied to other text types. It is presented, then, not as a definitive statement on response propositions, but in the hope that it will help

Table 7 Proposition Template for Summary 5

S1		
P1	Equivalent: BE (EQUAL), HALLOWEEN, FESTIVAL	+INF
P2	Specification: BE FOUNDED ON, FESTIVAL, TRAGEDY	××INF
P3	label: TRAGEDY, TYLENOL	TBP
S2		
P4	Additive: START AS, $, IT (FESTIVAL), REMINDER	××INF
P5	Purpose: TO PREVENT FROM, $, CHILDREN, (P6)	××INF
P6	EAT, CHILDREN, POISON	+INF
P7	label: POISON, TYLENOL	×INF
P8	manner: (P7), QUIETLY	EVAL

others who are interested in exploring inferencing and coherence phenomena see ways of classifying information found in response protocols that result from active reader interpretation. It is presented in the hope that as researchers continue to study the nature of prose comprehension, it will stimulate further refinements in text analysis techniques.

Finally, a taxonomy for representing text and response propositions is but one of the keys to furthering our understanding the role of coherence in contributing to comprehension. A general theory of text comprehension to guide researchers from the top down is even more essential. And, ultimately, the validity of prose comprehension studies, of research on inferencing and coherence, depends on selection and accurate description of naturally occurring, authentic texts and responses elicited in real-world contexts.

Note

[1]"The Tylenol Tragedy" is an excerpt from a news item that appeared in *Newsweek*, October 14, 1981.

Discussion Questions

1. Read the Connor and McCagg article (1984), cited by McCagg, on propositional analysis. Do you agree with McCagg that "the problem with scoring response protocols solely on the basis of the number of propositions common to both the response and the reading passage is that much of the information found in the response, information that often demonstrates a deeper or more complete level of comprehension, may not correspond directly to the test passage propositions"?

2. McCagg says that "there are several ways in which text information may covary, including conditionally, concurrently, and causally." Discuss possibilities for text in which propositions show causal covariance. How could we explain this covariance to students?

3. Think of examples in your own reading—or that of your students—in which inadequate or inappropriate prior knowledge interfered with comprehension of text. What did you—or they—lack? Are there ways that we can compensate in the English language classroom for what is missing?

4. Other than prior knowledge, what else makes summarizing difficult? For example, how many and what kinds of steps does the summarizing process require?

5. Read the Swales chapter in this volume, noting the four steps for introductions. Can you identify these steps in the McCagg chapter?

Where are they? How does McCagg mark the beginning of each step? Does McCagg's introduction mirror Swales' guidelines for writing each step?

Extension Exercises

1. Read Connor and McCagg (1984). Code two short texts (perhaps in the form of conceptual paragraphs) on related subjects using their methodology. Do the insights provided assist you in understanding how topic development should be taught to writing students? Why or why not?

2. McCagg notes in his Tylenol paragraph that "there are no rhetorical cohesive links [esp. conjunction and reference] that tie the sentences together" although there are some semantic links. Read an article about Halliday and Hasan's (1976) scheme for coding cohesion (e.g., Connor, 1984a; Johns, 1981). Then examine four paragraphs from the same genre by four different native speakers for the incidence of conjunctions and reference items. Are they frequent, or is lexical cohesion more common?

3. Using the McCagg discussion of Table 2, the analyzed text, and Connor and McCagg (1984), attempt the type of analysis McCagg describes. Were you successful? Why or why not?

4. Ask four native speaker expert readers to summarize a short passage of 250–500 words. Do you find that these summaries differ? Do they, for example, contain any of the additive or elaborative response propositions that McCagg lists?

III.   Studies of Student Writing

Types of Coherence Breaks in Swedish Student Writing: Misleading Paragraph Division

Eleanor Wikborg

University of Stockholm

Types of Coherence Breaks in
Swedish Student Writing:
Misleading Paragraph Division

This chapter is part of a larger study of what I have called coherence breaks in Swedish university-student essays. The chapter addresses misleading paragraph division, which is one of the 11 coherence breaks diagnosed in the sample. I start by briefly describing the larger investigation[1] whose purpose was (a) to define and classify types of coherence breaks and (b) to determine their relative frequencies, into which this one type of coherence break fits.

The sample consists of 144 essays and papers taken from five departments at the University of Stockholm: business administration, law, journalism, comparative literature, and English. The writers range from beginners to graduate students (i.e., four levels: three undergraduate and one graduate) because I wanted to see whether some coherence and structuring problems were more persistent than others. The results varied according to the subject area. The essays are in Swedish, except for those written by students of the English Department. All the example texts below have been translated into English. In this process, I have tried to refrain from improving on their style. However, I have corrected spelling and elementary grammar errors.

Coherence break is the term I use for what happens when the reader loses the thread of the argument while in the process of reading a text attentively. This may occur for any number of reasons, all of which are familiar to teachers. It may be that the reader cannot really figure out what the topic is or that there is a sudden and inexplicable change of topic. On a more local level, the reader may have trouble working out the logical relation between two sentences or there may be an inference that is difficult to follow. This type of disturbing factor I have called a coherence break because it interrupts the smooth processing of the flow of information in a text.

In my view, Widdowson (1978) offers the most helpful concept of coherence. According to him, a text is coherent when a reader understands the function of each succeeding unit of text in the development of its overall or global meaning. For example, the writer should make it possible for the reader to distinguish quickly between a specification of a point just made and the assertion of a new one, or between the elaboration of a point just made and the presentation of a contrasting one (cf. Lieber's functional roles, 1980, pp. 310-312). One of the sources of the breakdown of coherence in student texts is precisely the failure to make clear such functions of succeeding units of text.

Types of Coherence Breaks

The coherence breaks identified in the sample fell into two types, topic-structuring problems and cohesion problems, as follows:

I.   *Topic-Structuring Problems*
   1.   Unspecified topic
   2.   Unjustified change of/drift of topic
   3.   Misleading paragraph division
   4.   Misleading disposition (ordering of material)
   5.   Irrelevance (in the form of van Dijk's overcomplete-ness, 1977, p. 110)
   6.   Misleading headings
II. *Cohesion Problems*
   7.   Uncertain inference ties
   8.   Missing or misleading sentence connection
   9.   Malfunctioning cohesive tie (The type of cohesive tie does not actually hold, e.g., a contrast or illustration is signaled that is not borne out by the actual semantic relations established by the proposition[s].)
   10. Too great a distance between the cohesive items in a cohesive chain
   11. Misleading distribution of given and new information within the sentence

Of these 11 types, 5 turned out to be most frequent, accounting for 82% of the total number of coherence breaks counted (see Table 1).

Misleading Paragraph Division

This discussion will focus on the second most frequently appearing coherence break: the misleading paragraph division, which accounts for one-fifth of the total number of coherence breaks in the data. Though it is different in kind from the other types of coherence breaks, misleading paragraph division is similar in its effect on the reader, for, like the other types, it interrupts the reader's smooth processing of written discourse.

Table 1   The Five Most Frequent Types of Coherence Breaks

	% of total no. of breaks
1. Uncertain inference ties (214 instances)	27
2. Misleading paragraph division (172 instances)	21
3. Missing or misleading sentence connection (125 instances)	16
4. Unjustified change of / drift in topic (81 instances)	10
5. Unspecified topic (63 instances)	8
Total	82

Note 1–5 = 655 instances of a total of 801 coherence breaks.

(1) Neighborhood Center 90

. . .

¶1 One problem area which has also given rise to the neighborhood centers is the labor market's poor recruitment of the
disabled.

¶2 Neighborhood centers might provide them with job opportunities.

¶3 In the 1970's many companies moved out of center city, and
this meant an increase in the number of private cars. . . .

The use of the pronoun *them* in ¶2 emphasizes the fact that the two
sentences of 1 and 2 form one topic unit. It is the function of paragraph
divisions to mark the end of such units rather than to subdivide paragraphs
into single sentences as the student writer did in this section. Of course,
a paragraph break can have a rhetorical, rather than a topic-marking,
function (i.e., its purpose may be to give special emphasis to a particular
statement). However, if a paragraph break does not clearly have this
function (as in the case of text [1]), it misleads the reader into expecting
a new topic or a new aspect of the topic, when in fact no such change has
taken place.

Because misleading paragraph division is one of the major coherence
problems found in the student data (see Table 1) and because the factors
governing paragraph division are so complex, at this point I would like
to make some introductory comments on the role of paragraphing in the
structuring of well-formed texts.

Paragraphing in Texts

Despite the pioneering work done by Christensen (1967), Koen, Becker, and Young (1969), and Braddock (1974), formalized understanding of the factors that motivate paragraph decisions is in its infancy. The task of setting up criteria to distinguish between acceptable and unacceptable paragraphing is, at this stage, truly daunting. It is complicated, first of all, by the fact that the conventions vary from genre to genre. Second, even within the same genre, these conventions are only partly logical; they are determined by considerations of layout, register, and such rhetorical effects as personal tone, emphasis, and rhythm. (For discussions of these factors and of paragraph theory in general, see the three previous references and *Symposium*, 1966; Rodgers, 1966; Stern, 1976; Brown & Yule, 1983; Markels, 1984.)

There is thus a limited range of acceptable paragraphing alternatives available to writers. Outside of this range, there exist paragraphing practices that readers find dysfunctional, as can be seen in text [1]. The existence of constraints on paragraphing have been confirmed in experiments carried out by Koen, Becker, and Young (1969). Although these constraints have not yet been formally identified, it seems clear that unless readers perceive a rhetorical or layout reason for exceptions, they expect paragraph breaks to signal a change of topic or aspect of topic.

The importance of the contribution that paragraphing makes to the structure of a text varies according to the number of other structuring devices there are in a text. In some texts it merely adds a finishing touch to a structure that is communicated by other means. In texts with few alternative structuring devices, it is the paragraph divisions that are the central topic-shift markers. In such texts, their removal seriously impairs the coherence of the passage.

Alternative Structuring Devices

Let us start by identifying the repertoire of alternative structuring devices that can be observed in a well-formed text. In the following version of Bertrand Russell's (1951) Preface to his *Autobiography*, the original four paragraph divisions have been removed in order to highlight the powerful structuring function of (a) the metatextual pointers (capitalized) and (b) the cohesive ties established by repetition within the text's central cohesive chains (in italics).

> (2) THREE *passions*, simple but overwhelmingly strong, have
>   governed *my life*: the longing for *love*, the *search* for knowl-

edge, and unbearable *pity* for the suffering of mankind. These *passions*, like great winds, have blown me hither and thither, in a wayward course, over a deep ocean of anguish, reaching to the very verge of despair. I have *sought love*, FIRST, because it brings ecstasy—ecstasy so great that I would often have sacrificed all the rest of my life for a few hours of this joy. I have *sought* it, NEXT, because it relieves loneliness—that terrible loneliness in which one shivering consciousness looks over the rim of the world into the cold unfathomable lifeless abyss. I have *sought* it, FINALLY, because in the union of *love* I have seen, in a mystic miniature, the prefiguring vision of the heaven that saints and poets have imagined. This is what I *sought*, and though it might seem too good for human life, this is what at last—I have found. With equal *passion* I have *sought knowledge*. I have wished to understand the hearts of men. I have wished to know why the stars shine. And I have tried to apprehend the Pythagorean power by which number holds sway above the flux. A little of this, but not much, I have achieved. *Love* and *knowledge*, so far as they were possible, led upward toward the heavens. But always *pity* brought me back to earth. Echoes of cries of pain reverberate in my heart. Children in famine, victims tortured by oppressors, helpless old people a hated burden to their sons, and the whole world of loneliness, poverty, and pain make a mockery of what human life should be. I long to alleviate the evil, but I cannot, and I too suffer. This has been *my life*. I have found it worth living, and would gladly live it again if the chance were offered me. (pp. 3–4)

The devices marked in Russell's Preface are in turn supported by others. However, the first sentence alone, by explicitly naming the three topics to be developed, makes it clear that the following text will have a tripartite structure. This promise is so amply fulfilled by the other topic markers that it becomes less important to give them the additional support of paragraph division. The structural importance of paragraphing is thus inversely related to the number of alternative topic-structuring signals to be found in a text.

No doubt it is unfair to compare Russell's text with a paper written by a first-term student. However, to illustrate how important the structural function of the paragraph becomes in a text that has very few alternative topic shift markers, I have chosen this student analysis of an 18th century Swedish poem. The sentences have been numbered for easy reference.

(3) Kellgren's poem "To Frederica"

. . .

1. The poem can be schematically divided into three different stages. 2. The first deals with the poet's difficult relations with Frigga's friend, from the insistence "I am your
friend! I am Frigga's friend" to "tenderness in voice and
manner . . . ." 3. After that the poet attacks "those who
praise violence," and "those who worship gold" and he feels
"silent contempt" for them. 4. To him friendship means
everything and it is not to be shaken by anything. 5. He
says "Frigga's friendship is my laurel/ My treasure and my
power." 6. His only desire is that once, when "no one
Kellgren more remembers," "they shall say in my praise"/
" 'this page remains'." 7. And at the end of this the poet
says of himself: "he was one of Frigga's friends!" 8. But
suddenly there is a dramatic change of scene and he feels
strong self-doubt. 9. Here somewhere we also reach the
poem's peripety. 10. He says: "Now, why trembles this
hand / Why beats this heart? / The Happy bonds of friendship / Are they then fastened with pain?" 11. This is shown
clearly here in the poet's use of language. 12. But no answer
is given. 13. He obviously feels great inner anxiety after
"O lovely One! *Dare* I confess? *Dare* I?". 14. Does he reach
some kind of deliverance? 15. But, to make sure, he has to
repeat this "dare I" twice. 16. And thus he ends up by
losing the friendship of Frigga's friend. 17. Frigga is the
only mythological word I could find. 18. From this point it
is mostly a little rococo cupid who speaks for him. 19. The
cupid is introduced into the poem at "There appeared a
boy . . . ." 20. The poet somewhat reluctantly defends
himself against the cupid. . . .

Several factors contribute to the confusion of text (3), but one of the most important is the fact that only two of the poem's three stages, announced in the first sentence, are clearly identified in the text. The first stage is named in sentence 2 (S2) and the second in S3 ("after that . . ."), but it is difficult to know whether the third one has been forgotten or whether the author intends for the reader to recognize it at some other point in the text. Just as in Russell's Preface, the first sentence of text (3) prepares the reader for a three-part structure. However, the following propositions in the student text fail to fulfill the reader's expectations.

There are, moreover, very few signals in this text that clearly mark when a topic shift is intended. The "dramatic change of scene" in S8 marks a change in the poet's mood, and the introduction of the cupid in S18 brings in a new character. How, for example, is the reader to interpret the function of S4? The preceding sentences have led the reader to believe it would identify the poem's third stage, but it does not do this. Indeed, it returns to the topic of Frigga's friendship that was abandoned when S3 embarked on a new topic ("After that the poet attacks . . ., etc.). At first sight, the resumption of the friendship topic in S4 makes the reader wonder whether the sentence is simply out of place. Then one discovers that this topic is developed in the next 12 sentences, at which point the reader realizes that S4–S16 are intended as a unit containing a detailed discussion of the friendship topic. If the reader is to grasp, without a lot of hard work, that S4–S16 actually form a unit with this specific function, these sentences need to be set off from the rest of the text in a paragraph of their own.

Another way of clarifying the function of S4–S12 would be if S4 had introduced an explicit topic-shift marker of the type "But to return to the friendship theme . . . ." It is precisely in the absence of such alternative structuring devices that the topic-shift marking function of the paragraph becomes a central factor in the coherent structuring of a text.

In the preceding discussion I have presented the criteria for the various types of misleading paragraph division that I found in the student sample. Two types of misleading paragraph division were identified as:

1. cases in which there is a change of topic or topic-aspect within the orthographic paragraph (i.e., when there is a need to break up a long paragraph into several shorter ones as in text [3]), and
2. cases in which there is a change of orthographic paragraph without a corresponding change of topic or topic-aspect (i.e., when there is a need to combine several short paragraphs into one, as in text [1]).

Change of Topic Within the Paragraph

Most of the paragraph division problems in the sample were found to occur at the topic-aspect level. On the whole, students had no difficulty using the paragraph to mark the major topic shifts; their uncertainty manifested itself in connection with the subtopics of their texts. For the smooth processing of text, it is important that its subtopics also be clearly demarcated. If the structure of a text is not signaled at the lower levels, there will be stretches of text whose function is difficult to determine, as illustrated in text (3). However, it is not always easy for novice students to decide which of the many subtopics merit a paragraph of their own.

As far as I have been able to judge, there are at least three criteria that determine when a subtopic is set off in a paragraph of its own in well-formed texts. The first of these involves a shift in the level of generality from the more particular to the more general. Let us see what happens when a shift of this kind is not marked by a paragraph break. The following text is taken from a first year law student's paper. Sentences are numbered for the purposes of indentification and discussion.

> (4) The role of the counsel for the defense in the preliminary investigation and in the court proceedings for the issue of a warrant
>
> . . .
>
> 1. For the most part the preliminary investigation is carried out by the police. 2. Its purpose is to determine whether a crime has been committed or not, as well as to prepare for the trial in those cases which lead to prosecution. 3. As soon as someone is suspected on good grounds of having committed a crime, he is to be informed of the suspicions against him. 4. At the same time he is to be advised of his right to a lawyer in the preparation and implementation of his defense. 5. The counsel for the defense in a case should work toward elucidating the facts from the point of view of the suspect. 6. In order to carry out this task satisfactorily, it is required that he acquaint himself thoroughly with the case, as well as with the suspect and his background.
>
> In the preliminary investigation there are at least three ways to procure this information . . . .

S5 introduces a topic shift from the role of the police in the more specific preliminary investigation to the role of the counsel for the defense in the case as a whole. The new topic is thus more general than the old one. Many writers seem to perceive a shift in the level of generality as an appropriate demarcation point in a text, and it certainly makes it easier for the reader to grasp that S5 is the beginning of not only a new but a more all-encompassing topic if this fact is marked by a paragraph break. (cf. Christensen, 1967, for a discussion of the connection between paragraph division and shifts in the level or generality).

In addition to the shift of level of generality, there are two other criteria that determine when subtopics are given paragraphs of their own: the length of the subtopic in relation to the length of the other subtopics and the introduction of a contrast into the text, such as when the subtopic radically changes the direction of the argument.

In the final paragraph of the following first-term student's essay on another 18th century poet, each of the three subtopics warrants a paragraph of its own in accordance with the previously specified three criteria.

(5) An analysis of Olof von Dalin's poem "The Pleasures of the Serene Life"

. . . .

1. I interpret the "all-powerful being of truth and light" in the first line as the first verse's "simple trust in conscience and virtue." 2. The persona extols it as a miracle, as a god. 3. It casts down all its care (i.e., anxiety) even its whole world before this trust. 4. The persona also prays for help against arrogance and hubris, and says in line 6 that it only "values the joys of conscience." 5. Up to this point I think I can make out the poem, but the last two lines make me doubt what I thought before! 6. In the last two lines, despite everything he has said before, the persona seems to be defending contemporary morals, the contemporary way of life etc., which I see as lying behind the word "pleasure." 7. Though the persona is trying to live a high-principled and virtuous life, there is place within himself for this pleasure. 8. This can perhaps be explained by the title "The Pleasures of the Serene Life." 9. It gives the impression that there are various kinds of pleasure, serene and non-serene pleasures. 10. The non-serene pleasures are those that are explained in the second verse, the habits of that time are not good. 11. The serene pleasures are those of a good conscience. 12. The poem seems to be self-ironical. 13. Although the persona condemns the customs and pleasures of its time, it (the persona) does the same thing. 14. Maybe the persona means that in the end man's bad side wins over his good. 15. I interpret the poem to be saying that even though man can choose good, in the end he chooses evil.

Given its length and complexity, the reasoning in this piece cannot be easily processed unless its various turns are clearly marked off from each other. S5 is the beginning of an interpretation that stands in contrast to the previous one ("the last two lines make me doubt what I thought before"). Moreover, the discussion in S5–S11 of these last two lines is as long as the discussion of the preceding ones. Thus it constitutes an extensively developed subtopic that could very well form a paragraph of its own. S12 then moves to another subtopic that is more general than its predecessor. At this point the discussion definitely abandons its focus on the poem's last two lines in order to interpret the poem as a whole. As is typical for conclusions, S15 then summarizes the poem's message in a general statement. Because the shift upward in the level of generality from S7 to S11 is gradual (the poem's title, for example, is introduced in S8) and because there is no explicit transition to a concluding statement, it is particularly important that the writer use a new paragraph to clearly signal at what point she or he intends the essay to be embarking on its general conclusion.

I have discussed three criteria that determine when paragraphing is used to mark the transitions between subtopics:

1. The new subtopic must always be long enough, that is, it must be developed to the point where it forms an independent topical unit. Once this criterion has been met, one of the following may also apply:
2. The new subtopic introduces a contrast of some kind.
3. The new subtopic involves a shift to a higher level of generality.

There is, however, an exception to these criteria: a change of topic within the same paragraph is perfectly acceptable if it is stated explicitly. These explicit statements may occur at the beginning of a paragraph "There are both advantages and disadvantages to having a car," or "This problem has two aspects." Another example is the naming of the three passions in the opening sentence of Russell's Preface, text (2). On the other hand, they may be scattered throughout a passage, emphasizing the fact that several subtopics are being dealt with in the same paragraph. Topic-shift signals of this kind are enumerative sentence connectors (e.g., *first, next, finally*) and explicit contrast-markers like *On the one/other hand.* Contrast may also be announced by such explicit statements as "A different aspect of this issue is . . ." or "Apart from this consideration, there is also . . ."

This exception applies on the condition that the paragraph does not extend beyond the limit of a standard typewritten page (approx. 300 words). There is no doubt that this cut-off point is arbitrary. Nonetheless, it approximates an upper limit to the information many readers find themselves able to hold in their minds at once and thus perceive as a single topic. Indeed, it is likely that such a high upper limit is applicable only to texts that are exceptionally well structured such as the adapted Russell text (text [2]).

Unjustified Change of Paragraph

Earlier I discussed the first type of misleading paragraph division, change of topic within a paragraph, and reader confusion resulting from inappropriate signaling of topic changes. The second misleading type is the opposite of the first: an unjustified change of paragraph when it functions neither as a (sub)topic-shift marker nor as a rhetorical means of highlighting a statement or set of statements. This type accounts for 72% of the total number of instances of misleading paragraph division in the sample. It is particularly frequent in the essays written by the students of business administration (90%), law (85%), and journalism (70%). These texts often comprise a series of very short paragraphs, consisting of one or two short sentences, as in the following excerpt from a paper by a third-term business student.

(6) Svecia expands West-Germany
. . .

¶1 In the early 70's Svecia was having problems with its agent. Germany was then already a large market which Svecia believed in, and they got upset when their agent didn't do his job properly and didn't sell as well as he ought.

¶2 Therefore in 1973 Svecia started their own marketing company here. Local talent was recruited.

¶3 West-Germany is now one of Svecia's largest markets and in 1980 accounted for 15% of the company's sales.

¶4 The Germans succeeded in persuading Svecia's management to allow them to develop the Swiss and Austrian markets.

¶5 Svecia had to give up their former position that Germans should not be selling in Switzerland since they felt that there were real barriers between the various countries here (compare France and Belgium).

Single-sentence paragraphs are, of course, used in well-formed texts to give particular emphasis to a point; however this kind of rhetorical consideration does not explain the paragraph structure of this text. Rather, it is explained by a general feeling among many Swedish students that the shorter the paragraphs, the more readable the text. In this respect, they are following the conventions of popular journalism, in which very short paragraphs are the norm.

In texts that are both descriptive and narrative, writers may experience a conflict between paragraphing decisions based on chronology and those based on topic shifts. This seems to be the case in the first of three paragraphs of text (6). Each paragraph marks a different stage in the story of Svecia's involvement in Germany. In these paragraphs, chronology has been given precedence over grouping by topic.

It could be argued that, even within a single academic subject, conventions vary from genre to a greater extent than our teaching practices indicate. For example, two principles seem to determine many of the paragraphing decisions in journalism and business administration texts, reflecting a convention that may be specific to these two subject areas.

These texts are characterized by a series of single-sentence paragraphs that could just as well have been combined into one paragraph. This type of paragraphing seems to be governed by two considerations: (a) In an otherwise expository text, the new paragraph marks a change of time or place; this change is often emphasized by a contrastive sentence connector (e.g., *but, however*); and (b) the new paragraph marks the onset of a summarizing conclusion drawn from facts presented in the immediately preceding paragraph(s). Because of their frequency, I have not classified instances of these two principles as unjustified changes of paragraph.

These two principles are illustrated in the second and third paragraphs respectively of the following thesis proposal from a graduate-level student in business administration.

(7) Human resources in the cooperative movement
     . . .

¶1 The thesis work I have embarked upon therefore falls within the scope of an extensive problem area.

¶2 At the end of the 30's, as a young insurance agent I was surprised to see how little use the management made of the employees' pleasure in their work, the pride in their competence and the loyalty to the company which I observed all around me.

¶3 But it was not until the middle of the 60's that I fully realised the enormous waste that must be involved in not making use of the inherent qualities of these people.

¶4 In other words, a long time passed between my perception of the phenomenon and my awareness of its consequences.

¶5 Perhaps it will take even longer to move from an awareness of the problem to its final solution.

There is no topic shift between ¶2 and ¶3. On the contrary, "the inherent qualities of these people" in ¶3 refers directly to the "pleasure . . . ., pride . . . and loyalty . . . ." enumerated in ¶2. However, the new paragraph marks the time change from the 30s to the 60s—a change that is also emphasized by the use of the contrastive *but*. In ¶4, the *in other words* makes it clear that the function of this sentence is to draw a summarizing conclusion from the time lapse described in the two preceding paragraphs.

Though the single-sentence paragraphs from journalism and business administration described here are considered acceptable by experts in these disciplines, three other kinds of paragraph breaks that appear in the student data seem to be appropriate for writing in all disciplines. Though I make no claim that these three criteria cover all cases of unjustified paragraph changes, they represent what I believe to be the most basic of the intuitions that govern the paragraphing of well-formed texts.

The first criterion involves cases in which a new paragraph, in one or two short sentences, elaborates a point made in an equally brief preceding paragraph. The last two paragraphs of text (6) are an example:

> ¶4 The Germans succeeded in persuading Svecia's management to allow them to develop the Swiss and Austrian markets.
>
> ¶5 Svecia had to give up their former position that Germans should not be selling in Switzerland since they felt that there were real barriers between the various countries here (compare France and Belgium).

The two sentences of ¶4–5 deal with exactly the same topic. In these sentences, there is not even a time shift to explain the division into two units.

The second criterion is closely related to the first. It involves cases in which a paragraph break separates a topic sentence from one or two specifying sentences. The example text is an excerpt from an article written by a first-term journalism student.

> (8) Don't play it again, Sam
>
> . . . .
>
> ¶1 To stimulate an interest in European movies, we must above all do two things.
>
> ¶2 First of all, we should expand the teaching of film.
>
> ¶3 As early as grammar school, but later in High School too, film should be a subject on the timetable just as natural as, for example, Swedish is. Especially since school kids

nowadays go to the movies a lot more than they read literature.

¶4 Secondly, a lot more should be invested in the marketing
of European movies. The way things are now, large sums
of money are spent on advertising the opening of American
movies, but almost nothing on European products. In the
subway you see big poster campaigns for films like "Nine
to Five," and "The Shining" or "Firefox." But when did we
last see an ad for a movie by Alain Resnais or Luchiano
Visconti? Their films attract full houses in their own countries, but when they come here, they are hardly put on
before they disappear again.

The two sentences of ¶3 are a specification of the statement made in
the one sentence of ¶2, that is, "We should expand the teaching of film"
functions as a topic sentence governing ¶3.

In well-formed texts, topic sentences are, of course, frequently separated from long and complex specifications. However, I would argue that
when the specification is brief, as in the two sentences of ¶3, the reader
expects it, and the general statement that it develops, to form a single
unit. In ¶4 the student has actually applied this principle despite the fact
that the specification of the initial topic sentence in ¶4 is twice as long as
that in ¶3.

The third criterion involves cases in which the new paragraph does
mark a topic shift, but the new topic is too short to establish itself as an
independent topic or topic-aspect.

The example text is from a paper by a second-term student in business
administration. The paper, which is untitled, is about Adidas (the manu-
facturer of sports equipment).

(9) The shoe market
    . . .

¶1 Adidas stocks 115 different kinds of sports shoe, 35 of which
are for special purposes and only exist for service reasons.
Examples are fencing and shooting shoes.

¶2 The shoes are imported from factories in Germany and
Taiwan.

¶3 Adidas leads the market for high-priced shoes (170 crowns
and up).

¶4 Adidas' main competitors are the Finnish Karhu, from the
point of view of quality and sales volume. For jogging the
competitor is Nike, and for football, Patrick and Puma.

¶2 marks a definite topic shift from a description of Adidas' different sports shoe models to a description of the countries from which they are imported. There is no doubt that if the place-of-import topic had been developed at greater length, it could well have formed a topic of its own.

However, a single sentence does not carry enough weight to be able to establish itself as a topic in its own right except when used for purposes of special emphasis. To use van Dijk's terms in *Text and Context* (1977a, p. 139), a single sentence does not "acquire independent topical character." Undeveloped and unsupported , ¶2 functions as an extra piece of information and would therefore do far better as an addition to ¶1, as in the following revision of the two paragraphs.

> (10) Adidas stocks 115 different kinds of sports shoe imported
> from factories in Germany and Taiwan. 35 of them are
> for special purposes and only exist for service reasons.
> Examples are fencing and shooting shoes.

This criterion has a close relation to the definition of topic offered in Wikborg (1985b). One of the conditions for the presence of a topic is that if there is a series of statements, none of which is subordinate to any of the others, each statement must be developed before it can be said to acquire independent topical character.

The crux of the matter is, of course, the nature of topic development itself. Van Dijk mentions "a series of predicates" as the hallmark of a topic (1977a, p. 139). Actually, the development required for the establishment of a topic can be even slighter than that. Let us look at the following abbreviated version of text (9):

> (11)
>   . . .
> ¶1 Adidas stocks 115 different kinds of sports shoe. 35 of them
> are for special purposes.
> ¶2 Adidas leads the market for high-priced shoes (170 crowns
> and up). Its main competitors are Karhu and Nike.

The single-predicate specification provided by the second sentence in each paragraph is sufficient to confer independent topical character on each of the two paragraphs of this text. It would appear, then, that one additional predicate is sufficient to develop a statement into a topic. A whole series of such minimally developed topics would place the text in the border regions of coherence. Still, brief as they are, each of the two paragraphs of text (11) acquire topic status in a way that is not true of ¶2 and ¶3 in text (9).

There is no neat rule to specify the point at which a statement acquires topic status and thus can stand as a paragraph of its own. What we have instead is a scale from the clearly unacceptably short paragraph up through a large set of borderline cases to a standard length.

As teachers we can, however, start at the lowest end of this scale. Unacceptably short paragraphs were the most frequent of the two types of misleading paragraph division in the sample. This fact indicates that Swedish students are uncertain as to what the basic function of the paragraph is. This means that teachers can start with the students' own unacceptable short paragraphs and have them perform paragraph combining exercises on their own and each others' texts. Such activities make them aware very soon that a series of minimal paragraphs counteracts the paragraph's basic function, which is to signal topic and topic-aspect shifts at a level higher than the single predicate.

Notes

1. The complete study, which is now in press, will appear in Swedish. However, two of its chapters have been published in English (Wikborg, 1985b, 1987). A preliminary and much shorter version of the study, dealing with the English-language essays in the sample, has also appeared in English (Wikborg, 1985a).

2. The crux of the issue is, of course, to make the concept *topic* (or *subtopic*) as precise as possible. As Brown and Yule (1933) pointed out, topic is "the most frequently used, unexplained, term in the analysis of discourse" (p. 70). They have made a useful distinction between a *sentence topic* and a *discourse topic*. Whereas a *sentence topic* consists of a noun phrase (e.g. Adidas' shoes), a *discourse topic* consists of a proposition (e.g., Adidas' shoes are the best in the world).

Making use of this valuable distinction, a topic may be defined, then, as an explicitly stated or inferred proposition that governs and is developed by the other propositions in a given text unit. (cf. van Dijk, 1977a; van Dijk, 1980; Wikborg, 1985b.)

Discussion Questions

1. Compare the Wikborg discussion with the chapter by Harris on organizing sentences. Could the insights from these two discussions be combined for purposes of classroom teaching?

2. Do you agree with Wikborg's definition of coherence break? Is there anything you might add or delete from this definition? How would you restate it for classroom teaching, if necessary?

3. Expand on the reasons Wikborg gives for coherence breaks in the first pages of her chapter. Which of the reasons are most important, in your opinion? Which would you teach first? second? third? How would you teach the avoidance of these breaks?

4. The author uses her own intuitions to make decisions about acceptable

and unacceptable paragraphs. Do you agree with her intuitions? Why or why not?

5. In some disciplines, the conceptual paragraph is quite common. This concept refers to a series of paragraphs that are indented but continue on the same discourse topic. Have you come upon these types of paragraphs? If so, in the discourse of what disciplines?

Extension Activities

1. Select published articles from a number of disciplines. Turn to the Discussion section and select four or five indented paragraphs. Are there differences among the paragraphing practices in these Discussion sections? If so, what are these differences?

2. Select ESL essays written on the same topic by students speaking a number of different languages. Discard those essays written in the classic five paragraph form. After examining the essays that remain, decide what conclusions, if any, can be drawn about the paragraphing practices of the students writing these essays.

3. Read an article about the given/new contract (e.g., Weisberg, 1984). What are the differences between the given/new concept found in this and related articles and topic/focus, discussed in the Bardovi-Harlig chapter in this volume?

4. In her 1982 article, Carrell contends that "cohesion is not coherence." Yet cohesion is discussed by many text linguists as an important element in a coherence model. What types of cohesive features appear most frequently in your students' writing? Do your students employ these features successfully?

Building Hierarchy:
Learning the Language of the Science Domain, Ages 10–13

Suzanne Jacobs

University of Hawaii

Building Hierarchy: Learning the Language of the Science Domain, Ages 10–13

It has been argued in recent years that styles of verbal reasoning are artifacts of culture. In the case of cultures in which schooling is common, the style of verbal reasoning is said to be passed from one educated generation to the next by a tradition of literacy. Not just content, but whole paradigms of thinking are passed on by means of the written word (Bruner, 1985; Bazerman, 1981). Thinking clearly, speaking logically, and arguing rationally are processes that can hardly be defined without invoking the patterns of information created by expository writers. According to Scollon and Scollon (1981), Olson (1977), and Ong (1982), the conventions of verbal reasoning valued by schools are the conventions realized in a depersonalized and logically explicit language found in what we call *expository prose*. Therefore, it makes sense for the purpose of studying how children learn verbal reasoning to investigate how they learn the language of expository writers.

This learning can be viewed as the acquisition of a new language acquired, as second languages often are, in classrooms, not in homes. Vygotsky (1962) pointed out that children are presented in classrooms with a new language when the context for its use is far removed. In contrast, the context of language use in the home is at hand and clearly evoked. To use Donaldson's phrase (1978), the meaning of ordinary language is "embedded in human sense," attached by the learner to the here and now of human activity. A concern of second language instructors is whether the language of exposition is so depersonalized that the user is unable to attach meaning to it and will find the task of using it for classroom writing a lifeless exercise. This chapter deals with students from 10 to 13 years of age, an age range when reading matter is largely narrative rather than expository, but the traditional curriculum is increasingly devoted to the expository styles of science and social studies. This is an age when teachers feel uneasy about the gap between the written language of the domain and the language of the child.

This chapter focuses on the domain of science. In an effort to define what is foreign to many students but highly valued in academic discourse, this chapter examines its hierarchical structure. By age 11 some children are able to use language to build this structure; some are not. Recall protocols collected from a sixth grade classroom in Honolulu illustrate how children vary in their abilities to construct hierarchies. On the difficult question of how such skill is acquired and how teachers can arrange speaking and writing to encourage its acquisition, an argument is made for using a bilingual approach and placing value on both first and second languages.

Hierarchical Structure and Expository Text

Academic prose has a hierarchical structure, tall rather than wide. As illustrated by the following passage and Figure 1, certain propositions logically dominate other propositions. Higher propositions organize lower ones by showing how they are related to each other. Termed *rhetorical predicates* by Grimes (1974), the higher propositions may show that the lower ones are related by such rhetorico-logical notions as cause, classification, comparison, or illustration (D'Angelo, 1979; Fahnestock, 1983; Jacobs, 1981, 1982). Not only are such predicates part of the meaning of the passage, but they also show up as surface forms in vocabulary such as *example, cause,* and *difference;* in superordinate nouns such as *goals* and *methods;* and in connective language such as *if...then* or *the more X, the more Y.* An important task for students of academic discourse is to learn which predicates to place at the highest level of the hierarchy and to learn the lexicon for this top-level information.

The student in a science class learns to promote to the top, for example, predications of cause, especially when asked *why* questions. For example:

> Why is the side of a mountain facing the coast usually wetter than the side facing inland?

An answer that cognitivists Biggs and Collis (1982) would consider well reasoned is dense with the language of cause. Information about wind, rain, and condensation is lined up in subordinate fashion under top-level predicates in their suggested response:

> The prevailing winds are from the sea, which is why you call them sea breezes. They pick up moisture from the sea and as they meet the mountain, they're forced up and get colder because it's colder the higher you get from sea level. This makes the moisture condense which forms rain on the side going up. By the time the winds cross the mountains they are dry. (p. 4)

Let us look more closely at the part of the answer beginning *they're forced up and get colder.* Roughly speaking, this part of the answer (see Figure 1) tells the reader that the Sentence **X CAUSE Y** (something forces the winds up or causes them to rise) has a causal relationship with another sentence, that this sentence causes another sentence, and this sentence causes another sentence. The diagram is a tall structure, suggesting skills on the part of the writer in deciding which pieces of information belong in the hierarchy. The writer also shows skill in the use of causal language:

- *forced* is a causative verb (some agency made something happen)
- *because* shows cause
- *it's colder the higher you get from sea level* shows cause (two comparatives, one causing the other)
- the verb *makes* is causative
- the verb *forms*, a synonym of *makes*, functions as a causative.

The final sentence is related to the others by cause implicitly (the final result of a chain of causes), but otherwise the language of cause is explicit. A good answer to the original question is dense with causal relations expressed by vocabulary and syntax that make the causal meaning emphatic; information not fitting the causal hierarchy is not presented.

Contrast the preceding passage, written by the author of this chapter, with another answer to the same question, "Why is the side of the mountain facing the ocean usually wetter than the side facing inland?" The following answer has been constructed to reflect my experience with children's science writing and Biggs and Collis' (1982) description of immature reasoning. The answer is personalized, although held together by its relevance to the topic of wetness. In this case knowledge comes from authorities such as the child's father and is not presented as hierarchically organized information. Notions of causal relations are immature.

> The side next to the ocean is always wetter. It's damp and it rains a lot. I live in Hilo, Hawaii. There are mountains behind our town. Our house is down the mountain and a wet spot comes in our yard everytime it rains. Hilo is a wet town. My dad says it's because it evaporates a lot.

Deficit explanations of this answer point to what it does not have. The closing sentence, which touches on the answer to the question, has no developing details. The opening sentence repeats known information instead of providing an answer. The causal information sought by the reader is missing.

Is the deficit significant? One has only to examine measures of assessment for reading and writing to discover that skill in hierarchy building has value beyond the science classroom. This skill can aid in attaining high

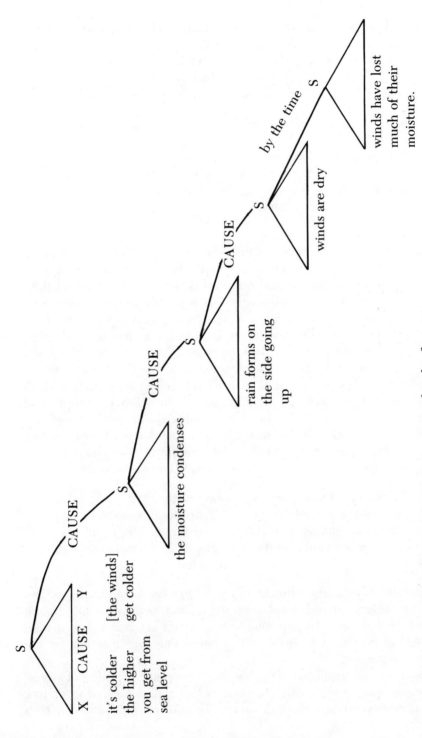

Figure 1. Hierarchy of propositions: Cause as top-level information.

test scores in reading comprehension, writing, and academic content, as indicated by several studies (e.g., Meyer, 1980; Langer, 1984).

Meyer (1980) showed that, when presented with a problem/solution text containing explicit rhetorical predicates, her skilled ninth grade subjects mentally constructed a hierarchy dominated by the proposition *X is a problem.* When given a reading test in which rhetorical predicates were absent, these skilled students' scores dropped dramatically. However, poorer readers were not as affected by the presence or absence of rhetorical predicates in readings. It can be concluded from this study that poor readers of exposition do not construct hierarchies from available evidence, presumably because they do not know what words and structures signal top-level information. In contrast to good readers, they are not in the habit of using rhetorical predicates to order propositions.

Langer (1984) found that 9- and 10-year-old writers were sharply divided in terms of their skill with top-level discourse. When judging student papers written in a comparison and contrast mode, expert readers selected as well organized those in which the knowledge was presented in hierarchical language. In these papers students employed the language of definition (*Congress is a body or a group that . . .*) or the language of comparison (*Congress is like Parliament. They both . . .*). By contrast, children judged as poor organizers and as less knowledgeable were those who phrased their knowledge of Congress in personalized terms (*I saw Congress on TV . . .*) or in a vague manner (*. . . important people*).

Teachers have reason for concern, therefore, when 10- to 13-year-olds seem content with personalized phrasing rather than the language of top-level information. Tests in school that rate academic performance are weighted positively toward the hierarchical uses of language, especially the use of top-level vocabulary, i.e., the language that indicates rhetorical predicates. The tests reflect the norms of our academic culture: They presume that the knowledge of greatest value is constructed with the use of vocabulary that indicates the top level of a discourse hierarchy.

Building Hierarchy: The Early Years

Knowledge of how the skill of creating hierarchies develops over time is sketchy. However, we do know that seven- and eight-year-olds rarely show evidence of using top-level language indicating the discourse mode (e.g., *x is a problem* or *x can be compared with y*) to organize their propositions. Their methods of organizing prose often employ the narrative, the mode with which they are most familiar. When they do choose expository structures, the evidence suggests that they choose a wide structure rather than a tall one such as that shown in Figure 1. Using a listing technique, they stay on a single plane, with no indication of the top-level structure, as shown by the following examples:

Chipmunks   by Nancy
A chipmunk lives in farms and meadows, gardens. They eat all kinds of nuts, you can feed them from your hand they have pouches in there mouths that they carry food in. Chipmunks make there homes in burrows.

(Langer, 1986)

Using a mode of coherence termed *attributive* (Huddleston, 1971), the child writer lists the attributes and routine acts of the topic of the discourse. Because the topic of the discourse is referred to in every statement, the passage overall is unified. The writer maintains tight control, which the reader senses. Researchers, however, have been apt to think that this mode of coherence is a kind of rote style, imitative of encyclopedia sources, devoid of original thinking, and responsive only to a teacher as examiner (Britton, Burgess, Martin, McLeod, & Rosen, 1975). Teachers often see such writing as an attempt to copy the language of the domain and deny the rich language resources used by children to make sense of things.

When children show even a hint of the ability to build propositional hierarchies, the reaction of researchers is more positive. Having a more complex style of language, the writer is considered a thinker. Consider, for example, the following segment. Ryan, the writer, was an exceptional achiever at the time of writing and continued to be so through grade 6 (when I last studied his progress). Notice in this passage the classification language he used to establish a class and membership relation. The topic of the segment is popping, a popular teenage style of break dancing in Honolulu.

Popping
Popping is fun. I know how too pop. And I konw three stiles of popping. One of them is the Robat and the king Cobar and the Old Man. Those were the three popping stiles I know. My brother is better than me he is going to teach me tow or five or six more stiles. One of the new ones is the tic and the wave and the whillpool and the king snake and the calaiforna snake and the number pop. My brother can do 300 stiles of popping. I don't know all the stiles that my brother knows. My brother is 16 years old. My other brother is 20 years old and my other brother is 21 years old. They all know how to do 100 each. And they are going to enter another poping contest and they are going to call there group the King Warriors.

The superordinate phrase, *styles of popping*, is the name of the class. Various other phrases maintain the superordinate to subordinate structure:

> three stiles of popping
> one of them is
> the three popping stiles I know
> tow or five or six more stiles
> one of the new ones is the tic

Ryan, unlike most children at his age, was learning how to construct reality according to the conventions valued in schools. Even his extracurricular interests are viewed in terms of categories and categorical relationships.

In the year that Ryan was in the sixth grade, I was often present in his classroom as a consultant for elementary school writing. One day the teacher, Mr. Gray, had the children working in pairs with small lizards in jars; the object was to predict the eating habits of the lizard, to observe the actual eating behavior, to draw conclusions about this behavior, and to speculate about why the lizard had chosen the particular food. Prediction, observation, and conclusion were the abstract elements of this paradigm. I was interested in the verbal responses given to me when I asked various children what they were doing and why. In most cases the responses were tied to the immediate and tangible (e.g., "I'm trying to get him into the jar") as expected, even for adults. Ryan's response, however, was tied to the paradigm: "I'm trying to find out what this lizard likes to eat." His language was precisely in line with the goals and purpose of the teacher, and these in turn were dictated by the experimental paradigm of the scientific method. Ryan had apparently internalized the paradigm to such an extent that his schoolroom hypothesis was his way of describing his present behavior.

Building Hierarchies: Grade 6

In the same setting, some children know how to build hierarchies and some do not. Within the domain of the science lesson, one year later, the children are observing crayfish instead of lizards. Will the children know enough of the paradigm—prediction, observation, conclusion—to describe what they are doing in these terms? If asked to say what they had done as they carried out their experiment, would they be able to construct an account of the experiment, organized hierarchically under the top-level vocabulary taught them by the teacher?

A simple recall protocol—a retelling—is a revealing means of finding out which children can build the verbal hierarchy and which cannot. The three children who were asked to do the retelling were part of a five-member group who began the year working together on their science observations at the same table. As measured by tests and grades, Helen was a high achiever; James generally scored below grade level; and Ben scored above average and was making accelerated progress. All three had been members of other small groups, each group collecting materials and making an aquarium. They talked informally, fed the animals, and generally tried to keep their aquarium or terrarium functioning. The teacher used the word *prediction* repeatedly throughout the curriculum. At the time of this study, the children had recently completed a journey through the formal experimental paradigm. Instead of finding out things about crayfish, their purpose had been redefined by Mr. Gray as drawing conclusions from observations, a change from thinking in list-like terms about the behaviors of animals to thinking in a hierarchical manner. The object was to direct their thinking toward hypothetico-deductive means of obtaining knowledge.

About a week prior to the recall protocol, the children had been taught the top-level language of the paradigm. Mr. Gray wrote five words on the board:

> Hypothesis (or prediction or question)
> Materials
> Procedures
> Observations
> Conclusions

He handed out an extended outline with these words as headings, then with a clear plastic mini-aquarium in front of each small group, he had the groups rehearse the language by applying it to the rock and the crayfish in front of them. *Prediction, materials*, and the other words were specifically defined for this situation.

The experiment recalled for the protocol was slightly more complicated than the rock and crayfish exercise. For this experiment, each group was provided with various kinds of food that a crayfish might find enticing. Hypotheses were invited: Which food would be chosen? Why? Like the rain and wetness question, this one demanded a patterned response, hierarchically ordered and dominated by particular top-level predicates.

The investigator phrased the request as follows: "Try to tell me what happened as you did your experiment. But tell me in a special way. Follow the format of your lab report. Like start at the top of the lab report and go on from there." The children, sitting at their own desks while other children in the room carried out a variety of verbal and nonverbal activities, were neither shy nor uncertain. They talked without prompting for several minutes.

The recall protocols showed the three children to be at different levels of learning in building hierarchies. Helen, the high achiever, told the story of the experimental procedure in exactly the form of the lab report, using all five terms of the top-level vocabulary as guideposts that helped her remember the experience and construct the reality of the experience in terms of the conventional paradigm. The top-level words and their synonyms, of whose importance she was obviously aware, are shown in boldface in the following passage to draw the reader's attention to them. In spite of all the starts, stops, and repairs in this recall, the speaker is skilled in the use of schoolroom language. Apparently part of her strategy for learning vocabulary is remembering the definitions of the top-level words. (Note her use of defining phrases for the words *hypothesis* and *conclusion*.)

> The first thing was the **hypothesis** . . . hmm. . would be to state what you think is gonna happen . . . in the experiment, how the crayfish will react. After that is the **materials**. We used elodia, a frozen guppy, a dead crayfish, and tetramin fish food. And the **procedure** was to put food, to put the food in, four different parts of the tank, the terrarium, and place the crayfish in the middle, to see what he would eat first and how he would eat it. And after that, we stuck in, we put in two crayfish about the same size to see what would happen, if they would fight or stay in one corner . . . n . . . We **observed** and we saw that the crayfish ate the other, dead crayfish first before it ate anything else and it ate by putting the food in its mouth with . . . pincers that are right near it. And . . . it had looked at all the other food before it went and ate one [unclear]. And we **found out** they were cannibals because they ate the crayfish. When we put the two crayfish in, the crayfish went into one corner then they came together and they were crawling around. The jumped across the tank. And after that we had **conclusions**, to tell what we learned. And I learned that . . . how the crayfish eats by putting the food in its mouth with the paws near it and and I learned it was a cannibal, and I thought it would eat fish, I mean the plants more, because it was used to it, but it didn't. And it probably ate the the meat because it has protein in it. . . . That's it.

If this looks like an easy exercise in simple repetition, we have only to look at the protocol of James to appreciate Helen's skill. James shows a grasp of the first part of the paradigm, the predicting and hypothesizing, but little awareness of the latter part, the observing and concluding that help the predicter confirm or disconfirm the prediction. James heard Helen recite, was eager to do well but could not create the verbal hierarchy. The following is a portion of the recall, highlighting the single occasion when he uses a top-level word.

> [We wanted to see if] they were friendly or enemies if they were gonna fight, and to see the food, if they would go for it and see if you had a **prediction** . . if you . . what . . they would go for first and if they would go for the seaweed, then the meat. After, Mr. Gray told us that it would go for the meat first because it has protein in it . . . and go for mostly the protein so it could live . . . [unclear] . . . so it could live and be more healthier and . . . it wouldn't die . . . well, it's not that old yet . . . well, that's all.

James did not remember the top-level words except for *prediction*, which he uses without meaning or connection to the other information. He did not appear to have acquired the sequence and logic of the paradigm as a whole. Although Mr. Gray is cited as the provider of his knowledge, James' own observations apparently had little to do with knowledge. His interesting conclusion, unlinked to the earlier prediction, consists of the common sense, proverbial notions that eating makes for health and that dying comes with old age. Not only did he omit the word *conclusions*, but he also omitted all reference to *finding out* anything; he did not mention that the observations *showed* anything. The first recaller used the verb *found out*, and Ben uses *shows*. Both of these children, unlike James, internalized the conventional mode of reasoning; they learned the language of the paradigm.

Ben's protocol may be the most interesting. Not nearly as high an achiever as Helen, Ben was nevertheless willing to go along. When the teacher asks him to pose his own questions and make predictions, he complies. He looks ahead, imagines, and anticipates. His protocol is successful in terms of his memory for top-level vocabulary, even if more rambling and more fragmented than Helen's protocol. In fact, memory and language work both ways: Ben remembers the top-level language, and the language in turn helps him reconstruct and organize the experience. The top-level words are successfully tied to subordinate information, with the exception of *procedures*. Investigator responses are shown in brackets.

> First we wrote . . . Mr. Gray gave us a little summary of what we were gonna do and then after that we wrote our **hypothesis**.

One of mine was . . . uh . . . cause it had 3 types of food, so
. . . elodia, let's see . . . elodia, tetra . . food . . and crayfish
and guppy. So **I predicted** that we, that he would eat the elodia
. . . cause I thought he was gonna eat it because in the . . .
that's the only thing they have in there to eat besides fish, but
the fish are too fast, so I thought that this . . . that was what
he was gonna eat. [un huh] And uh another **question** was . . .
uh . . . cannibalistic or not, going to eat its same kind. So I
thought it was going to eat something else besides the crayfish,
but it ate the crayfish tail . . . and then after that the . . .
put the crayfish in and tested all these out, wrote out, uh,
procedures and the crayfish, we were just **testing** the crayfish,
we had two baby crayfish, so we didn't have the big ones so
all they did was just, uh, walk around and play around like
little kids [chuckle from investigator] and like, so, . . . and
then after that . . . and we wrote our observations while we
were doing that. Some of them were: they just went by the
food, ate it for a little while and then they didn't . . . didn't
. . . just left to a corner, cause they . . . these two crayfish are
fighting because they just sat kind of together and they didn't
fight or anything for their territory . . . hmmm . . . so it took
him about six minutes to eat the crayfish tail, and then after
that they just started playing again and going in corners, but
they didn't eat any of the elodia, guppy, or tetramin, so that
shows they want to be . . . uh . . . their own kind cause the
meat was . . . it was like the meat had protein in it, so it was
. . . they picked . . . uh . . . the, their own kind instead of any
other fish or, so, it was cannibalistic and I thought it wasn't.

Investigator: Hmmm . . . wow . . . OK . . . The End?

And then, no, the end was . . . we . . . our **conclusions** were
to me . . . I just learned that the crayfish doesn't fight for its
territory, and the crayfish doesn't . . . and then uh they took
the . . . they didn't take the elodia . . . they took the crayfish
tail so they picked the crayfish tail over all the rest of the . . .
uh . . . foods they could've picked . . . hm . . . right.

Ben rambled and at some points sounded incoherent, but his mind was
clearly on the guideposts provided by Mr. Gray's top-level words. At the
forefront of his consciousness, as seen at the beginning of the recall, is
the *little summary of what we were gonna do*. Holding tight to the

summary was Ben's way of fixing information into a hierarchical structure, bunching up what he remembered around the given words.

Comparison of Abilities

Ben personalizes much of his information. The narrative and conversational situation calls for the pronouns *I* and *we*, but Ben uses first person to refer to *hypotheses* (*one of mine was . . .*) and personalizes the *conclusions* (*our conclusions were . . . to me . . . I just learned that . . .*). He refers to his state of mind several times, and we notice his active remembering:

> let's see . . . I thought he was gonna eat it . . . I thought that was what he was gonna eat . . . so it was cannibalistic and I thought it wasn't.

Ben uses language as if he were playing the role of scientist. This investigation is his. Within the conventional paradigm of reasoning taught him by Mr. Gray (and perhaps other sources), he has used his own personalizing style. Far from being a hindrance to his learning, the style seems to have stimulated his thinking and assisted him in using the appropriate vocabulary to build the necessary discourse.

Ben's protocol and the paragraph on wetness by a child from Hilo that appeared earlier indicate that learners need a personalized store of information to organize. However, Ben went much further than the child from Hilo, using his personalized information to organize his knowledge and develop exposition.

This point brings us to James, whose account of the experiment is impersonal. Little of what happened in the experimental situation seems to belong to him. The knowledge resulting from the experiment is represented as *What Mr. Gray said.* In a part of the protocol not printed, James refers to the people who carried out the experiment as *they*:

> [unclear] first did the crayfish experiment they were writing about what does a crayfish eat and how does it . . . and if it makes friends with other crayfish or does it attack its enemy.

Somewhat later he refers to the experimenters with the general *you*:

> When you put . . . ummm . . . tetramin, grass, and guppy and meat of the crayfish and you put 'em in four corners and you see which one they go for first.

Did James consider this someone else's project and see no role for himself in it? The excerpts just quoted are accurate in terms of what the children did and follow the paradigm, but soon after this point in the recall James lost the continuity and finished with everything he remembered with no stake in confirming or disconfirming a prediction.

Building Hierarchy: The First Language First

James's detached air throughout the interview is not only attitudinal. Being interested, playing a role, being mentally alert, and participating energetically are more than affective states. In this part of the chapter, I present arguments to suggest that such mental activity is spurred by using the first language, usually the most familiar.

In both language acquisition and verbal reasoning, researchers use the terms *embedded* and *disembedded* to apply to stages in the learning process (e.g., Donaldson, 1978; Piper, 1985). The terms point to the degree of understanding with which children use new language. Children often utter words without an awareness of what they refer to or the effect they have on other people. Words can be used with an elaborate understanding of their meaning or hardly any understanding at all. When new language is embedded, the child sees how the words are attached to the familiar elements of a known situation. A clear example is Church's (1966) discussion of the one-year-old toddler who responded to the word *bath* by a sequence of actions: running to the bathroom, taking off her clothes, turning the handle on the bathtub, and so on. At this point, the word had meaning related to a social routine in which the learner was a participant. However, meaning was not yet disembedded, that is, removed from the daily episode in which she played a major role. She could not at this point apply the word to a variety of situations or at a time outside the context of the social routine.

Donaldson (1978) makes a similar point about verbal reasoning. Reasoning accurately means thinking one's way through to logical outcomes when certain premises are given and certain conditions shift. Even very young children can do this when the world (Piper, 1985) about which they are asked to reason has been made familiar to them. They can reason accurately about the events and characters of stories, about stamps and envelopes, or cars and garages. Failed attempts to reason logically when confronted with more abstract problems, however, indicate that their reasoning skill is tied to the specifics of situations. Reasoning is embedded rather than disembedded.

In schools, disembedded reasoning is preferred to reasoning embedded in contexts and situations. An obvious point should be added, however: The value we place on disembedded language, in this case the top-level language of the science paradigm, should not blind us to the usefulness of language used for purposes of embedding. Embedding is necessary for learning the meaning of new language, and by the accounts of teachers (see, especially, Chittenden, 1982; Heath, 1983), embedding needs to be given a prominent place in the school day.

Mr. Gray's classroom aquarium project is a case in point. The project required two phases: the familiarizing phase, during which the world of the crayfish was realized by the children's construction of the aquarium environment; and the academic language phase, during which the science paradigm was introduced, explained, and used as a means of thinking and writing. The familiarizing phase took more than a week to accomplish. In Ben's case, this was time well spent: Ben embedded the academic language in the familiar world. The academic words in the protocol are attached to the crayfish and to the thinking and remembering activities in which he played the role of scientist. The paradigm had meaning as it related to self and to the moving, interesting creature in front of him.

Britton et al. (1975) argued that the embedded or familiar language, as a bridge to the disembedded, academic language, should be better exploited in the classroom than it usually is. Arguing from research in writing and learning, they claim that academic learning should be supported by the use of language structures closely approximating the child's informal idiom, especially among 10- to 13-year-olds. To refer to this idiom, Britton et al. have used the term *expressive*. In the discussion that follows, I will continue to use the term *first language* to refer to the familiar, embedded language that Ben and others used to make the scientific knowledge and discourse hierarchy their own. Five traits of this language, believed to make it a bridge to the second, are listed:

1. episodic structure
2. reference to the self
3. emphasis on feeling
4. speculative, inquiring, and metacognitive qualities ("I think . . . I wonder . . . I bet . . .")
5. talky, interpersonal quality, assuming a comfortable relationship with the audience

Such language provides a way for learners to lay claim to knowledge and make it their own.

Returning briefly to James, who seems only to have attached a part of the academic paradigm to the crayfish world, we note that his language is characterized by its episodic structure. Within this structure, he has retained a memory of the experimental situation. Unfortunately, his language shows none of the other first-language qualities that may lead children to adopt the logical paradigms taught by Mr. Gray. James' knowledge is encapsulated within an authoritarian structure (Mr. Gray is the source). He fails to personalize, to express judgments, or to speculate. James should be doing more of the recalling that the investigator asked him to do, but without the constraints of the lab report format, which seem to have inhibited his recall and failed to encourage the personalizing of information. In his case, the embedding process has hardly begun. He cannot employ the second, or disembedded, language until he has personalized the knowledge and scientific method of his classroom. For now, first language resources are what James has to work with, and he should be making more use of them.

The hypothesis offered here and illustrated by way of the children's recall protocols is that the first, personalized, embedded language is necessary in working through knowledge before the disembedded, academic language can be successfully employed. At 10 to 13 years of age, these students use the first language to varying degrees to assist them in understanding the scientific process discussed by Mr. Gray. For Helen, the need for personalized language is minimal; she has already discovered how to employ the top-level vocabulary that indicates the expository structures valued in schools. But for the other children, the personalized first language is still necessary, for it helps them to make the knowledge of schools their own.

There is space in this chapter only to suggest, hardly to demonstrate, that Britton et al.'s (1975) view of the value of the first, personalized language is correct. This view indicates that disembedded academic idiom and the hierarchical structure dictated by expository prose resemble a second language for children at the developmental level of Ben and James. While learning the vocabulary and organization of academic discourse is central to achievement in schools, it requires the use of personalized language and the familiar world as a prerequisite. Children must embed meaning before disembedding can occur.

The personalized first language is instrumental in learning in two ways. First, this language, in combination with seeing and touching the object of study, makes the topic more real and familiar to the learner; and second, the language provides a holding place for information that the learner can then attach, however loosely, to newly introduced schoolroom concepts. Both first and second languages are important. In our hurry to teach and measure the second, it is perhaps too easy to overlook the importance of the first.

Discussion Questions

1. Both Jacobs and Johns make the point that styles of reasoning are artifacts of culture. Think of examples in which you—or your stu-

dents—used reasoning inappropriate to a target culture to solve a problem or make an argument. How did members of the target culture respond?

2. Do you agree with Jacobs that a bilingual approach should be employed when encouraging language acquisition? What is your experience in using your first language when attempting to acquire a second?

3. Note that both Jacobs and McCagg discuss rhetorical predicates. Are their discussions comparable? How would you explain the value and application of this concept to students?

4. Jacobs mentions immature reasoning among children. In what ways is reasoning among children—or among those unfamiliar with a particular discourse context—immature? Give examples, if possible.

5. The author mentions that students organize their prose through narratives. Is there some method through which we can exploit narrative use in developing other types of writing (e.g., expository or persuasive prose)?

Extension Activities

1. Examine the use of protocol analysis for various purposes (e.g., learning about students' writing processes; Flower & Hayes, 1981), studying reading recalls (Connor & McCagg, 1984), examining student summaries (Johns, 1985), or analyzing students' retellings of a science experiment, as is done in this chapter. What are the strengths and weaknesses of this method? Ask students to complete 100 word recall protocols of an expository passage. What are the important features of these protocols? How do they differ?

2. Using the summary protocols collected for Extension 1, complete an analysis employing the system described by either McCagg or Bardovi-Harlig. What do these analyses indicate about the protocols and about the methods of analysis employed?

3. One skill students must learn in order to succeed in academic life is argumentation or persuasion. Read Connor and Lauer's (1985) article. How might you apply this discussion to moving students out of the narrative into argumentation? Do Connor and Lauer suggest some midpoints between persuasion and narration that might assist students?

4. Employ Jacobs' hierarchy of top-level propositions to analyze the prose of a science textbook written for children. How can this scale be employed to assist students in understanding higher order propositions?

Pointers to Superstructure in Student Writing

Lars Sigfred Evensen

University of Trondheim

Pointers to Superstructure in Student Writing

Based on the distinction between local and global coherence, this chapter first presents a justification for a taxonomy of pragmatically de-fined linguistic items signaling rhetorical superstructure in written discourse. Then, a tentative taxonomy is offered, and, third, the chapter presents results from exploratory analyses of upper secondary English as a foreign language (EFL) students' narrative writing within the Scandinavian NORDWRITE project.[1] Finally, the implications of this research are discussed for the purposes of improved instruction in EFL writing.

Justification for the Concept of Pointers to Superstructure

Many researchers have pointed out the significance of marking local logical structure in texts by connectors (i.e., conjunctions and sequential sentence adverbials, cf. Quirk, Greenbaum, Leech, & Svarlvik, 1972; Tommola, 1982). This marking has been found to be a sign of development in writing abilities throughout primary school (McCutchen & Perfetti, 1982), and connectors have been found to be more frequent and diversified in EFL texts produced by advanced students than in texts written by less advanced students (Evensen, 1985a; Rygh, 1986).

Most discourse analyses following Halliday and Hasan's (1976) pioneering study, however, have recognized a distinction between surface cohesion and underlying coherence (cf. Enkvist, 1978; Widdowson, 1978). Recent research has also pointed out a distinction between local and global coherence (see Ferrara, 1985; van Dijk, 1985a), attaching importance to a textual mesolevel (episodes or conceptual paragraphs; see Lackstrom, Selinker, & Trimble, 1973; van Dijk, 1982, 1985a). These less local views of coherence help explain how underlying coherence and surface signals of that coherence interact in the construction of meaning. Certain kinds of surface markers, or connectors, are important for the reader in the process of assigning mesolevel or global coherence to a text during processing.

The influence of the surface marking of textual superstructure[2] on assigned coherence has important implications for the teaching of writing. Many immature student writers rely too heavily on implicit coherence, with too-large demands made on the readers' inferencing capabilities (cf. Flower, 1981, on writer-based prose); others rely heavily on local

171

coherence strategies (Lesgold & Perfetti, 1978) or very simple global coherence strategies (e.g., clinging to the time dimension in narratives, cf. Lagerqvist, 1980; or using an associative strategy, cf. Scardamalia & Bereiter, 1987).

Empirical analyses have made it clear, however, that the connector category has a fuzzy textual scope in discourse (Evensen, 1985b). Whereas the lower bound seems relatively closely tied to the interclausal function (cf. Winter, 1977), the upper bound is not clearly defined. Sometimes an item like *therefore* may be used to conclude a very long argumentative section; sometimes it plays a strictly local role connecting neighboring clauses or sentences. Below are observations that point to the complex relation between local and global functions of some signaling mechanisms.

1. When connectors are used with large textual scope, they are typically used anaphorically. It seems that large cataphoric scope is blocked.[3] An item like *therefore* may signal the conclusion of a complex argumentation, but it will not normally link a large subsequent section with this complex argumentation. On the other hand, some surface signals (e.g., *In this book I am going to . . .*) have unlimited cataphoric scope within a text.

2. When connectors are used to signal mesolevel units of discourse, they may trigger shifts in verb form sequence.[4] A sequence from one of the EFL texts in the Trondheim Corpus of Applied Linguistics (Evensen, 1982) illustrates this interaction between a global signal and shift in verb form sequence. Note that the local connector *because* does not trigger such a shift. The composition, "Describe the Place Where You Live," was written by a boy in the 10th grade.

(1) . . . I *work* at a sports-shop, which *sales* lot of bicycles. *Last year hadn't* the shop enough bicycles to it's customers, *because* the bicyclefactory *couldn't produce* enough bicycles for the growing market. . . .

Every year a trim-club *arrange* a cycle-trip around Orland. . . .

3. Some surface markers seem to interact with the notion of conceptual paragraphs underlying indenting conventions in written, monologic communication (Lackstrom, Selinker, & Trimble, 1973; cf. also van Dijk, 1981, 1985a on the related mesolevel notion of "episodes"). In narratives, paragraph-initial frames (in the sense of Coulthard, 1977) such as *now* or temporal adverbials such as *two years ago* are sometimes used to signal the shift from backgrounded orientation (including setting) to foregrounded

narrative action (on the superstructure of narratives cf. Labov & Waletzky, 1967; Labov, 1972).

4. Certain anaphoric items such as *as already mentioned* (or *as pointed out above*) seem to require one or more intervening paragraph boundaries between them and their referents. Thus there are surface signals that may have an interesting theoretical role to play in delimiting a conceptual paragraph level in writing (probably also in monological speech; cf. Longacre, 1979, on morphological marking of spoken paragraphs in some languages).

5. Winter (1977) observed that certain lexical items (e.g., *cause/problem/question* and *effect/solution/answer*), often in semiformulaic but paraphrasable lexical phrases (e.g., *the reason for this . . .*), are used to signal the same kinds of logical relations in texts as do conjunctions. These items form a semiopen set functioning as a link between grammaticalized and lexical means of creating cohesion. Some of the items, furthermore, are categorized as "items of the meta-structure," thus suggesting a possible superstructural signaling function of some items that might otherwise be attributed the same local discourse function as connectors (Winter, 1977, p. 18f).

6. Analyses of student compositions at different levels of quality in Norwegian upper secondary L1 writing have pointed out that certain items with large textual scope seem to go with high quality. Zwicky (1982) claimed that lexical items such as *dette gjør at* (*this causes*) and *dette fører oss over til* (*this leads us over to*) are typically found only in texts written by cleverer students at this age level.

The six observations above motivated a search for a taxonomy of discourse markers that may better reflect the multilevel aspect of coherence in discourse and that may eventually allow for higher reliability in composition analysis. The search has so far resulted in a tentative category of pointers to superstructure (henceforth referred to as *pointers*), as distinct from connectors fulfilling the local role of making logical relations between neighboring clauses or sentences explicit (see Evensen, 1985b).

A Tentative Taxonomy of Pointers to Superstructure

Signals of superstructure are functionally derived in genuine communication. It is their use in discourse rather than their linguistic form that establishes their status. For purposes of empirical analysis, however, it is desirable to establish some formal or at least semiformal criteria. *Pointers* are a subset of a larger functional category in which the subset has some elements of conventional linguistic form. Nonetheless, the semiopen, semilexical nature emphasized by Winter (1977) has been recognized in my analyses to the extent that the items counted as pointers often contain variables (i.e., they can be paraphrased), and the pointer function of certain items can be guessed.

In skilled writing, pointers will often occur in paragraph-initial or paragraph-final positions. This observation is a very loose, analytical criterion, but may be relevant in distinguishing between connector and pointer functions of an item such as *therefore*. It may also be relevant in deciding when a frame such as *now* or a temporal adverbial such as *two years ago* functions as a pointer.

In English, syntactic position may be used to describe some pointers such as *firstly*, which occur mainly in sentence-initial position. Their pointer function is, however, often made clear by lexical cohesion in that they are later referred to by means of near synonyms (e.g., *first* or *primary*) used in collocation with lexical items like *point* or *consideration*.

Position is not a good criterion to characterize Winter's (1977) lexical items of the metastructure. *Problem* or *solution* and *cause* or *consequence* are not positionally bound, but derive their superstructure potential mainly from their lexical content. Their linguistic status as lexical items also makes them different from sentence adverbials with related lexical content, and a pointer function is more likely than a local logical function.

Some pointers are register-sensitive collocations including metatextual reference. The phrase *this article will report on* is not fixed or idiomatic in any strict sense. *Article* may be replaced by *paper* with no effect on the pointer function, and other paraphrases are easily conceivable. Nonetheless, the phrase is collocational to the extent that any skilled reader of scientific articles will recognize it as exemplifying a small, semiopen set of conventional superstructural statements. This fact is related both in linguistic form (future verb) and to probability in use— metatexual reference normally has a superstructural purpose even if this is not necessarily the case.

The previous discussion has shown that, whereas pointers in the last resort are a functionally defined category (items used as signals of textual superstructure), a subset of items may be further characterized with the aid of syntactic or lexical criteria. To make the distinction between pointers and connectors operational, however, it is necessary to make it more accessible to scrutiny by presenting a tentative classification with examples. The classification includes the following categories: metatextual deixis, internal logical structure, topic markers, temporal pointers, and connectors used as pointers.

Metatextual Deixis

Kurzon (1984, 1985) analyzed items with a metatextual, deictical function. These items often include adverbials such as *above* or *below*, or demonstrative *this* in combination with lexical items like *section, story, article,* or *book.* Kurzon also counted section and chapter headings in this category along with tables of content.

Kurzon did not elaborate on the discriminatory power of this category in relation to text quality. It seems reasonable to hypothesize, however, that metatextual deixis adds to clarity of exposition and readability and thus is a feature of high-level texts, at least in some text types.

Internal Logical Structure

Deictical elements such as *below* may easily be conflated with *firstly* and *secondly.* The latter do not, however, belong in a category of metatextual deixis; they refer more abstractly to the internal logical structure of parts of discourse. For this reason, items like the ones in the following classes should be treated as a separate category.

A first subcategory, *enumerators,* consists of items like *first, second,* and so forth or sequences such as *for one thing . . . another thing is . . . .* The items in this subcategory are taken to reflect a quantitative text strategy whereas the items in the next category are taken to reflect sequential text structure itself.

A second subcategory, *sequential relaters,* reflects traditional rhetorical principles of dividing a text into an introduction, a text body, and a conclusion. Among the items are *I want to begin by saying that, to begin with, next, my next point is, then, furthermore* (after paragraph division), *last, finally, the final point is, to conclude, in all,* and *in a word.*

Some of the items referring to the text body have relatively local scope and might be analyzed at the same level as connectors. Nonetheless, their main function within the present context seems to be that they help to bring out structural relations larger than those at the interclausal or intersentential levels. In communicative terms, these items also help to make rhetorical text structure explicit, contributing to making a text more readable. It is thus reasonable to predict that they are more frequent in texts written by more highly proficient students.

A third subcategory, *lexical dyads,* contains lexical signals of superstructure such as *cause, effect, question, answer, problem,* and *solution.* This category reflects sequential structure more indirectly than the sequential relaters, as the focus is on hierarchical logical relations between parts of discourse subsumed under the items, and not on logical sequence itself. The items in this category are paraphrasable.

Topic Markers

Several attempts to define coherence in discourse have relied on the notion of discourse topic (cf. van Dijk, 1985a). In ordinary discourse, several semiformulaic expressions are used to nominate, uphold, and change topics during discourse (cf. Källgren, 1981; Evensen, 1983).

Explicit marking of topical focus and structure may aid both coherence-assigning processes and memory retrieval when local structure fulfills reader expectations (cf. Bock, 1980). In the present taxonomy, titles and subtitles go into the first subcategory under topic markers, *topic nomination*, along with syntactic frames such as *how about?* or subtopic markers *as for* and *with respect to*.

During discourse it is sometimes preferable to change topic, and a second subcategory, *topic shifters*, may be used to signal such changes. In accounting for text strategies reflected in the use of conventional signals of topic change, it seems justified to make a distinction between signals of planned shift of topic (e.g., *to turn now to* and *but first*) and signals of on-the-spot association or digression (e.g., *before I forget, talking of, that reminds me, by the way*, and *incidentally*). The latter are common in oral, unplanned discourse (and are used in informal letters) whereas the former are more typical in less personal written discourse. When the latter are used in student compositions, they may be a sign of what Flower (1981) termed "writer-based prose" (cf. Aarek, 1984).

Temporal Pointers

As discussed in the justification for a pointer category, paragraph-initial temporal adverbials may sometimes have functions as markers of episode boundaries and triggers of shifts in verb form. For this reason certain temporals are analyzed as temporal pointers. In this category are paragraph-initial items such as *now, one day*, and *years ago*. One also finds sequences of markers signaling temporal sequence, such as *originally . . . later . . . recently* and *presently . . . soon* (cf. Werlich, 1976).

The formulaic expression *once upon a time* might be analyzed as a temporal discourse marker, but it has come to be a genre marker rather than a temporal pointer. Such genre markers seem to be relatively rare and are not here given the status of a separate category. Further studies may, however, justify establishing a separate category of genre markers that have a strong signaling effect (cf. another example below).

Connectors Used as Pointers

Earlier in this chapter it was pointed out that connectors have a multi-functional nature. Recognition of this multifunctionality may lead to a more insightful interpretation of empirical results from research on student writing. The discrimination found between poor writers and more skilled writers in connector use may be related in part to differences in textual scope. Poorer students may rely on local uses of conjunctions and sequential sentence adverbials, whereas more proficient students also exploit the more global, superstructural potential of such items.

Empirical analysis of conjunctions and sequential sentence adverbials used as pointers may rely on connector taxonomies like the one reported in Evensen (1985a) and Evensen and Rygh (in press). These taxonomies include classes of items like additive, temporal, causal, adversative, alternative, conditional, concessive, inferential, comparative, specifying, and illustrative connectors. Examples of additive connectors are *and, also, too, in addition, besides, furthermore,* and *moreover.*

An Exploratory Study

To illustrate the usefulness of the suggested taxonomy for the analysis of EFL writing, a small-scale study of two classes of pointers was carried out as part of the exploratory analyses within the NORDWRITE project (1987). This study is reported below. A later, more comprehensive study will be reported in *NORDWRITE, Reports II.*

Data

The data for the present analyses consisted of nine narratives written by Swedish learners of EFL. The corpus is a nonrandom sample of data collected by NORDWRITE researcher Moira Linnarud for her doctoral thesis (see Linnarud, 1986, p. 40). The learners were all in the 11th grade (upper secondary school) and were near the end of the 9th year of EFL study at the time of writing.

A picture story of six episodes adapted from Bergh and Ljungmark (1973) was given as the stimulus for a writing session of 40 minutes (see Figure 1). The story line is simple. A man, probably bald, falls in love with a girl who has beautiful long hair. A relationship develops and they marry. In the last picture, however, the man ends up with her hair in his soup.

The compositions were typed and rated holistically by three sets of evaluators. Average marks within a 5-point scale were computed for each category of evaluators, and on this basis the texts were divided into three quality groups—a HI group, a MID group, and a LO group. Within each of these groups, three compositions were selected for the present study.

Figure 1. A picture story given as the stimulus for a writing session. From *Mots et Images* by L. Birgh and E. Lyungmark, 1973, Stockholm: Esselle.

Metatextual Deixis in Student Compositions

The use of metatextual deixis (e.g., *above* and *below*, *this story*) is very rare in narratives produced by learners at this level. Only four occurrences appeared in this material. Their distribution, however, reveals a striking pattern. Metatextual deixis does not occur at all in texts in the LO group. In the MID group there is one inappropriate case—a text ending with the phrase *The End*.

This item might be included in a short list of unambiguous genre markers (here: film). It sometimes occurs in student compositions but should normally not be analyzed as an error of genre. From a process-oriented point of view it is more appropriately read as a sign of student satisfaction with having completed another boring writing assignment (the exclamation mark, in fact, sometimes penetrating the paper on which the text is written). In this particular case, however, the picture-based stimulus might have influenced the student writer.

Appropriate use of metatextual deixis may be exemplified by the opening sentence of the text that was given the best average mark:

(2) This is the story about Mr. Frank Coopersmith and a girl with long, blond hair.

The few cases of appropriate metatextual deixis that occur in the material are all in the HI group. At the upper secondary level of student development, then, metatextual deixis may be an indicator of multilevel, global discourse strategies.

Temporal Pointers

In contrast to metatextual deixis, temporal pointers (i.e., paragraph initial temporal adverbials) are quite frequent throughout the material, making it necessary to standardize the results to adjust for differences in text length. In the present analysis this was done with a second aim in mind—finding out to what extent students rely on temporal marking as a discourse strategy in narrative writing. For this reason, the number of temporal pointers was divided by the number of locally used connectors and pointers. The results were 0.17, 0.31, and 0.21 for the LO, MID, and HI groups, respectively.

Evidently there is a weak tendency toward more frequent use of temporal pointers with increase in skill. However, this tendency is far from linear. Use of temporal pointers is characteristic particularly of the MID group, suggesting a possible difference in productive strategies; the MID group may cling to the chronological dimension as a major structuring principle in their narratives whereas members of the HI group have other coherence strategies at their disposal.

The LO group has the lowest score, which may indicate that poorer student writers may not yet have acquired the full resources of a temporal strategy in narrative production. They may rely on more unmarked means for creating text productivity, like the local, multifunctional additive strategy that is so common in child language. This strategy does not introduce and relate clear structures of larger episodes or text modules (cf. Scinto, 1984), but adds proposition to proposition in a sequential, semiassociative way (cf. knowledge-telling strategy, Scardamalia & Bereiter, 1987).

Further analyses of connector use seem to be consistent with this assumption. Texts in the LO group are shorter than texts in the MID or HI groups. Impressionistic analyses also seem to indicate that the connector *and* is very common in the LO group and that temporal adverbials are used less often in this group than in the other groups.

The analysis of temporal pointers has revealed what may be a qualitative difference in writing strategies between subjects in the MID and HI groups. Writers in the MID group may signal an episode that is never realized as more than a single sentence. Mesolevel structures are sometimes announced, but not elaborated, as in this excerpt from the poorest text in the MID group:

> (3) *When a year had passed* Colin finally asked her to marry him. Dolores gave him imiadetly the answer:yes. Both looked forward to the wedding, and they spend the time together waiting.
>
> *At last* the day came when the wedding was supposed to be.
>
> *Some time after the wedding* Colin had changed his mind about long hair . . . .

The text seems to illustrate a problem some student writers have in adhering to global and local coherence simultaneously. In this text global coherence seems to have been achieved at the expense of local coherence, illustrating an unsuccessful attempt at creating the multilevel, hierarchical coherence typically found in skilled writing.

These exploratory results expand on several remarks I made in the introduction on the problems with the connector category. To reanalyze conflicting results, it seems necessary both to take both the connector versus pointer distinction into account and to bring the mesolevel of conceptual paragraph or episode into the analysis.

Concluding Remarks

Exploratory analyses within the NORDWRITE project have shown that there are some relatively new linguistic parameters that may help us understand the development of writing quality in somewhat advanced EFL learners.

The differential characteristics of particular skill levels observed in this study may have implications for language teaching, even if they will have to be tested by further research. The different productive strategies assumed in the chapter seem to imply that a local, multifunctional additive strategy may be very helpful to students only at introductory or low intermediate levels (cf. Lindell, Lundquist, Martinsson, Nordland, & Petterson, 1978, on text productivity as an objective at lower levels). At higher levels its potential is too limited. Here, a temporal strategy may be one useful transition to more varied global strategies.

The results of the study discussed in this chapter need to be interpreted carefully in light of the small sample size. Future research needs to focus on the complete taxonomy of pointers within a larger sample of student essays. In fact, such research is a major aspect of the continuing research in the second stage of the NORDWRITE project.

However, it already seems clear that pointers do play a role in the writing of relatively advanced EFL learners. At these relatively high levels there may be some profit to be gained from focusing on pointers in teaching (cf. Carrell, 1987, for a semidirect approach, using the rhetorical structures proposed by Meyer, 1975). It may be even more important to select stimulating reading materials in which pointers occur and to give students the opportunity (a) to rewrite preliminary drafts in text production, (b) to help each other during text production, (c) to write for different audiences in different text types, and (d) to experiment with new discourse features without fear of premature negative evaluation (cf. indirect teaching programs like the ones being developed within the American *National Writing Project*; see Ingram, 1985; Olson, 1986).

Author's Note

The research for this chapter was funded by a grant from the Norwegian Research Council for Science and the Humanities (NAVF). I want to thank Thorstein Fretheim for several rewarding discussions. I am also grateful to Moira Linnarud and the editors of this volume for helpful comments on an earlier version of the manuscript.

Notes

[1]In 1986 a joint Nordic research project on EFL writing in schools was initiated with the financial support of NOS-H, the joint committee of the Nordic research councils

for the humanities. The focus of the three-year NORDWRITE project (see Evensen, 1986a) is on discourse-level performance analyses of EFL compositions written by students in four Nordic countries (Finland, Sweden, Denmark, and Norway). In the main stage of the project, national samples of about 200 texts from each of the four countries are being analyzed in an attempt to illuminate aspects of discourse competence acquired at intermediate and advanced levels of education.

[2]Superstructure is viewed here as the macrolevel (sequential or hierarchical) result of text strategies employed for some rhetorical purpose given a definite sender and a definite receiver-audience.

[3]This fact was first pointed out to me by Thorstein Fretheim, University of Trondheim.

[4]This pattern was first observed by Irmgard Lintermann-Rygh.

Discussion Questions

1. Evensen speaks of the importance of distinguishing between local and global coherence of texts. What constitutes local coherence, according to him? What constitutes global coherence? Which is more important, in your opinion, for the successful understanding of written texts? Or are they of equal importance? Compare your view with the notions of some of the authors in this volume, for example, Bardovi-Harlig, Harris, and Swales. If you had to choose to teach one coherence, that is, global or local, before the other to your students, which would you choose? Are there ways to teach them both simultaneously?

2. Evensen classifies superstructure pointers (i.e., pointers, signals of global coherence) into five types: metatextual deixis, internal logical structure, topic markers, temporal pointers, and connectors used as pointers. Are these meaningful categories in your opinion? Do they cover most important superstructure relations? How universal do you think these categories are? In other words, do all languages use signals similar to Evensen's superstructure pointers?

3. Evensen found that metatextual deixis does not occur at all in the essays written by the low group in his small study. Connor and McCagg (1984) also found that ESL learners in their reading recall summaries did not provide what Connor and McCagg called the "pragmaic condition" of the task; in their study it meant saying things like "the article I just read" or "the article." Speculate on reasons for Evensen's finding. Discuss the importance of the strategy (metatextual deixis or pragmatic condition) for enhancing reading comprehension and suggest ways to teach it to students for writing a variety of texts.

4. Compare Evensen's superstructure pointer taxonomy to Halliday and Hasan's (1976) taxonomy of cohesion. There is overlap between Halliday and Hasan's taxonomy and Evensen's. What, if any, is the differ-

ence between the premises underlying these taxonomies? What is Evensen's contribution to the field?

Extension Activities

1. Ask five students or friends to write an essay based on the stimulus in Evensen's Figure 1. Analyze the writings using Evensen's taxonomy and compare your results with his. What did you find? In your sample, were all types of superstructure pointers found? Was the use of super-structure pointers related to writing quality? Is the task conducive for producing all types of superstructure pointers or does it favor some? If so, which does it favor? Would you use this type of task for teaching purposes? If so, how would you do so and at what level?

2. Take the same stimulus and ask five different students or friends to tell the story it depicts. Analyze their accounts and compare the results with the written samples gathered earlier. Do you find any differences in the use of superstructure pointers between the two samples? Discuss reasons for your findings. Based on your findings, do you believe that the taxonomy is useful for spoken language analysis? Is it useful for teaching oral language skills to students?

3. Compare Evensen's *metatextual deixis* and Swales' *introduction of present research*. Is Swales' term a subcategory of Evensen's that is suitable for a particular genre? Use Evensen's term in the specific sense suggested by Swales and analyze this particular superstructure pointer in the chapters in this volume. Does each chapter include it? Is there any pattern in the location?

4. Evensen states that "it seems clear that pointers do have a role to play in the writing of relatively advanced EFL learners" and recommends teaching them at "these relatively high levels." Do you agree that pointers should be taught at higher levels only? Are there pointers that would be useful for writers of all levels? Read Carrell (1987), mentioned by Evensen, for the teaching of top-level rhetorical struc-ture and signaling the text's organizational structure. Consider the timing of this instruction in the writing process that considers the recursive nature of writing and encourages multiple drafts. At what stage in the writing process do these top-level structures appear? Could they serve as heuristics to help the writer generate and organize ideas?

IV. Pedagogical Approaches

Nonnative Speaker Graduate Engineering Students and Their Introductions: Global Coherence and Local Management

John Swales

The University of Michigan

Nonnative Speaker Graduate Engineering Students and Their Introductions: Global Coherence and Local Management

Coherence has proved notoriously difficult to pin down, both in the sense of where it resides and what it consists of (Johns, 1986c). Even so, the prevailing view would seem to be that *coherence* is a property that a reader ascribes to a text (in some varying degree) while *cohesion* is a property that a text possesses (in some varying degree) (Halliday & Hasan, 1976). A definition of coherence along these lines is that of Williams (1985):

> In terms of discourse pragmatics, coherence is a property ascribed to a discourse when the decoder judges that it success-fully executes the encoder's intentions and that it meets the decoder's expectations of what the discourse should be, given his perception of the context, goals and intentions underlying the language event. (p. 474)

Williams goes on to observe that the reader-decoder has to rely heavily on the text itself, whereas the listener-decoder, especially in conversation, has opportunities to negotiate meaning with the encoder. The most obviously missing element in this definition is any indication of how "the decoder's expectations of what the discourse should be" arise; indeed Williams, if only by default, seems to imply that expectations will (or will not) be instantiated simply on the basis of the particular text being read. Such a zero-sum account would seem implausible, even though the underlying concept of coherence as a matching of expectations is an attractive one. I take the view here that discoursal expectations are socioculturally established and are of two main types: global and local. Global expectations relate to such matters as purpose, content, and schemata, and are thus concerned with what the reader expects to find in a text *in grosso modo*.

Discoursal Expectations

Purposive expectations find expression in the reader's anticipation of the writer's underlying purpose. Readers use their purposive expectations to distinguish parody from "the real thing," anecdote from parable, and in cases in which there may be doubt, fiction from nonfiction. Expectations with regard to content are self-evident.

Schematic expectations derive from two types of schemata: reader-based content schemata that derive from previous experience of the world and reader-based formal schemata that derive from previous experience of texts (Carrell, 1983). Although there is much that is uncertain here with regard to the relationship between the two types of schema and to the mental representation of schemata, there is little doubt that schematic expectations are a key element in rapid and efficient textual processing (Bazerman, 1985).

Local expectations relate to the on-line, chunk-by-chunk processing of the text by the reader. There may be, for example, expectations about topic maintenance (Connor & Farmer, 1985), the "given-new" contract (Clark & Haviland, 1977), the fulfillment of predictive structures and the use of metadiscoursal elements (Tadros, 1985; Johns, 1986c), and the employment of the principle of local interpretation (Brown & Yule, 1983). There are also expectations at the local level about the selection of language; in particular, expectations about the avoidance of "off-register" items (Halliday, 1978; Gregory, 1985). As Lemke (1985) observed, the register system of a speech community systematically deploys certain of the resources of its language for particular purposes in specific situational contexts and certain other resources for other purposes in other contexts. Thus readers expect contracted modals in personal letters but not in formal papers; readers expect the proportion of lexical items of Graeco–Latin origin to increase as the educational maturity of the audience is presumed to increase and the abstractness of the topic increases (Corson, 1982).

Often when readers process a text that perfectly fulfills all their expectations, they find themselves recognizing a genre that is familiar to them. This close match provides a powerful boost to coherence for the reader and a powerful boost to organization for the writer. It does so because a genre "is a rhetorical means for mediating private intentions and social exigence; it motivates by connecting the private with the public, the singular with the recurrent" (Miller, 1984, p. 163).

In this chapter, I discuss a sample of nonnative speaker (NNS) student introductions to research papers. The research paper is a relatively well-known genre and the characteristics of its introductory section have been relatively well studied (see Swales, 1987b, for a review). I suggest that a taught appreciation of the elements that make a research paper introduction coherent to genre-experienced readers has, in alliance with students' expertise in their individual content areas, created a set of texts to which we can ascribe a sufficient amount of global coherence to compensate for processing difficulties at the local level.

Educational Setting

In Fall 1986 I taught (with three assistants) a 20-hour class on Writing for Academic Purposes to nonnative speakers, the great majority of whom had recently enrolled in degree programs at the University of Michigan. I had taught a similar class in Fall 1985, but in 1986 enrollment doubled from 32 to 65 as a result of a more effective system of English reevaluation. In 1986, 80% of the class were graduate students.

The required material for the class consisted of a 70-page course pack comprising four units and a number of appendices dealing with the English article system, the forms of references, and so on. The opening unit presented and illustrated a five-component approach to effective writing (audience, organization, style, flow, and accuracy). The next unit dealt with a number of paragraph types such as general-specific, problem-solution, and data-comment. The third unit dealt with types of academic text, but there was time to cover only "Introductions to Research Papers" (the topic of this chapter). The fourth unit was titled "Perspectives on Research Writing," and its use is discussed in Swales (1987b).

The basic pattern of the weekly 90-minute class was the first half in plenary format (orchestrated by myself) and the second half divided into four groups based principally on disciplinary area. I took the largest of these groups, 25 graduate engineers: 18 from the Far East, 3 from the Middle East, and 2 each from the Subcontinent and Latin America. During the semester the students were asked to submit 12 pieces of writing (mostly quite short). About half of these were set pieces and about half were free choice. For example, for the data-comment component, all the students were asked to write a commentary on a set of nonverbal data provided in the course pack and additionally a commentary on a set of nonverbal data they had chosen themselves.

The aims, which underlay the somewhat variable methodology, were essentially five:

1. The class was to be encouraged to believe that academic and research writing is typically a recursive process.
2. The class was to be shown that academic-research writing is not simple or straightforward reportage but, like most other writing, ultimately persuasive, despite surface indications to the contrary.
3. The class was to be helped to see what mature academic writing consists of and helped to understand how that maturity is achieved.
4. The class was to be involved in rhetorical analysis, both of given texts and of their own and their peers' writing.

5. The class was to be offered "caricatures" of text types, and, as far as possible, these models were to reflect what we know of texts·in the real world.

The course as currently conceived thus utilizes both process and product elements (Horowitz, 1986) in its attempt to help these apprentice writers in English match the perceivable expectations of their readers.

Introduction to Research Papers

The one and a half sessions on introductions to research papers took place about two-thirds of the way through the course. The first session opened with a small group task requiring the reassembly of an introduction to an article. As is my usual experience, this task was not well done because the students were operating with an incorrect schema (i.e., they wanted to place the statement introducing the authors' present research too early; Swales, 1984). This activity was followed by an outline of a Create a Research Space for Yourself model:

Step 1: What do I need to do to establish my research area at the outset? (field establishment)

Step 2: How can I organize my description of previous research? (description of previous research)

Step 3: How can I show that there is a *space* or *hole* in the previous research? (gap indication)

Step 4: How do I make it clear that I am going to try and *fill* that space or hole? (introduction of present research).

This outline was followed by an analysis of a series of texts that either fitted or did not fit the model; some of the texts used were those submitted by the 1985 class. Other activities in the sessions involved work on typical ways of establishing fields; on syntactic patterns and tense choice in the description of previous research (including introspection on individual and disciplinary preferences); on adversative connectors at the outset of Step 3, the use of negative quantifiers such as *little* and verbs of negative import such as *restrict* and *neglect*; on typical realizations of Step 4; and on close exercises and searching for "interesting" introductions out of class.

In the following week students were asked to submit introductions to their own research. Twenty of the engineering students did so on time and overachieved (at least in the sense that they averaged about 80% on this assignment as opposed to a general average of 60–70% on other writing tasks). Of the 20 timely submissions, one was a revised version of a qualifying research paper that already had been discussed with the student; one was sufficiently at odds with the student's normal writing style to raise a suspicion of plagiarism; and one was by a student who had failed to understand the assignment, offering an essay introduction instead. These three papers have been excluded from the following analysis. The remaining 17 drafts are, as far as I can ascertain, examples of fresh writing.

Analysis of Global Coherence

The 17 introductions were quite short; they varied between 120 and 300 words with an average length of about 175 words. The average number of sentences was 8.3, and the average sentence length was 21 words (a little under the norms for published scientific prose; Barber, 1962; Huddleston, 1971). The following texts are exactly as they were submitted except that sentence numbers have been added for ease of reference. Because a majority of the introductions were written on a word processor, a number of the spelling mistakes are "typos."

Eleven of the 17 introductions follow the model in terms of the four-step sequence. Three had no Step 2 (describing previous research) and one had no gap (Step 3), but, as we shall see, these omissions may be well motivated. The remaining two are, for a number of reasons, problematic and will be discussed in some detail.

Introduction J can serve as a clear example of explicit global structure, particularly as its content is more generally accessible than many of the others.

Like most of the introductions in the sample, J is not an ineffective piece of writing. Although there are occasional off-register elements such as *made a research about* in S3, the overall text moves smoothly and authoritatively toward the expression of the research topic in the closing sentence. For all its merit as a piece of writing by a Japanese with no prior English-medium academic experience and only 2 months into a master's program, the introduction nonetheless remains somewhat flat in the second half. It fails (or so it seems to me) to emphasize sufficiently the gap between surmise and substantiated opinion, between a qualitative present and an anticipated quantitative future. Consider these three alternative versions of the last three sentences (modifications in italics).

S4a. However, the low maximum speed limit *presumably* imposes a *certain amount* of burden on drivers and social economy.

S5a. *In particular*, the additional traveling time caused by

Introduction J

I	(1) The 55 mph National Maximum Speed Limit on highways was decided and became effective after the historic Arab oil embargo in 1974. (2) Though it was originally a temporary measure to conserve energy the government decided to make it permanent because of its great contribution to highway safety.
II	(3) In 1984, after a decade had passed, the Transportation Research Board made a research about the 55 mph speed limit, and recommended that the federal government continue the low speed limitation because of its safety benefit.
III	(4) However, the low maximum speed limit imposes some burdens on drivers and social economy. (5) The additional travelling time caused by the lower speed limit increases costs of freight transportation, especially in rural states where average length of trips is longer.
IV	(6) The purpose of this research is to find out the gross national economic defects of the 55 mph National maximum Speed Limit on highways.

> the lower speed limit *can be expected* to increase costs
> of . . . .
>
> S6a.   The purpose of this research is to *arrive at a preliminary*
> *estimate* of the . . . .

The increasing "modulation" (Latour & Woolgar, 1979) highlights more effectively both the justification of the research and its precise focus.

If the author of J is somewhat above the class average in command of the English language per se, the author of Q, a Mexican, is probably the weakest member of the sample when it comes to grammar, lexical choice, and sentence construction.

The surface-level problems in this text are apparent enough: problems in agreement, aspect, and the article system. Apart from a somewhat reader-inconsiderate opening (resistance to what? loads?) and confusion about the scope and applicability of the present research compounded by the long S5, the reader is still able to process this text without undue difficulty. For instance, global expectations allow the reader to interpret the "Spanglish" formulations at the beginnings of S4 and S5:

> S4.   However, it is far the day . . .
> S5.   The report pretends to give . . .

Introduction Q

I	(1) Nowadays the strengthening of building is a economical option for those buildings that have lost the original resistance or because the new codes require more resistance in the existing buildings. (2) Because the strengthening of a building requires more ac-knowledge than the design of a new one, in the last 20 years a few Universities around the world and, mainly in the United States and Japan, have spend a lot of time and money trying to know deeply the different procedures of strengthening.
II	(3) Every year new research projects are opened, their results are published in the most recent journals, and this contributions are applied to real buildings.
III	(4) However, it is far the day when the optimum strengthening process be found.
IV	(5) The report pretends to give information about scale models tested in the laboratory, which were strengthened with the tradi-tional techniques, but trying to keep the original characteristics of the construction in Mexico city, which corresponds to the characteristics of the middle east of the United States. Therefore, this report contribute specifically to that zones and its results may be extrapolated to other zones.

Even so, a problem with the scale models remains:

S5a(?)   These models replicate the construction characteris-
         tics of older buildings in Mexico City.

The final sentence looks very tired—excessively compressed and possibly contradictory. Is *extrapolation* that simple? Is that *may* capacity or possi-bility? When I was reviewing the paper with Q, we came up with the following revision, but I believe we both suspected that we had not fully understood each other:

S6a(?)   Therefore, this report attempts to make a contribution
         to Civil Engineering techniques in those geographical
         areas; it is possible that its findings may be applicable
         to other regions.

These problems aside, introduction Q would seem to be an interesting instance of a text that maintains global coherence despite severe difficul-ties in managing local meaning and retaining stylistic appropriateness.

I now turn to the two texts that present processing problems, especially on first reading. The first is text A:

(a) A large difference between the ionization coefficients for electrons and holes is essential requirement for low noise avlanche photodiode. Silicon has an ionization rate ration K >20 and there is an ideal AOD at wavelengths < 1.06 um. (2) However, the conventional silicon detector has too low internal quantum efficiency and therefore the development of new detectors with both high ionization rate ratio and high internal quantum efficiency is greatly needed.

(3) Three typies of detector systems for this requirements have been considered. (4) (1) III-V compound semiconductor alloy heterojuction avalanche detectors (2) III-V compound semiconductor schottky barrier avalnche detectors (3) dynamic cross-field photomultipliers. (5) Unfortunately, most III-v compound semiconductors have not ionization rate ratio high enough to be used for low noise avlanche photodiode. (6) It is, therefore, of great interest to explore the possibility of artificially increasing the ionization rate ratio by using new device structures.

(7) Then, some of optical properties of the superlattice APD are described in detail.

As the reader processes introduction A, two possible schematic interpretations may come to mind, as shown in the following diagram:

		I (steps)	II (steps)
Para 1	S1	1	1
	S2	1	1
Para 2	S3	4	2
	S4	4	2
	S5	3	3
	S6	3	4
Para 3	S7	4	4

The diagram shows that the first paragraph is unequivocal; indeed, the field establishment is competently done via embedding rhetorical evaluations within the highly technical substate:

S1   . . . a large difference is *essential requirement*
S2   . . . the *conventional* . . . has *too low* . . . therefore the development . . . is *greatly needed.*

The first problem arises with identifying an underlying agent in S3:

> S3a.   Three types of detector systems . . . have been consid-
>   ered by previous investigators. (Step 2)
> S3b.   Three types of detector systems . . . have been consid-
>   ered by me in this study. (Step 4)

The ambiguity is not fully resolved by S4 because the following sentence is a straightforward exemplification of S3, even though the wide scope of the survey now leads the reader to prefer the II-type interpretation. This interpretation would seem to be confirmed by a clear Step 3 gap indication in S5. However, no sooner is the reader's sense of the passage retrospectively resolved in S5 than the reader encounters another problem with S6. Is the sixth sentence a further elaboration of the gap, or is it some oblique announcement of the present research topic (Step 4)? By the end of S7 the reader can again see that S6 must be a Step 4 (despite the paragraph break) because the phrase *are described in detail* looks more like an elaboration than an initial statement.

Thus it would seem that readers of introduction A experience difficulties in real-time processing—difficulties that are only resolvable by retrospective analysis. However, introduction A is likely to prove coherent if it is subjected to the following two local revisions:

> S3a.   Three types of detector systems . . . have been consid-
>   ered in the *literature*.
> S6a.   (New paragraph) This paper therefore explores the in-
>   teresting possibility of . . .

Introduction O is the other text with an uncertain macrostructure. O is one of the longer introductions (240 words) and is divided into two paragraphs. The first six-sentence paragraph is a field establishment of the state of current knowledge type (Swales, 1981) and develops the following topic sentence:

> S1: The structure of a horizontally homogeneous and steady
>   turbulent boundary layer is fairly well understood.

Here is the second paragraph:

> (7) It still seems impossible to develop a theory describing
> statistical effects due to these pertubations. (8) We have inves-
> tigated the structure of the boundary layer above waves by
> direct mathematical modelling, which allows the simulation
> of the interaction between an arbitrary wave surface and a
> developed turbulence flow. (9) This approach has been formu-

lated in general terms simultaneously by Chalikov (1976) and Taylor (1976) and somewhat later, but independently, by Simonov (1979). (10) These papers to be enumerated later have demonstrated that the method allowing for the simulation of individual motions in the boundary layer is quite effective in investigation of many problems of wind-wave interaction. (11) The main advantage of the suggested approach is the possibility of using initial nonlinear equations of motion, which allow for the effects of turbulence almost completely.

This paragraph illustrates the common phenomenon of a Step 2 being embedded in another step (Bazerman, 1985; Crookes, 1986; Dudley-Evans, 1986).

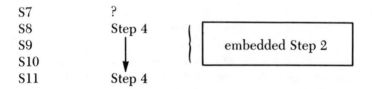

S7	?	
S8	Step 4	
S9		embedded Step 2
S10		
S11	Step 4	

The problematic feature of the paragraph is its opening sentence; as it stands, it seems to produce the effect of the author "shooting himself in the foot." Even when readers readily concur with the observation about "the many problems of wind-wave interaction" in sentence 10, they still expect that the author of O will create a research space for himself in S7 rather than immediately concede the field of battle. What O needs is some statement of the form:

> S7a. Although a complete statistical theory accounting for these perturbatory effects is still some way off, progress can be made in solving certain aspects of the problem.

The four remaining introductions in the sample can be more briefly discussed. Three of them lack mention of previous research. In two cases the students introduce research topics dealing with the development of computer software. According to Cooper (1985), published technical reports in this area tend not to refer to previous research papers but rather to deal with the evolution of hardware and software products; in her phrase, they are "thing-oriented." In the third case, the author makes it clear that there is little research available.

> Text B (S4)   Unfortunately, construction productivity data for nation-wide use is not available. The Bureau of

> Labor Statistics productivity data for construc-
> tion, unlike the data for other industries is con-
> sidered unreliable by the Bureau unrelible(?)
> and is not published.

The 17th introduction (P) does not offer a gap as much as build on previous research (a pattern that is common in the hard sciences; Swales, 1981; Crookes, 1986). The author of P offers the following (italics mine).

> S13. It is highly absorbing with an absorption constant greater than 10^5 cm $^{-1}$ has been considered as an *attractive candidate* for use as the absorbing layer in solar cell[6].

The phrase *an attractive candidate* is a sufficiently marked authorial comment (Adams Smith, 1984) for the reader to have clear expectations of how the research topic is going to be developed. After all, it is unlikely that the reader would encounter at S14 a sentence such as the following:

> S14a. However, this paper will examine another possibility.

Local Management

It is likely that the comparatively good quality of the writing sample is due to a number of factors:

1. The writers knew the subjects about which they were writing.
2. They had considerable intellectual interest in their topics.
3. They apparently recognized the face validity of the pre-sented model as a means of leading the readership up to their particular research topics.
4. They were acquiring a formal schema for processing re-search introductions.

As a consequence of these favorable circumstances, they generally managed to match expectations with the reader with regard to both organization and level of technical sophistication. In this section I examine three areas of local management (tactics rather than strategy): (a) performance in establishing a field, (b) performance in creating a space, and (c) performance in introducing present research.

Field Establishment

A number of field-establishment tactics were discussed and illustrated in class. They included (a) demonstrating that the research area was important, interesting, or problematic; (b) demonstrating that research interest in the field was strong and continuing; or (c) outlining the current state of knowledge. Interestingly, the students responded to these hints highly selectively. Although (a) proved quite popular, none chose (b) and only one (the author of introduction O) selected (c). Several went their own independent way.

Four students opened by indicating a problem of need (italics mine).

1. A *large difference* between the ionization coefficients for electrons and holes is *essential requirement* for low noise avlanche photodiodes. (text A)
2. *Most* robots have their own positioning and orientation *errors*. (C)
3. The effect of air pollution from the stacks of industrial plants has become *a serious problem* nowadays. (G)
4. The *decline* of productivity in the construction industry during the past decade *has led to the recognition* that *better ways* of measuring construction productivity are *needed*. (B)

In my judgment, all of these four openings are effective field establishments, and the last, in nonnative speaker terms, is superb.

Six graduate students opened by placing the research area within some historical or developmental setting. Two have already been illustrated in the larger context (J and Q); the other four are as follows (italics mine):

1. The aid of computers to the architect in the design process that is known as Computer-aided Architectural Design (CAAD) is *a very rapid growing field*. (D)
2. *Almost a decade has passed since* the fifth generation of computer was talked about. (H)
3. Artificial intelligence is a *new breath* of computer science related with developing intelligent computer systems . . . . (K)
4. The digital control system, as proposed by TRW in 1955, *has proved to be versatile* in control industry. (N)

On the whole, this group of field establishments is less successful than the problem-need group. Example 1 has some linguistic weakness, example 2 opens well but limps home; while example 3 shows the difficulty of hitting the right conceptual level when opening with a generalized definitional statement that the reader associates more with a textbook than with a research paper.

Third, there is a group of four statements of facts, two of which are flat generalizations:

1. Radar homing missiles use a space stabilized seeker antenna in order to get and follow the target. (E)
2. In the steel-making process the top and bottom blowing processes imply different oxygen transfer mechanisms to metal and slag. (F)

The other two open with fronted prepositional phrases that signal to the reader the challenge to come (italics mine):

3. *In our common sense*, organic materials fall under the category of electric insulator, (P). (But in fact . . .)
4. *In the past*, the use of robots was primarily limited to environments which were harmful to workers. (But today . . .)

Apart from minor infelicities (*get* in 1), the repetition of *process* in example 2 and the choice of opening preposition in example 3, the four statements of this type all communicate effectively and convincingly.

Two unclassified statements remain, although both assert centrality in some way (italics mine):

1. The *advantage* of Finite Impulse Response (FIR) design is that FIR filters have linear phase (I)
2. Knowing how to choose to CPU-Control Process Unit will *profoundly affect* the performance of a control system. (M)

In the latter, the hands-on opening detracts from the rhetorical strength of *profoundly affect*. If the verbal-style subject is replaced by a more contextually typical extraposition, M is much improved:

2a. It has become clear that the choice of a CPU . . . .

Opening sentences are notoriously difficult to write, but in the present sample the difficulty would seem on the whole to have been surmounted; only those who opted for a developmental opening statement experienced problems of "impression management."

Tactics Used to Create a Space

The uncertainties that the authors of texts O and P encountered in creating a gap or space have already been discussed and will not be mentioned further. All except one of the remaining 15 student writers offered a contrast at the earliest possible moment by placing the adversative connector or subordinator in sentence initial position. The figures are as follows:

However	10
Although	2
Unfortunately	2	(not mentioned in class)

The exception is text F, whose author places the subordinate clause second. The unfortunate effect of this postponement can be seen in the following pair of sentences.

1. Metallurgists have observed these facts through qualitative studies while quantitative evaluations are only a few (original).
1a. Although metallurgists have observed these facts through qualitative studies, quantitative work in this area remains scarce (modified).

The 14 statements following the opening contrast are not on the whole successful instances of local management. In my estimation, only four (A, B, E, and L) achieve their communicative aim with grace and competence; the remainder, while schematically clear, run into local problems. Here are some examples in skeletal form:

2. One issue concerned is that it needs . . . . (I)
   These comparisons concern only about areas in which . . . . (M)
   Reading of these nine sensors required engineers substantial time . . . . (C)
   It needs much effort of . . . engineers to develop these systems (H)
   It is for the day when the optimum . . . . (Q)
   All work in AI are still in laboratory . . . . (K)

Finally, one student apparently took the model more literally than intended:

3. However, with the development of VSLI, . . ., there is some *space* between the control theory and the application of microcomputers. (N)

In general, handling Step 3 caused more problems in language management than at any other juncture in this sample of NNS introductions. Perhaps this finding is not surprising given the fact that Step 3 requires a rhetorical maneuver of some sensitivity; certainly, the finding suggests that further applied research and pedagogical experimentation would be advantageous.

Local Tactics in Introducing Present Research

The problematic nature of the Step 4 in introduction A was discussed in the preceding section. With one exception, the remaining 16 student writers performed either successfully or creditably. A particular successful group were those six authors who chose an aim/purpose format.

1. The aim of this paper is to suggest...................... (H)
   The aim of this paper is to introduce .... (I)
   The aim of this paper is to find out .... (J)
   The purpose of this paper is to examine .... (G)
   The purpose of this paper is to develop .... (P)
   The purpose of this paper is to drive (derive) .... (E)

It is worth noting that no student opted for the alternative of *the present paper*, offered an alternative to *paper*, or was persuaded to use the past tense.

Two students (F and M) used a passive format (perhaps motivated by theme-rheme considerations). One opened, *In this study* (P), and two switched to first person:

2. Our studies show that..................................... (B)
   We have investigated...................................... (O)

Four students opted for placing *this paper* in subject position, a decision that, on present evidence, offers more of a challenge:

3. This paper presents .... (C)
   Therefore, this study is conducted to produce .... (D)
   This paper uses.. (L)
   Therefore this report contributes specifically .... (Q)

All in all, the writers in the sample handled the final step in the model very competently, both in terms of clarifying that they moved on to their own research and in terms of coming up with an appropriate and accepted phraseology. There is, alas, an exception; poor author K, although succeeding in the first objective, abjectly failed in the second by abandoning his earlier determination to maintain an academic style:

Step 3. However, all work in AI are still in laboratory except a little part being implemented on expert systems.
Step 4. Especially, the intelligent robot which combines AI

and robotics interests me to do this research. I develop the robot with AI to search and work by itself.

Discussion

In this chapter I have undertaken a performance analysis of genre-
specific writing fragments produced by a group of nonnative speaker
graduate students who had been required to take a writing class as a
result of an English test. I have adopted Miller's position that "a rhetorically sound definition of genre must be centered not on the substance or
the form of discourse but on the action it is used to accomplish" (1984, p.
151). I have suggested that one possible characterization of the rhetorical
action accomplished in research paper introductions is that it is designed
to create a research space for the writer-researcher. This goal, even when
imperfectly perceived by encoders and decoders, gives rise to a number
of expectations. The expectations are global, for example, there is a
patterned information structure, and local, that is, the procedural steps
that articulate the information structure are self-evident and syntactic and
lexical resources are appropriately selected. If these expectations are met,
then the text is deemed to be coherent. As nonnative speakers cannot be
expected to be able to match registral and grammatical expectations with
any great reliability, it becomes particularly important for them to succeed
on the other local level—to signpost unerringly—even by overincorporat-
ing metadiscourse items (Johns, 1986c).

A conscious appreciation of this need is somewhat akin to the classical
Greek architect's use of *entasis*. The classical Greek architect knew that
it was necessary to swell the temple columns in the middle so that
they would appear straight to the casual observer on ground level. The
equivalent rhetorical illusion for the disadvantaged NNS writer is to
maintain normal expectations of coherence by exaggerating metadiscoursal signals to compensate for the anticipated semantic and registral
uncertainties.

In the writing samples discussed in this chapter, there is some evidence
of such a process in action. Certainly the texts in the sample suffer from
few of the orientation problems in introductions noticed by Scarcella
(1984); in particular, these texts do not contain unnecessary background
information, insufficient use of attention-getting and clarifying devices,
or insufficient "linking of concluding statements to preceding subtopics
of the problem" (Connor, 1984a, p. 301). Rather, their deficiencies are
as much lexical as anything else and lie in a restricted ability to use
paraphrase. In the following text, for instance, part of the reader's diffi-

culties lie in interpreting the meaning of *works* (operations?) and in the fourfold repetition of the work *problem*:

> Text L
>
> In the past, the use of robots was primarily limited to environments which were harmful to workers. Today the implementation of robots are increasing in almost every industrial area. However, the problem of endpoint position accuracy has restricted their applications to works which are error tolerant. Many works require error tolerance on the order of 0.01 mm. Existing manipulators can perform only on the order of 0.1 mm. The problems are related to the transmission mechanisms and the structure deformation. A direct drive arm is used by Asada [1] to solve transmission problem Kuntze and Jacubusch [2] also discussed this problem.
>
> However, few research papers concentrated on structure problems, especially on dynamic effects of the distributed link flexibility. This paper uses an assumed modes method to model the flexible motion of robot arms. We can then investigate the relationships between the arm structural flexibility and a linear controller for the rigid body motion.

Text L was written by a South Korean student who was thought to be "at risk" because of weaknesses in English (he was taking other ESL courses beside this writing class). The student had little confidence in his English ability, which found expression in his determination to write short sentences. Nevertheless, Text L is an effective piece of writing; the movement of thought from the opening to the closing sentence is coherent, appropriately paced, and authoritative.

Conclusion

It is certainly the case that the performance analysis presented here is small-scale, carried out by a single individual without recourse to corroborative support, and targeted on a localized piece of writing. However, the analysis is fairly complete, at least in the sense that it provides a description of all the textual data rather than a judiciously advantageous selection of that data. Moreover, research paper introductions are by no means components of an obscure or highly specialized genre. Published examples of the genre amount to several million a year (Swales, 1985), and there is reason to believe that those researchers who cannot make their contributions in English are increasingly threatened with invisibility. Further, there is reason to suspect that a typical composing practice for NNS scholars in writing their introductions is to lift phrases and expressions from a variety of printed sources (St. John, 1987; Manfred Gerbert, personal communication). Instructors *ought* to be able to offer an alternative to such match and mix techniques—one that mirrors the rhetorical insights, processes, and competencies of skilled LI writers.

Author's Note

I would like to thank Liz Hamp-Lyons, Ann Johns, and Larry Selinker for valuable comments on a preliminary version of this paper. Remaining deficiencies are entirely my responsibility.

Discussion Questions

1. According to Swales, one of the three types of global expectations that influence a reader's judgment of text coherence is *purpose*. What purposes do writers have other than those that Swales mentions? How do we teach students to announce or obscure their purposes in their writing?
2. Swales takes his definition of schemata from Carrell's (1983) article in *Reading in a Foreign Language*. Read this article and decide whether you would like to expand the definition of *formal schemata* found there. What is the relationship between formal schemata as discussed by Carrell and traditional rhetorical modes (e.g., comparison and contrast) discussed in the literature?
3. When Swales discusses his five-component approach to teaching research writing, he mentions that one of these components is *flow*. Using your own insight and readings in this volume, discuss a definition of *flow* that could be understood and implemented by teachers and students.
4. Composition instructors often refer to *style* as important to writing; Swales also mentions this feature as one of the components in his approach. How can style be defined? Is style coterminous with *register*? If not, what are the differences between the two? Is the research writing that Swales describes an example of register? What are the constituents of its style?
5. Swales argues that "like most other writing, [academic research writing] is ultimately persuasive." Do you agree? Support your argument with examples from various genres.

Extension Activities

1. Select a text that perfectly fulfills your expectations because it is from a genre that is familiar to you. Answer the following questions about

this text. Why is it familiar to you? What are the essential content and formal features of this text that you have previously seen and perhaps employed?

2. Imagine that you have students who need to develop a familiarity with the genre type discussed in Activity 1. Write two exercises that might assist students in developing this familiarity. Take Swales' stance that "a taught appreciation of the elements . . . (that exemplify) coherence to genre-experienced readers has, in alliance with student expertise in their individual content areas, created a set of texts to which we can ascribe a sufficient amount of global coherence to compensate for the processing difficulties at the local level."

3. Like many researchers in linguistics and rhetoric, Swales' judgments of the student introductions are introspective. However, introspection is not the only—or even the best—method for research. Teach your students Swales' four-step introduction, then ask them to produce introductions in content areas with which they are familiar. Submit these introductions to faculty in the appropriate disciplines and request evaluation. You might ask the faculty to use a three-point scale, with *1* as *inadequate* and *3* as *good*. Follow up on these evaluations by asking why the scores were awarded in each case.

4. Ask two students to peer-evaluate each of the texts written by their fellow students, using the four-step system as the criterion. Do the two students agree with each others' evaluations? Does agreement depend upon the content areas with which they are familiar? What comments do students make about the strengths and weaknesses of the introductions?

Coherence as a Cultural Phenomenon: Employing Ethnographic Principles in the Academic Milieu

Ann M. Johns

San Diego State University

Coherence as a Cultural Phenomenon: Employing Ethnographic Principles in the Academic Milieu

One reason that coherence is of concern to teachers and researchers is that it is a complex phenomenon, involving a multitude of features within the text as well as requiring an integration of reader expectations and text realization (see, e.g., Carrell, 1982; Johns, 1986c). Most contributions to this volume (e.g., Wikborg, Hinds, Harris, Evensen, Bardovi-Harlig) have dealt principally with text features and referred only in passing to the effect of discourse on readers. When readers are mentioned, they are experienced teacher-readers, those already initiated into academic discourse communities.

The focus of this chapter is considerably different. Whereas text will be discussed, it is the novice academic readers and writers who are the primary focus. What will be discussed here are the problems students face within the academic community, especially at the college and university levels, in becoming effective readers and producers of text, in identifying and developing the accepted linguistic, intellectual, and social conventions characteristic of the academic community, the rules of use employed by the community members often without conscious attention (Hymes, 1980). Guthrie (1985) has suggested that some principles of ethnography, especially those that require researchers to be participants and observers simultaneously, are effective in developing students' objectivity about academic reading and writing and in developing their understanding of what it means to be pragmatically competent within the academic culture. Following the lead of Guthrie (1985) and others, I have devoted this chapter to student exploration of pragmatic competence and to how this competence relates to broader issues of coherence within an academic context.

Pragmatic competence has been defined as "the knowledge and skills that are necessary for membership in a society or community" (Mehan, 1980, p. 131). In any culture, this competence is "indicated by [a participant's] ability to interact effectively on [the culture's] terms with others who are already competent" (Goodenough, 1976, pp. 3–4). Traditional societies encourage practices that specifically initiate the young into the culture. In a society that values the use of proverbs, for example, older children lead younger ones in proverb-completion games (Diaz, 1986). By providing opportunities for children to be initiated, older members of the society encourage the young to learn gradually to interact effectively with those who are already pragmatically competent (Vygotsky, 1978). In societies in which a number of cultures are represented, young people require initiation into several cultures in order to develop a "cultural repertoire" (Guthrie & Hall, 1981), an ability to move from culture to culture with relative ease.

Unfortunately for students in English-medium colleges and universities, opportunities for direct initiation into academic culture are few and the demands of the already-competent within the culture are many. There is little chance for the necessary conversation among participants that provides a bridge into the culture, a conversation that can lead to authentic interaction within the community and to the development of the private thinking and appropriate writing necessary for academic success (Bruffee, 1984).

Students enter a university in which environments are unidirectional—the entire agenda is set by the faculty members, with little or no input from students. In the vast majority of college classes, especially in the larger universities, instructors provide few opportunities for real conversation and partnership or for other practices that might initiate these novices into the culture. Of necessity, these instructors generally make all the rules for classroom behavior; and students who do not conform are ostracized, often without knowing why. The instructors lecture or lead controlled discussions and expect students to take notes, even if students have never taken notes previously. The instructors write and grade the examinations, often returning them without comment. At few points in this prototypical teaching process is there room for instructor feedback or conversation with students, or for the imposition of student agenda, negotiation, self-expression, or practice (Myers, 1986). When students attempt to negotiate their grades, the content of the class, or the teaching environment, they are considered cultural outsiders. When students ask questions that do not conform to the turn-taking norms of the lecture-discussion, their questions are considered annoyances that interrupt the development of the lecture discourse (McKenna, 1987). When students inappropriately personalize their experience for their university instructors, especially in writing, they are classed as cognitively underdeveloped, still in Piaget's egocentric stage (see Lunsford, 1980).

Therefore the English-medium university setting does not often allow for initiative practices led by the instructor or role model. New students must face a communicative context "severely bound by institutional constraints" (Perelman, 1986, p. 472) without much assistance. To succeed in this milieu, they have to come to terms with the cultural rules of the university (Bizzell, 1986) and be equal to the cognitive demands that the institution imposes (Bizzell, 1982). In this effort they often must sacrifice some of the world view of their native cultures and of the academic cultures in which they were previously educated to gain acceptance into the English-medium university culture, a milieu that is often quite foreign and unappealing to them (Bizzell, 1986).

Compounding the adjustment difficulties are the requirements of university classes, both in reading and writing (Johns, 1981, 1986a). In terms of the latter, many first-year students have completed very little writing beyond the paragraph (Applebee, 1981). The little they have written is generally in the narrative, completed in English classes in which the audience is limited to an English teacher or the students' peers.

Students are ill-prepared for the conventions or the volume of reading and writing assignments of their academic classes, taught by instructors who over years of academic cultural orientation have developed a tacit knowledge of the rules for writing and reading in their own disciplines: methods for examining and evaluating information (Perelman, 1986), for special uses of lexicon and grammar (Tarone, Dwyer, Gilette, & Icke, 1981), and for intergrating information from various sources (Jacobs, 1982). University instructors often expect students to intuit these rules while providing little practice in using them.

Assistance in Academic Initiation

The writing-across-the-curriculum movement, which in English as a second language (ESL) and English as a foreign language (EFL) has traditionally been subsumed under the English for academic purposes (EAP) rubric (Strevens, 1977; Widdowson, 1983), was established to assist students in coming to terms with the linguistic features of academic discourse communities. EAP researchers attempt to determine the nature of academic institutional discourse through needs assessments and task analyses (Chambers, 1980; Kennedy, 1985; Munby, 1978) and to describe, among other things, the sociolinguistic context (Markee, 1986) and the nature of the writing tasks students must perform (Bridgeman & Carlson, 1984; Horowitz, 1986; Johns, 1981). Huddleston (1971) and Johns (1980) completed discourse analyses that focused on some of the syntactic and linguistic features of academic writing. Swales (1984) completed analyses of the moves in introductions to scientific articles, and Tadros (1984, 1985) built a taxonomy of predictive devices in selected academic discourse.

There are at least two problems that the EAP teacher faces, however, that cannot be readily solved through prior needs analyses. Although experts in a discipline (e.g., history professors) practice the "accepted reader and writer roles and the social purposes for writing [and other activities] in their disciplines" (Herrington, 1985, p. 35), these rules are often not articulated because the knowledge is generally tacit and rules of use are applied without conscious attention (Hymes, 1980), and therefore are not identified through a needs assessment. As a result, professors often cannot explain the institutional or discipline-specific conventions of their disciplines to students, writing teachers, or researchers, nor can they provide the practice that leads to understanding these conventions. For these reasons, writing teachers find it difficult to help students to "engage in social cognition, representing to themselves and to their audiences the interests, values, prior knowledge and experiential associations" of the disciplines (Kantor, 1984, p. 86) that they are studying. Yet students' writing and other academic activities will not become successful until appropriate interaction with this academic culture is accomplished (Perelman, 1986).

In addition to institutional roles, university professors are also subject to their own idiosyncracies. They often choose to create a classroom context that is somewhat different from other university contexts, even within their own departments. The idiosyncratic nature of a single academic context is also difficult for EAP instructors to predict through a precourse needs assessment.

Therefore, despite the plethora of task analyses completed by researchers, students continue to be faced with dilemmas and obstacles in an academic culture that are often neither articulated nor predictable. It is the task of EAP teachers to devote their courses to assisting students to recognize the conventions of academic disciplines and to understand the idiosyncrasies of individual faculty with whom they come into contact. One of the most effective methods for providing assistance is to train students in the principles of ethnography, especially in the research roles that require those involved to be participants and observers at the same time:

> the [student] researchers must adopt a dual role—that of both participant and observer. As participants, researchers try to develop an empathetic relationship with the individuals they are studying. Researchers must try to see things from these individuals' point of view, becoming—at least vicariously— participants in the life of the group to which the individuals belong. Researchers, however, must also be able to distance themselves, to look at phenomena from an outsider's point of view. (Doheny-Farina & Odell, 1985, p. 508)

The Academic Journalog

One technique for assisting students in their ethnographic pursuits is the use of the academic journalog (or learning log). Journals of various types have been important elements in ESL classrooms for several years. They have been used as diaries, as instruments for increasing writing fluency (Urzúa, 1984), for indirect correction of English, and for dialogue with instructors (Staton, Shuy, Kreeft, & Reed, 1982). In EAP classrooms, journalog responses are focused on academic tasks and topics (Johns, 1986b; Nower, 1986; Simmons, 1983). In contrast to product-based assignments, no journalog is graded for grammar, spelling, or mechanical errors; the concern is more for student exploration and discovery than for right or wrong answers.

The journalog is valuable for a number of reasons. It requires each student to become involved, it allows for individual dialogue between teacher and students, it promotes fluency in writing, and it permits digression and allows for the privacy most students desire when struggling with new ideas and concepts. In a journalog, students can be themselves. With their peers in a classroom, they are often constrained by their desire to conform.

In addition, the journalog embodies the three advantages of all writing. It requires the physical act of putting something on paper, focusing student attention and making learning active and individual; it is visible, allowing a dialogue with self and providing a forum for analysis and digression; and it is personal, committing an individual writer to a position, that is, making biases clear, clarifying values, revealing what the writer does and does not know (Fulweiler, 1986).

The Academic Context

At San Diego State University about 300 freshmen, principally from ethnic groups (Hispanic, Black, Filipino, American Indian, and Indo-Chinese) that are underrepresented in universities are assigned to an academic "package" in the Intensive Learning Experience Program (ILE) at the Academic Skills Center, an English adjunct program designed to assist students in bridging the gap between high school and university. Each group of 20 ILE students is assigned to academic writing and reading adjunct classes, a general education class in which other students are also enrolled (e.g., freshman history, biology, Afro-American studies, religious studies), a study skills course, and a study group. Journalogs are required in each of the package writing classes.

This chapter discusses journalogs as they are employed in one writing adjunct class attached to a general education class entitled Western Civilization. Students in this class were very advanced in that most could produce a fairly good personal narrative or personal response to a question. However, their understanding of university academic culture was slight. Therefore, the principal purpose for assigning the journalogs was to examine the features of the Western civilization class in order to increase the pragmatic competence of the student writers-ethnographers. Because the development of an understanding of the academic context is a long process, this discussion will focus on the exploratory stage, the stage in which these freshmen, first exposed to this culture, were beginning to come to terms with the conventions of the academic classroom and to assess their roles in this context.

Since these students were first-time freshmen, it was important for them to begin at the beginning, as participant-observer, with topics and questions for entries in their journalogs that could give them insights into their first academic experience as well as the experiences that followed. During the first semester, then, they were asked to answer questions about the roles they and the professors play in the conventional university classroom; to identify the major topics with which the class would deal and their relation to each other within the organization and structure of the course; to begin to understand some of the conventions of academic writing, at least for this classroom; and to develop some approaches to this writing, especially how to exploit the assigned reading to produce a paper. These topics were selected not only because they are central to understanding the academic community, but because they might lead to student production of a prose that is coherent for this context, i.e., prose that might be sufficiently academic to satisfy the professor-reader. As Enkvist, in this volume, points out, "text is a trigger releasing a process of interpretation, which depends [for coherence] on the situation and on the interpreter" (p. xxx).

In the discussion that follows, all students are quoted authentically; entries included are exactly as they were written in the journals, complete with the graphological, morphological, and syntactical errors. It is not the purpose here to focus on sentence-level error but on meaning and insight, and on students' attempts to understand the rules of the culture, especially as these rules affected them in their efforts to achieve coherence in their reading and writing.

Roles in the communicative context.   One of the first goals in the use of journalogs was for students to explore the roles that they and the professor play in this particular academic context, for "intelligence is a kind of social relation" (Calhoun, 1970, p. 28). Although some aspects of these roles were determined by the discipline and institution (e.g., note taking), others were unique to this classroom and professor. In their first entries in the journalogs, the students were asked to assess the role and personality of their professor and his expectations for class behavior. The questions were (a) what does the instructor want to be called, (b) what kind of a person is he, and (c) what does he expect of students?

The following are some typical journalog entries.

One student dealt with the rules of classroom protocol in this manner:

> Joe [the professor told the students that he wanted to be addressed by his first name; "it made him feel younger"] expect the class to be pretty much on time and present on the days of class. He also think that notes should be taken and that your attention will be on him during the lectures. He will tolerate drinking [soft drinks] in class as long as your careful not to tip the glass over and that it is not played with during discussions.

Another had more difficulty dealing with the professor's dual personality:

> My biggest problem in Dr. X's class is figuring out what he's really like. I often wonder if he strict as he seems to be or maybe its just a front to scare people into working. I've talked to him personally twice and he seems to be an ordinary guy, but in class he acts like "dirty Harry."

A third student decided to take a more personal approach:

> I went to see Dr. X. At first, I thought he was a very strict teacher; but, last Friday, I talked to him after class and he seems to be a nice person. I didn't really talk to him about the class, but confirmed if he was the professor who was in the meeting last spring regarding the discussion of Marcos' fall, as the leader of the Philippines.

One of the problems for the students in this particular context was the mixed signals that this professor gave. In the first days of class he was seen as acting like "Dirty Harry," yet he asked to be addressed by his first name and was very kind when students spoke to him individually. In time the students learned to be alert but generally silent in class and to approach the professor with real questions during his office hours.

Topics. The second goal of the journalog questions was to identify the topics that were to be of importance in the class. Most of the students were unable to separate the "forest from the trees." They thought that they had to study everything, to read and give equal value to every word in the textbooks and lectures. They also had great difficulty understanding the relations between topics presented.

Because Western civilization is a very broad topic, the purpose of the journalog questions was to identify the subtopics that were most important for the class and their relation to each other and, eventually, to the writing required. Students were asked (a) which topics are going to be emphasized in this course, (b) which of these are important, (c) how are they related to each other, and (d) how will they be dealt with in the class?

One student's entry began:

> Dr. X's class goes very quickly, he gives us information on so many topics all at once. He mentions agriculture and then on to war. I guess it all goes together . . . but it needs to be defined a little better.

Another said:

> Reasons, it seems Western Civilization beginnings had to do with this. We are going to be centering on France and England. Napoleon is very interesting guy. Renaissance, Age of Enlightenment, the Industrial Period, Science, very important topics, probably how it evolved.

A third was honestly mystified:

> I don't understand his class very well. He sometimes confuse about some historical facts. He also jump from one event to another without even stopping to see if we have any question . . . .

And a fourth:

> He likes to get all the information that he has fast! He's basically going to teach us about the economic and social aspects of Western Civilization. He gets off the subject matter quickly and he'll start talking about his personal life.

Although the students were able to identify most of the important topics, they had difficulty, as can be seen from the first and third entries, understanding how topics would be connected, either for the purposes of the introductory lectures or for the course and its examinations. The second entry is particularly interesting because the student was beginning to explore the rhetorical context for the topics presented. Would reasons provide support for a knowledge claim? Was evolution of the Ages (e.g., the Enlightenment and Industrial Revolution) an important concept?

One of the major problems that the students faced as they dealt with topics was the speed with which they were presented in the class. The students' lack of experience with note taking and their inability to sort out what is important and what is not contributed to their confusion and frustration. Professors often complain that students don't take notes; these journal entries indicate that the problem may be that they have no experience with note taking and therefore give up when they cannot write with sufficient speed.

Conventions of written discourse.   Students faced a number of problems when grappling with the conventions of the discourse they were to produce in papers and on essay examinations. Although about half of the students in the class had little previous writing experience, the other half had written extensively in high school English classes and occasionally in their other academic classes. Increasingly aware of the differences between the demands of their high schools and the university, the more experienced group believed that the conventions of their high school English classes were not transferable to other university academic classes. They had been taught—and had produced—a thesis; yet when asked to write on a topic in history, no thesis was present. They often failed to paragraph for their history teacher, although they had worked on paragraphing. Although a few had studied what we called *signal words*, such as conjunction and metalanguage to lead the reader through text, they generally failed to produce these as well.

Because many of these basic rules are transferable to most academic writing, journalog questions were posed to encourage discovery of possible transfer. As the semester progressed, students were asked to evaluate themselves as academic writers with questions such as (a) what did you learn about your writing from this assignment, and (b) for those who had completed essays in high school, what particular characteristics of writing for history are like the writing you have done before?

Here is how one student responded to the first graded writing assignment:

> I learn that my writing is weak in organizational grammatical style. My style in organization lack a system of topic sentence and then supporting it with alot of good details. My writing seem to me need a solid topic . . . not a short statement sentences that are not clear in its relations to the details. Furthermore my conclusion leave the reader hang on the question that I previously answer. This is what my English teacher expect too.

For most of these students, the principal emphasis in their earlier English class writing had been process approaches in which students were "to develop their own ideas in writing [after which] considerations of organization and logical development [were to] come into play" (Zamel, 1984, p. 154). Because meaning preceded form and organization in most of their previously written prose, they had had little practice in responding to essay questions requiring a prespecified form and examples from external sources. Therefore, journalog entries after the first in-class history examination were devoted to answering questions that would indicate some of their frustrations such as (a) what did you do well in answering the essay questions (i.e., how well did you meet the professor's expectations for coherent text) and (b) what could you do better?

One student responded:

> After looking over my paper, I discovered that I need to spend more time in analyzing the question being asked. When I write my papers, I tend to touch around the question, without answering directly. This is an extremely bad quality, for on an exam the teachers going to want to focus on the main idea of that paper. Not just ideas that touch around that main theme.

In addition to the issues of transfer and responding to essay examinations, journalog questions dealt with exploration of the "types of knowledge claims they could make and what counts as a good reason to support those knowledge claims" (Herrington, 1985, p. 355), that is, the principles of argumentation within the discipline. These students, with little experience in using sources for constructing an argument, had difficulty deciding what they could and could not claim, what evidence they would need to support their claims, and in what prose this evidence should be couched. When asked in an early journalog question to compare the absolute monarchy of Louis XIV's France and the constitutional monarchy of England during that period, a typical student began in this manner:

> The monarchies of France and England were different. France was an absolute monarchy and England was a constitutional monarchy. Both monarchies had different goals and direction. France was said to be "Supreme in Europe," with an absolute king, but England did not know where it was going. England compared to France, was weak in government.

After obtaining permission from the student to present this entry to her peers, I distributed it and asked if it was appropriate for a response in the history class. The students generally judged this writing as "very good" because "it doesn't have too much detail" and "it is something we can write." However, in this student's writing there are overly general and repeated knowledge claims ("monarchies of England and France were different"), claims that the history professor would discount as lacking depth and insight. The supporting details, that France was "supreme in Europe" and England "didn't know where it was going," are somewhat inaccurate, although they might be acceptable if they were supported adequately. A third inaccuracy is student confusion of English government with the monarchy. As this example shows, students tended to be general, to make knowledge claims that were inaccurate, unsupported, and therefore lacking in coherence for the target audience.

Later, students understood better how to make knowledge claims and, fully as important, how to use appropriate detail to support these claims. When asked "What is the importance of detail in your essay response?" one student responded:

> I realize that my main problem is to go back and look at my notes and re-read the book. Although I have some good points in my essay, I cannot really support it because I don't have the facts or proof to make my points valid. I need to concentrate on people and places and understand their relation with time or events.

Finally, the class explored the rules for the use of quotations from sources. Some quotes were acceptable to the professor if enclosed in quotation marks; however, memorizing long segments of text and repeating them on the examination or a written assignment was not considered appropriate. After one student had this experience, he said "I learned about my writing . . . that I should try to do the assignment in my own words and that I need to be more pacific [sic] about answering questions."

Approach to an assignment.   Early in the semester students began to realize that they would not be led through the course as they often had been in high school. They learned that, instead, they would have to take the intellectual initiative. As one student put it, "The syllabus that instructors give you doesn't really include or explain what and why they expect you to do the work written in the syllabus."

When the professor assigned a paper on Louis XIV, students had to come to terms with the fact that he would not provide guidance for them on how to go about writing that paper in terms of what pages to read in the textbook, what details they should select, or how the paper should be organized. They were not being asked to scan the textbook for isolated facts; instead they had to read for relation, for specific information that answered the questions.

One student, after some frustration, said:

> We have a two page report due next Tuesday in Western
> Civilization about Louis XIV. I've been doing alot of reading
> and so far I haven't come across the answers to the questions
> we're supposed to answer. I am reading the right pages in the
> right books but I'm not finding the right information. Maybe
> I'm reading the right stuff but not understanding what I'm
> reading. I guess I should go to the library and get some books.

Another, after completing the assignment, attributed his difficulties to
poor reading skills and his own laziness:

> More intense reading of the chapter is desperately needed.
> I can read it the first time and I'm not sure exactly what was
> contained in the paragraph. Also I should look up words that
> I'm not sure about [actually, most key words were defined in
> the text], sometimes I am just too lazy. I had a hard time doing
> part of the assignment because some of the details escaped
> me . . . .

For those who had little writing practice in high school, the task was
particularly onerous. One such student wrote:

> Dr. X wanted us to make a two-page report on Louis XIV
> by Tuesday. I haven't done a written report since 9th grade.
> Also then I was copying out of the encyclopedia. I'm worried
> about this report also because I don't know where to start,
> what to read. I'm also wondering if I would be able to write it
> long enough and have it still make sense.

With little practice and guidance from their history instructor, students
faced multiple problems in completing the assignment. They experienced
difficulties with reading (e.g., defining vocabulary), with organizing their
paper, with selecting appropriate details, and (for the last student cited)
with producing a paper in their own words that was coherent, i.e., that
would make sense to their professor-reader.

Conclusion

The journalogs had a number of salutary effects on these culturally
diverse freshman students new to the university. The primary goal of the
questions posed was to train students to be participant-observers in their
academic classrooms, by enabling them to understand academic conventions better and to produce text considered coherent by their professor.

The discoveries made by students while answering these questions transferred to other academic classrooms, in which students could again ask questions about the important features of the sociolinguistic context (see Johns, 1986c). A second goal was to promote students' self-assessment as potential members of the target culture of the university. As the journalog entries indicate, they were continuously involved in this activity even when it was not a specific focus of the journalog questions. They discussed their weaknesses as academic writers and commented on how they hoped to improve. They noticed their failure to respond directly and completely to a prompt; they realized their need to express and support their knowledge claims more adequately. They were frustrated by their reading strategies as they attempted to approach an academic assignment.

To extend the writing assignments beyond what had been previously discussed, the journals were exploited in two major ways.

1. Certain journal entries were designated as "shared" before they were assigned. Usually these entries dealt with discoveries about the conventions of academic discourse rather than about students' own self-discovery. Students came to class with their entries, discussed them in groups, and attempted to come up with agreed-upon "rules of use" realized in a particular reading or written assignment. One journal assignment, for example, focused on a list of take-home midterm examination questions, some of which the students were to answer. Students were asked to select two questions, then analyze in their journals features of the task realized in these questions: the principal organizational patterns demanded (e.g., comparison or contrast), the way in which the argument should be structured, the kinds of information necessary to support the argument, the essential terms to be employed, and the sources from which the argument should be drawn. When students met in the group, they not only discussed the elements of specific questions, but they also looked for generalizations that they could make about a number of questions in the list. They examined how these related to the conventions of the discipline that were realized in lectures and the readings. These analyses of brief essay questions were one of the most valuable group aspects of the program, because they not only assisted students in becoming more comfortable with the rules of use in academic discourse but also in selecting questions that they understood and could answer well.

2. The more personal, self-discovery journalog responses were often dealt with in conferences with instructors, conferences that were illuminating for both parties concerned. During the conferences the instructors often asked, "What do you mean by this?" and "How do you think the professor responds when you write in this way?" Through joint analysis with the instructor of their weaknesses and strengths in understanding

and responding to their professor, students began to grasp what it meant to produce prose that this new audience considered coherent, prose both the same as and different from what they produce in their writing classrooms or in classes at lower levels of academic work.

In classroom discussion, lecture, and conferences, the instructor's position was that of listener and guide. As students worked through their discoveries, the instructor remained fairly silent, offering a leading question or two. When students veered off course or they were wrong about their assumptions, it was the instructor's responsibility to steer them back to the realities and to assist them in discovering not only what they understood to be the conventions but also what they actually are.

In terms of developing pragmatic competence, then, the journalogs provided a two-pronged approach: methods for analysis of the language and task demands of the university and for self-analysis as a potential member of that context. In this class the results were encouraging. The grade point average of this group of underprepared students was slightly higher than that of the Western civilization class as a whole.

Comments from the students about the value of the use of journalogs were positive without exception. Students mentioned the virtue of focused questions:

> Asking questions is the best way to start writing about something because you can answer them in your writing. It is also a way of organizing your work better. Most of all, it makes the subject more interesting.

Some mentioned the improved understanding of the conventions of the discipline:

> I have learned to distance myself when writing. Yes, being that this course is being taken together with a history class, it has taught me to write more about facts instead of my opinion, which I used to.

Others mentioned the value of the questions about topics: "I now understand what the critical questions about the subject are."

The journalog, a classroom technique that is employed by students in their effort to discover the rules of use of the academic culture to which they are foreign, has been discussed here. The setting in which these particular journalog entries were written is ideal: All of the students were enrolled in both the academic class and the adjunct English class. What does the writing teacher in less ideal circumstances (i.e., who is teaching general academic English to students from a number of disciplines) have to learn from this discussion? First, that teachers can begin training students to think of the instructor as audience very early by asking them to analyze teachers as audiences and to look at the conventions of writing in new ways. When students are also enrolled in academic classes, teachers can ask them to answer ethnographic questions about the academic classes for which they must read or write, and those can be dealt with on an individual basis in student conferences. Although teachers cannot access the terminology from each discipline to teach to the class, they can focus heavily on the general academic terms employed across disciplines and the types of assignments and prompts that seem to cross disciplines (see, e.g., Horowitz, 1986).

Despite these suggestions, the many teachers who must teach some kind of general academic English are faced with a dilemma. Most modern discussions of academic register and task demands (e.g., Huckin, 1987; Swales, 1987a) focus on the particular features of specific disciplines. They may therefore discover that the only way for students to come to terms with academic culture is through the discourse of each of their classes. If there is any way for direct contact with and discussion about content classes to take place, as it does in the program mentioned here, then more ideal teaching and learning circumstances can result.

Discussion Questions

1. Pragmatic competence is defined in this chapter as "the knowledge and skills that are necessary for membership in a society or community" (Mehan, 1980, 131). This chapter suggests that coherence requires pragmatic competence in a target discourse community. Does this competence differ considerably between secondary and university communities, as this chapter claims?

2. Johns mentions that the tacit knowledge held by initiated members of a discourse community includes rules for the conventions of writing, for important terms, for topics and concepts and their relation to each other, and for the required approaches to academic assignments. What other knowledge (e.g., of formal and content schemata) do initiated members share?

3. Johns employed a journalog to determine student perceptions of the target discourse community. What other media or methods might be used to obtain this information from students?

4. Do you believe that "intelligence is a kind of social relation" (Calhoun, 1970, p. 28)? How does this definition of intelligence, as discussed by Johns, differ from other current definitions (e.g., IQ)?

5. What other questions about coherence and rules of use in the targeted academic classroom might Johns have asked?

Extension Activities

1. Examine a discourse community in which you feel comfortable. What are some of the writing (i.e., coherence) requirements of this community? What have you noticed about the topics discussed, the writing conventions, the uses of argument? What do audiences in this context feel is important to writing?

2. Interview students who are new to the discourse community because they are functioning in a new language or operating in a new milieu. What do these students perceive as the rules for writing in this community? Are these rules different from those in their previous writing communities?

3. Keep a journal recording your writing experiences for different audiences. How can coherence be established between writer and reader in each of these contexts? One basic element of coherence is reader expectations. How do these differ when audiences change?

4. This chapter describes how students are guided in identifying the rules of use in the academic context. Attempt to gain a faculty perspective in an identified discourse community by determining criteria for good written work, examining essay prompts and other assignments, and discussing writing in this context with the faculty member, thereby establishing the coherence rules for the discipline as perceived by an "expert."

Improving Coherence by Using
Computer-Assisted Instruction

Constance S. Cerniglia

Karen L. Medsker

Ulla Connor

Indiana University in Indianapolis

Improving Coherence by Using
Computer-Assisted Instruction

Although most teachers consider coherence an essential element of good writing, it remains difficult to teach. Teachers acclaim its benefits, demonstrate its effects, and exemplify good models, but students still do not know how to write coherently. English as a second language (ESL) students have particular difficulty in writing coherent English texts. In most cases, they consider their writing coherent if it discusses the same subject, even if it continually shifts focus. For example, when asked to write a coherent paragraph, an advanced ESL composition student wrote the following:

> It is very cold when it is snowing. In the winter time, it is very often cold, especially at the northern side of America. Most people need to have a coat for the winter time. It looks so pretty when it is snowing. The children like to go out to play in the snow. But not the adults because it is not safe when you have to drive on the snow to go to work every day.

The student described the paragraph as coherent because every sentence had *snow* in it, but the paragraph lacks coherence because the central themes of the sentences are different from each other.

Handbooks and textbooks offer little help. Most agree that coherent texts have clear and smooth connections among sentences and paragraphs. For example, Bander (1983) said that a paragraph is coherent "when its ideas are clearly related to each other in orderly sequence" (p. 6). Lauer, Montague, Munsford, and Emig (1985) asserted: "Coherence is a matter of putting the selected material in the right order with the right connectives" (p. 94). These definitions are too abstract for concrete application and thus do little to help an inexperienced writer achieve coherence through revision.

Coherence has also been of increasing interest to researchers around the world (e.g., de Beaugrande, 1980; Carrell, 1982; Enkvist, 1985; Kintsch & van Dijk, 1978). Researchers now are less concerned about distinguishing between coherence and cohesion than they are about finding an adequate definition of coherence. A few text linguists have described coherence using linguistic features from the text in their attempts to operationalize theoretical concepts of coherence (Connor, 1984a;

Evensen, this volume; Lindeberg, 1985a; Wikborg, 1985a, this volume). Following the theory of functional sentence perspective, Lautamatti (1987), developed a particularly promising attempt to describe coherence. "Successful integration," she claimed, refers to the semantic relation that exists between sentence topics and the discourse topic. Through topical structure analysis, these relations can be studied by looking at sequences of sentences and examining how the sentence topics work through the text to build meaning progressively. Topical structure analysis offers a sound, analytical approach to teaching coherence.

This chapter has two purposes. One purpose is to show that topical structure analysis can be taught to ESL students as a tool for improving coherence in their writing. Our experience indicates that students enjoy learning about topical structure analysis and that relatively brief instruction in topical structure analysis enhances their ability to assess passage coherence. The other purpose is to describe an innovative systems model we used to develop a computer-assisted lesson in topical structure analysis. We believe our experience has implications for other faculty involved in computer-assisted instructional development.

Topical Structure Analysis

Topical structure analysis, originally developed by Lautamatti (1987) for the purpose of describing coherence in texts, focuses on the semantic relation between the sentence topics and the discourse topic. Working on the theory of functional sentence perspective (Danes, 1974), Lautamatti analyzed the relation of topic and comment in sentences. *Topic* is simply the main idea of the sentence, which often, but not always, coincides with the grammatical subject of the sentence. One noun or noun phrase usually expresses the topic, and it can appear in one of several places in a sentence—beginning, middle, or end. *Comment* is what is being said about the topic.

Lautamatti (1987) identified three possible progressions of sentence topics: parallel, sequential, and extended parallel, illustrated in the student text that follows:

> (a) Since *teenagers* are the target audience for slasher films the victims in them are almost always independent, fun-loving, just-out-of-high-school partyers. (b) Could it be that the filmmakers believe that *the teenage audience* somehow identifies with other youths being decapitated, knifed, and electrocuted? (c) But *the kids* portrayed in the movies die so quickly that

viewers don't get much chance to learn about them, much less identify with them. (d) The *girls* all love to take latenight strolls alone through the woods or skinny-dip at midnight in a murky lake. (e) The *boys*, eager to impress these girls, prove their manhood by descending alone into musty cellars to restart broken generators or chasing psychotic killers into haylofts and attics. (f) Entering dark and gloomy houses, *men and women* alike decide suddenly that now's a good time to save a few bucks on the end-of-the-month electric bill—so they leave the lights off. (g) After hearing a noise within the house, *they* always foolishly decide to investigate, thinking it's one of their many missing friends or pets. (h) Disregarding the "safety in numbers" theory, *they* branch off in separate directions, never to see each other again. (i) Or the *teenagers* fall into the common slasher-movie habit of walking backwards, which naturally leads them right into you-know-who. (j) Confronted by the axe-wielding maniac, the *senseless youths* lose their will to survive, close their eyes, and scream.

In parallel progression, the topics in a number of successive sentences are identical or synonymous (see sentences a–c, f–h, and ı–j). In sequential progression, the comment of one sentence becomes the topic of the next or the topics differ as the paragraph is developed with examples (see sentences d–f). Finally, in extended parallel progression the first and last topics are parallel but are interrupted with some sequential progression (see sentences a–c, j). In the student text the topic of the first three sentences is teenagers; the topics of the subsequent sentences shift to girls, boys, and men and women before turning back to teenagers at the end of the passage. Topical structure analysis, as operationalized by Lautamatti, provides a means to identify systematically the sequence of sentence topics and to examine how sentences work to develop the discourse topic.

Topical structure analysis was also used by Witte (1983) to study patterns in freshman level students' writing and to compare them with the quality ratings of their essays. He found topical structure analysis to be a fair predictor of writing quality; however, he was not concerned about topical structure analysis as a teaching tool.

More recently, Connor and Farmer (in press) have investigated topical structure analysis as a revision tool and coherence check in intermediate and advanced ESL classes. They have adapted the ideas of Lautamatti and Witte to show students how to identify sentence topics, systematically chart topic progression, evaluate passage coherence, and employ revision strategies to improve the writing. Preliminary results show improved coherence in student essays.

Our current project extends the work of Connor and Farmer (in press) by developing a systematic instructional sequence to teach topical structure analysis by computer. Studying Topical Analysis to Revise (STAR) a computer-assisted instructional program especially suited for the ESL and basic writer, presents the fundamentals of topical structure analysis. The lesson first shows how to identify the topic of a sentence. Then it explains the three types of progression and asks the student to identify the types of progression used in a number of passages. The student is then instructed how to diagram the topical progression and evaluate the passage coherence. Finally, the lesson explains revision strategies that could be used to improve incoherent writing. These concepts lead students to analyze their own work and improve their writing through constructive revision.

Development of STAR

The development team for STAR was composed of a linguist (Connor), a writing instructor (Cerniglia), an instructional designer (Medsker), and a computer programmer (Dan Hart). About 280 person-hours were devoted to the planning, design, and writing of the 20-minute lesson. The linguist served as content expert and coauthor on the project. The writing instructor, experienced in teaching basic writers and ESL students, coauthored the text and exercises and coordinated the lesson testing, data collection, and revision. The instructional designer developed the lesson structure and participated in the writing and revision. Although some computer-assisted instruction (CAI) developers describe the work of an instructional designer as "polishing the screen design," the development team advocates a continuous and more substantial role for the instructional designer, who is vital in decisions about teaching strategy, lesson flow, testing, and so forth. The computer programmer translated the lesson into the PC Pilot authoring language, created graphics, revised screen design, and ensured that the lesson logic worked correctly. He also made extensive revisions during the testing phase. Our experience on this project underscores the importance of all team members, each with a particular expertise; a sole developer would usually lack some of the required skills. Furthermore, a CAI project is a major undertaking that requires the time and attention of more than a single developer.

Systems Model

STAR was developed using a basic systems model (see Figure 1). In this model, the objectives and scope of the project are defined first. Next, the lesson is designed using principles and techniques derived from learning theory and research. An instructional product is then developed based on the design requirements. That product is tested to see if it meets its objectives, and necessary revisions are made. The following sections describe how we applied the systems model in this project.

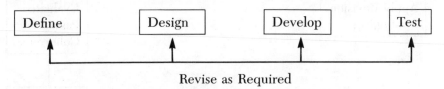

Revise as Required

Figure 1. Systems model for instructional development.

Definition phase.   Topical structure analysis involves a set of structured skills that can be taught in a straightforward tutorial fashion; however, teaching these skills in the writing classroom can be slow and repetitive. Some students understand easily; others need several examples and continued practice. Because students in our writing program were already using microcomputers for various aspects of their writing and language instruction, a self-paced computer lesson appeared to be an ideal solution.

While the fundamental concepts of topical structure analysis and the skill of analyzing a passage can be taught by computer, the more complex skills of evaluation and revision should be taught by a teacher. Thus the objectives of the computer lesson were limited to identifying sentence topics, diagramming topical structure, and identifying the type of topical progression. Only an introduction to evaluating passage coherence and revising were included in STAR.

Design development phase: learning hierarchy.   A learning hierarchy was constructed according to the model of Gagné (1977). The result of this learning analysis is presented in Figure 2. Each box in the hierarchy represents a skill that is hypothesized to contribute to the final performance. The analysis proceeds from the top down, from complex to simple skills. One performs this type of analysis by repeatedly asking the question, What must the student learn before he or she can learn this? The advantages of such a hierarchy are that no critical prerequisite skills

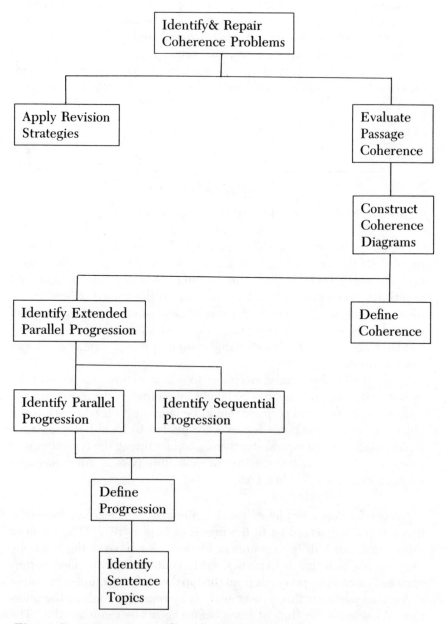

Figure 2. Learning map for coherence lesson.

are omitted and that no unnecessary material is included. Further, the hierarchy provides a guide for sequencing the lesson. Learning proceeds from bottom to top, from simple to complex skills.

Teaching strategy.   A deductive teaching strategy is chosen for STAR in which each new concept is explained, examples are provided, and exercises and feedback are given to allow the student to practice. Students are expected to master each skill in the hierarchy before proceeding to the next level.

In any CAI lesson, it is important to maximize the amount of interaction, keeping the student engaged in appropriate practice with corrective feedback; otherwise, the computer is just an "electronic page turner." STAR is very interactive; students respond frequently to several types of questions, including multiple choice questions, constructed responses, and fill-in-the-blank items, for which the computer uses pattern matching to judge corrections.

One advantage of CAI is that it allows "branching" based on variable student responses. If students get one or several exercises wrong, they can be branched to a remedial explanation and exercise. If students demonstrate prior knowledge of a skill, they can skip ahead to avoid boredom. Little branching was included in the initial STAR design because the content would be new to nearly all the students. Trial data were used to decide where remedial loops were needed. For example, when identifying sentence topics proved difficult for some students, an optional exercise set was added.

Learning Sequence.   In the first section of STAR, coherence is defined, and coherent and incoherent passages are shown. Next, students learn to identify sentence topics. Sentence topics are nouns or noun phrases in 95% of the sentences, and most often sentence topics are the grammatical subjects of the sentences. Occasionally, though, an adjective or a question word might express what the sentence is about more accurately than a noun or noun phrase. In the lesson, students are shown a number of sentences with topics located in various parts of the sentence. The sample sentences that follow show topics at the beginning, middle, and end of sentences.

Dorm life is not as drab as I had first imagined.

There are many *changes* coming to Purdue from such a small town like Danville, Indiana.

> Although Purdue and Owen Hall are wonderful places to be
> at times, they also have their *disadvantages.*

Students are reminded that the context determines the sentence topics
in many cases; occasionally more than one sentence topic may be correct.
However, students should not belabor the decision over the sentence
topic because a certain amount of impressionistic intuitiveness is required. Next, as the exercises that follow illustrate, students are asked to
identify sentence topics first in isolated sentences and then in passages.
When reading passages, students are asked to read the whole passage
and tell what it is about in order to link the sentence topics with the
discourse topics. They are given instructional feedback whether they
answer correctly or incorrectly.

> What is the sentence topic here?
> The briefcase bulged with unfinished paperwork so that the
> seams nearly split open.
> Type in the sentence topic: (briefcase)*

> What is the sentence topic here?
> It seemed as if her work would never be finished.
> Type in the sentence topic: (her work)*

> What is the sentence topic here?
> Although Bob and Alice were unfair and cruel parents, their
> daughter still took care of them.
> Type in the sentence topic: (Bob and Alice or parents)*

> Football fans used to go to football games to watch football.
> Now there is more action in the stands than there is on the
> field. Rowdy crowds at games have developed their own sport.
> There should be a class in how to avoid toilet paper or how to
> intercept beer cans. Obviously, many spectators wish that
> football fans would watch football, not play it in the stands.

> What is this passage about?
> a. More football fans should become football players.
> b. There is too much action in the stands from fan rowdiness.
> c. Football games are too dangerous.

> Answer: (b. There is too much action in the stands from fan
> rowdiness.)

> Identify the sentence topic:
> Sentence 1. (fans)
> Sentence 2. (action)

Sentence 3. (crowds)
Sentence 4. (class)
Sentence 5. (fans)

*The correct answer is indicated in parentheses.

Following the identification of sentence topics, students learn to identify three types of progression: parallel, sequential, and extended parallel. The program explains, shows examples, and tests students' abilities to identify each type. The exercise below shows two examples of passages given to students:

STUDENT PARKING

Parking on the IUPUI campus is a real hassle. *Students* rush to campus hoping to have an educational experience. *Hiking boots* are a necessity to trek from car to class. On rainy days *everyone* gets soaked to the skin.
A. Parallel   B. Sequential   C. Extended Parallel
What type of progression is illustrated above?
    (B. Sequential)

MICROWAVE OVEN

Microwave ovens have changed the role of the modern woman. No longer does a *housewife* stand over a hot stove cooking pots of stew. Today *she* works at a career, manages her family, and prepares satisfying meals in minutes. The *microwave oven* has given her freedom from her traditional role.
A. Parallel   B. Sequential   C. Extended Parallel
What type of progression is illustrated above?
    (C. Extended Parallel.)

In the first one, the sentence topics *parking, students, hiking boots*, and *everyone* are highlighted, clarifying to the student that the topics are different and the progression is sequential. In the second example, the progression is extended parallel since the passage starts with *microwave ovens*, moves away to *housewife* and *she*, and then returns to *microwave ovens*. In the lesson, students first differentiate between parallel and sequential progression, and then they differentiate among all three types of progression.

In the third section, students learn to construct diagrams of sentence topic progression. Sentence topics with parallel progression are placed directly below each other. Sequential topics are indented two spaces, and an extended parallel topic is placed in line with the parallel topic to which it refers. The program first shows students a number of coherence diagrams, and then the students construct diagrams for passages. A correct diagram is shown to the students to check their answers. The diagrams provide a visual means of assessing the overall pattern of progression, help students identify the type, and later help in evaluating passage coherence. A sample STAR screen is shown below. The topics are synonymous; therefore, they are placed directly below each other indicating parallel progression.

> Construct a coherence diagram from this passage of text:
> Chocolates are a national craving. They are sold in huge quantities—1 1/2 pounds per capita per year. Designer chocolates often sell for nearly $30/lb. These candies are America's number one choice.

> Type in your diagram here, using the space bar if needed:
> 1.
> 2.
> 3.
> 4.

> (1. Chocolates
> 2. They
> 3. Designer chocolates
> 4. These candies)

In the final section, students are introduced to the evaluation of passage coherence based on topical structure analysis. The lesson explains that parallel progression helps reinforce an idea in the reader's mind, but too much repetition can become tiresome. In addition, using sequential progression helps develop a topic, but too many new topics may distract the reader from the main idea. Using extended parallel progression often develops an idea well but also brings the reader back to the main idea to achieve a closure. The students are then given a passage for which they must identify topics, develop a coherence diagram, and then evaluate coherence. A sample exercise follows. In the sample passage, all the topics are different with no development of any one topic; the passage, therefore, has too much sequential progression.

Dorm Life

Dorm life is not as drab as I had first imagined. My room is large enough for two girls. My roommate and I can also decorate our home to our satisfaction. The food is a step above the high school cafeteria-style lunches I was accustomed to in the past. The bathroom facilities accommodate all of the girls' needs at various times.

How would you evaluate the coherence of the above text?
A. too much parallel progression
B. too much sequential progression
C. adequate extended parallel progression.
Type either "A", "B", or "C":
    (B. too much sequential progression)

Test phase. The lesson was first tried out on paper with a student in a one-on-one meeting with the writing instructor. This procedure is a recommended first step in formative evaluation (Dick, 1977) because it fosters a clinical atmosphere in which the student's thinking can be monitored and trouble spots can be precisely pinpointed. The instructor can try different explanations and examples, making lesson improvements on the spot. After this informal trial, several revisions were made, including minor changes in sequence and clearer explanations of concepts. We found this step to be extremely valuable and highly recommend early one-on-one trials.

Next, the lesson was tested with an entire class. The purpose was to refine instructional strategies and wording. The group setting allowed for discussion of strengths and weaknesses and corrected for idiosyncratic responses. At this stage, revisions included changed examples, improved feedback, and streamlined screen format. Some passages were too complex for ESL students, who were struggling to understand the text rather than to identify sentence topics. Some students progressed very quickly; others wanted to review frequently, so we added a review feature to the program.

Computer Trials

Once the lesson was programmed, we conducted trials with 29 ESL writing students. We found that most of the students were able to identify sentence topics, construct a coherence diagram, and evaluate coherence after going through STAR. Those who could not do topical structure analysis after STAR were able to do it after minimal teacher intervention. Information from these trials was used to make final revisions to the lesson.

An attitude survey based on Selfe (1986) was administered following

the student trials. Student attitudes were favorable: 48% of the trial
students rated the program *highly interesting,* with the remaining 52%
rating it from *medium to highly interesting.* Because coherence is a
difficult topic to learn, students appreciate the specificity and directness of
the computer lesson. They especially like learning to identify progression
because it provides a common vocabulary for discussing their writing.
Eighty-six percent of the students felt they had learned something new,
and 66% felt they could use topical structure analysis to improve their
writing.

Concurrently, the computer lesson was shown to several other subject
matter experts, linguists, and writing teachers familiar with ESL education and with topical structure analysis. They were generally positive
about the lesson, seeing a number of applications for it and suggesting
minor revisions. Interestingly, the teachers saw use for the program in
all the writing classes they taught, far outreaching our original intent for
the program.

Conclusions and Implications

STAR is now used in our ESL writing classes at Indiana University–
Purdue University at Indianapolis to teach coherence. With the specific
strategies STAR introduces, we feel that students are able to determine
the focus of their writing more clearly and develop their subtopics more
logically. STAR helps them organize and connect their ideas in a more
effective manner.

Our team continues to examine how STAR can best be integrated into
other writing courses. Our experience has shown that an instructor should
use STAR after students have some introduction to coherence. Students
need to understand that coherence is only one aspect of good writing and
only one consideration in the revision process. After completing the STAR
lesson, students often need peer and teacher assistance to be sure they
understand the concepts clearly, and they often need help evaluating
coherence and using revision strategies. We found that students especially needed follow–up when evaluating their *own* writing. Collaborative
activities in coherence mapping or text revisions often help students
overcome their weaknesses.

In writing classes, a variety of activities can be used to encourage
student collaboration and text revision. STAR, though, allows students
to analyze writing specifically for coherence. With teacher and peer
assistance, topical structure analysis provides a systematic method for
students to plan and revise their writing.

Author's Note

This project was partly funded by a grant from the Lilly Endowment, Inc.

Discussion Questions

1. The authors use as an example of incoherence in a paragraph on snow on p. 229. How are the sentences in this paragraph different from each other? Do you agree with the authors that incoherence is the result?
2. The authors mention that textbooks do not do a very good job discussing or teaching coherence. After reading much of this volume, what information or exercises would you include in the coherence section in an ESL writing book that are not ordinarily present?
3. The most typical position for the *topic* in a sentence is sentence initial. This typical position is often held by both *topic* and *subject*, which are then identical. Where else can a topic be found? Why do writers choose to delay mentioning the *topic*?
4. Why do the authors argue for a team approach to CAI? Have you had experiences with CAI development? If so, did you work with computer experts? What information or expertise do these experts lack when approaching the development of CAI materials?
5. STAR teaching strategy is deductive. What are the advantages of deductive and inductive teaching approaches? How might topic structure analysis have been approached inductively?

Extension Activities

1. Take a paragraph that you consider coherent and analyze it according to the system of topical structure analysis developed by Lautamatti and explained in this chapter. Did this analysis assist you in understanding coherence? As a teacher, how would you employ this technique with students?
2. There has been a great deal of talk about how computers assist students in writing. Examine the CAI literature to determine in what ways this issue has been studied and what conclusions can be drawn from the research.
3. Examine the commercial CAI materials available for ESL writing. How would you classify them? Which are most useful in terms of developing coherence?
4. The authors provide a learning map for the coherence lesson they have designed. Using Gagné's (1977) categories or Bloom's (1956) famous taxonomy, design a learning map for another coherence feature, for example, McCagg's rhetorical predicates.

References

References

Aarek, L. (1984). *17 mai: Innholdsstruktur og tidsuttrykk i elevtekster fra barneskolen.* Unpublished master's thesis, Department of Nordic Languages and Literature, University of Oslo, Norway.

Adams Smith, D. E. (1984). Medical discourse: Aspects of author's comment. *ESP Journal, 3,* 25–36.

Applebee, A. N. (1981). *Writing in the secondary school: English and the content areas.* Urbana, IL: National Council of Teachers of English.

Bander, R. B. (1983). *American English rhetoric* (3rd ed.). New York: Holt, Rinehart and Winston.

Barber, C. L. (1962). Some measurable characteristics of modern scientific prose. In C. L. Barber, F. Behre, U. Ohlander, Y. Olsson, S. Stubelius, J. Soderlind, & P. Zandvoort (Eds.), *Contributions to English syntax and phonology* (pp. 21–44). Göteborg, Sweden: Almqvist & Wiksell.

Bardovi-Harlig, K. (Ed.). (1983). *Papers from the parasession in the interplay of phonology, morphology, and syntax.* Chicago: Chicago Linguistics Society.

Bardovi-Harlig, K. (1986). *Discourse determinants of English sentence stress.* Bloomington, IN: Indiana University Linguistics Club.

Barnes, D. (1976). *From communication to curriculum.* Hammondsworth, England: Penguin.

Bazerman, C. (1981). What written knowledge does: Three examples of academic discourse. *Philosophy of Social Science, 11,* 361–387.

Bazerman, C. (1985). Physicists reading physics: Schema-laden purposes and purpose-laden schema. *Written Communication, 2,* 3–23.

Bergh, L., & Ljungmark, E. (1973). *Mots et images.* Stockholm: Esselte.

Biggs, J. B., & Collis, K. F. (1982). *Evaluating the quality of learning: The SOLO taxonomy.* New York: Academic Press.

Bizzell, P. (1982). Cognition, convention and certainty: What we need to know about writing. *Pre/text, 3,* 213–243.

Bizzell, P. (1986). What happens when basic writers come to college? *College Composition and Communication, 27,* 294–301.

Bloom, H. S. (Ed.). (1956). *Taxonomy of educational objectives by a committee of college and university examiners.* New York: D. McKay.

Bock, M. (1980). Some effects of titles on building and recalling text structures. *Discourse Processes, 3,* 301–311.

Bond, S. J., & Hayes, J. R. (1984). Cues people use in paragraph text. *Research in the Teaching of English, 18,* 147–167.

Bovair, S., & Kieras, D. (Eds.). (1981). *A guide to propositional analysis for research on technical prose* (Technical Report No. 8). Tucson: Department of Psychology, University of Arizona.

Braddock, R. (1974). The frequency and placement of topic sentences in expository prose. *Research in the Teaching of English, 8,* 287–302.

Bridgeman, B., & Carlson, S. B. (1984). Survey of academic writing tasks. *Written Communication, 1,* 247–280.

Britton, J., Burgess, T., Martin, N., McLeod, A., & Rosen, H. (1975). *The development of writing abilities (11–18).* London: Macmillan Education.

Brown, G., & Yule, Y. (1983). *Discourse analysis.* Cambridge: Cambridge University Press.

Bruffee, K. A. (1984). Collaborative learning and the "Conversation of Mankind." *College English, 46,* 635–652.

Bruner, J. S. (1985). Narrative and paradigmatic modes of thought. In E. Eisner (Ed.), *Learning and teaching ways of knowing.* Chicago: University of Chicago Press.

Calhoun, D. (1970). *The intelligence of people.* Princeton, NJ: Princeton University Press.

Carrell, P. L. (1982). Cohesion is not coherence. *TESOL Quarterly, 16,* 479–488.

Carrell, P. L. (1983). Some issues in studying the role of schemata, or background knowledge, in second language comprehension. *Reading in a Foreign Language, 2,* 81–92.

Carrell, P. L. (1987). Text as interaction: Some implications of text analysis and reading research for ESL composition. In U. Connor & R. B. Kaplan (Eds.), *Writing across languages: Analysis of L2 texts* (pp. 47–56). Reading, MA: Addison-Wesley.

Chambers, F. (1980). A re-evaluation of needs analysis in ESP. *The ESP Journal,* 25–34.

Cheng, P. G. (1985). *An analysis of contrastive rhetoric: English and Chinese expository prose, pedagogical implications, and strategies for the ESL teacher in a ninth-grade curriculum.* Unpublished doctoral dissertation, The Pennsylvania State University, State College.

Chittenden, L. (1982). What if all the whales are gone before we become friends? In M. Barr, P. D'Archy, & M. K. Healy (Eds.), *Language/learning episodes in British and American classrooms, grades 4–13* (pp. 36–51). Montclair, NJ: Boynton/Cook.

Christensen, F. (1967). A generative rhetoric of the paragraph. In F. Christensen (Ed.), *Notes toward a new rhetoric* (pp. 51–82). New York: Harper and Row.

Church, J. (1966). *Three babies.* New York: Random House.

Clark, H. H., & Haviland, S. (1977). Comprehension and the given-new contract. In R. O. Freedle (Ed.), *Discourse production and comprehension* (pp. 1–40). Norwood, NJ: Ablex.

Connor, U. (1984a). A study of cohesion and coherence in English as a second language students' writing. Papers in Linguistics *International Journal of Human Communication, 17,* 301–316.

Connor, U. (1984b). Recall of text: Differences between first and second language readers. *TESOL Quarterly, 18,* 239–255.

Connor, U., & Farmer, M. (1985, April). *The teaching of topical structure analysis as a revision strategy: An exploratory study.* Paper presented at the American Educational Research Association Conference, Chicago.

Connor, U., & Farmer, M. (in press). The teaching of topical structure analysis as a revision strategy for ESL writers. In B. Kroll (Ed.), *Current issues in second language writing research.* New York: Cambridge University Press.

Connor, U., & Kaplan, R. B. (1987). *Writing across languages: Analysis of L2 texts.* Reading, MA: Addison-Wesley.

Connor, U., & Lauer, J. M. (1985). Understanding persuasive essay writing: Linguistic/rhetorical approach. *Text, 5,* 309–326.

Connor, U., & McCagg, P. (1984). Cross-cultural differences and perceived quality in written paraphrases of English expository prose. *Applied Linguistics, 4,* 259–268.

Cooper, C. (1985). *Aspects of article introductions in IEEE publications.* Master of science thesis, University of Aston, Birmingham, England.

Coppieters, R. (1987). Competence differences between native and non-native speakers. *Language, 63,* 544–573.

Corbet, E. J. (1987). *The little English handbook* (5th ed.). Glenview, IL: Scott, Foresman.

Corson, D. J. (1982). The Graeco-Latin (G-L) instrument: A new measure of semantic complexity in oral and written English. *Language and Speech, 25,* 1–10.

Coseriu, E. (1985). Linguistic competence: What is it really? *Modern Language Review, 80*(4), xxv–xxxv.

Coulthard, M. (1977). *An introduction to discourse analysis.* London: Longman.

Crookes, G. (1986). Towards a validated analysis of scientific text structure. *Applied Linguistics, 7,* 57–70.

Crothers, E. (1979). *Paragraph structure inference.* Norwood, NJ: Ablex.

D'Angelo, F. A. (1979). Paradigms as structural components of Topoi. In D. McQuade (Ed.), *Linguistics, stylistics, and the teaching of composition* (pp. 41–51). Akron, OH: University of Akron Press.

Dahl, Ö. (1974). Topic-comment structure revisited. In Ö. Dahl (Ed.), *Topic and comment, contextual boundedness and focus (Papiere zur textlinguistik, 6)* (pp. 1–24). Hamburg: Helmut Buske Verlag.

Daneš, F. (1974). Functional sentence perspective and the organization of the text. In F. Daneš (Ed.), *Papers on functional sentence perspective* (pp. 106–128). The Hague: Mouton.

de Beaugrande, R. (1980). *Text, discourse and process.* Hilldale, NJ: Lawrence Erlbaum.

de Beaugrande, R., & Dressler, W. (1981). *Introduction to text linguistics.* London: Longman.

de Villiers, J., & de Villiers, P. (1978). *Language acquisition.* Cambridge, MA: Harvard University Press.

Diaz, E. (1986, October). *Making native language skills and cultural experience an asset in second language learning.* Paper presented at the California Teachers of English to Speakers of Other Languages Regional Conference, San Diego, CA.

Dick, W. (1977). Formative evaluation. In L. J. Briggs (Ed.), *Instructional design: Principles and applications* (pp. 311–336). Englewood Cliffs, NJ: Educational Technology Publications.

Doheny-Farina, S., & Odell, L. (1985). Ethnographic research on writing: Assumptions and methodology. In L. Odell & D. Goswami (Eds.), *Writing in non-academic settings* (pp. 475–510). New York: Guilford Press.

Donaldson, M. (1978). *Children's minds.* London: Croom Helm.

Dooley, R. A. (1982). Options in the pragmatic structuring of Guarani sentences. *Language, 58,* 307–331.

Doyle, A. C. (1917). *His last bow: A reminiscence of Sherlock Holmes.* New York: Review of Reviews Co.

Dudley-Evans, T. (1986). Genre analysis: An investigation of the introduction and discussion sections of M. Sc. dissertations. In M. Coulthard (Ed.), *Talking about text* (pp. 128–145). Birmingham, England: English Language Research, University of Birmingham.

Ebbitt, W., & Ebbitt, D. (1982). *Writer's guide and index to English* (3rd ed.). Glenview, IL: Scott, Foresman.

Eggington, W. G. (1987). Written academic discourse in Korean: Implications for effective communication. In U. Connor & R. B. Kaplan (Eds.), *Writing across languages: Analysis of L2 texts* (pp. 153–168). Reading, MA: Addison-Wesley.

Enkvist, N. E. (1973). Should we count errors to measure success? In J. Svartvik (Ed.), *Errata: Papers in error analysis* (pp. 16–23). Lund, Sweden: Lund Publishers.

Enkvist, N. E. (1975). *Tekstilingvistiikan peruskäsitteitä.* Helsinki: Gaudeamus.

Enkvist, N. E. (1978). Coherence, pseudo-coherence and non-coherence. In J. O. Östman (Ed.), *Semantics and cohesion* (pp. 109–128). Åbo, Finland: Åbo Akademi.

Enkvist, N. E. (1981). Experimental iconicism in text strategy. *TEXT, 1*, 97–111.

Enkvist, N. E. (Ed.). (1985). *Coherence and composition: A symposium.* Publications of the Research Institute of the Åbo Akademi Foundation 101. Åbo, Finland: Åbo Akademi.

Enkvist, N. E. (1987a). A note towards the definition of text strategy. *Zeitschrift fuer Phonetik, Sprachwissenschaft und Kommunikationsforschung, 40*(1), 19–27.

Enkvist, N. E. (1987b). Text linguistics and the applier: An orientation. In U. Connor & R. B. Kaplan (Eds.), *Writing across languages: Analysis of L2 text* (pp. 23–43). Reading, MA: Addison-Wesley.

Evensen, L. S. (1982). Data om språkundervisning. *Humanistiske Data, 9*, 4–11.

Evensen, L. S. (1983). Tekstlingvistikk i norsk for innvandrere? *Norsk Lingvistisk Tidsskrift, 1*, 131–148.

Evensen, L. S. (1985a). Discourse-level interlanguage studies. In N. E. Enkvist (Ed.), *Coherence and composition: A symposium* (pp. 39–65). Åbo, Finland: Åbo Akademi.

Evensen, L. S. (1985b). Connectors in student writing: A methodological note. *NORDTEXT Newsletter, 4*, 1–6.

Evensen, L. S. (1986a). Nordic cooperation on discourse-level performance analyses. *Trondheim Papers in Applied Linguistics (TRANS), 2*, 1–10.

Evensen, L. S. (Ed.). (1986b). *Nordic research in text linguistics and discourse analysis.* Trondheim, Norway: Tapir.

Evensen, L. S. (1987). *Den vet best hvor sko(l)en trykker . . .* Unpublished doctoral dissertation, University of Trondheim, Norway.

Evensen, L. S., & Rygh, I. L. (in press). Connecting L1 and FL in discourse-level performance analysis. *Papers and Studies in Contrastive Linguistics, 22.*

Fahnestock, J. (1983). Semantic and lexical coherence. *College Composition and Communication, 34*, 400–416.

Ferrara, A. (1985). Pragmatics. In T. A. van Dijk (Ed.), *Handbook of discourse analysis* (pp. 137–157). London: Academic Press.

Fillmore, C. (1977). The case for case reopened. In P. Cole & J. Sadock (Eds.), *Syntax and semantics: Vol. 8, Grammatical relations* (pp. 59–81). New York: Academic Press.

Firbas, J. (1961). On the communicative value of the modern English finite verb. *Brno Studies in English, 3*, 79–101.

Firbas, J. (1979). A functional view of 'Ordo Naturalists.' *Brno Studies in English, 13*, 29–59.

Firbas, J. (1982). Has every sentence a theme and a rheme? In J. Anderson (Ed.), *Language form and linguistic variation: Papers dedicated to Augus McIntosh* (pp. 97–115). Amsterdam: John Benjamins.

Flower, L. (1981). Writer-based prose: A cognitive basis for problems in writing. In D. Tate & E. P. Corbett (Eds.), *The writing teacher's sourcebook* (pp. 268–292). Oxford: Oxford University Press.

Flower, L. S., & Hayes, J. R. (1981). A cognitive process theory of writing. *College Composition and Communication, 35,* 365–387.

Frederiksen, C. (1979). Discourse comprehension and early reading. In L. B. Resnich & P. A. Weaver (Eds.). *Theory and practice of early reading* (Vol. 1, pp. 155–186). Hillsdale, NJ: Lawrence Erlbaum.

Fulweiler, T. (1986, October), *Managing a writing-across-the-curriculum program.* Presentation for the San Diego Teachers of English, University of San Diego, CA.

Gagné, R. M. (1977). *The conditions of learning* (2nd ed.). New York: Holt, Rinehart, and Winston.

Genette, G. (1972). *Figures III: Discours du récit.* Paris: Seuil.

Givón, T. (Ed.). (1979). *Syntax and semantics 12: Discourse and syntax.* New York: Academic Press.

Glahn, E. (Ed.). (1985). Datamatstottet undervisning i fraemmedsprogrogsfagene. *SAML, 11,* 131–139.

Goodenough, W. (1976). Multiculturalism as the normal human experience. *Anthropology and Education Quarterly, 7*(4), 4–6.

Gregersen, K. (Ed.). (1978). *Papers from the fourth Scandinavian conference of linguistics.* Odense, Denmark: Odense University Press.

Gregory, M. (1985). Towards 'communication' linguistics: A framework. In J. D. Bensen & W. S. Greaves (Eds.), *Systemic perspectives on discourse* (Vol. 1, pp. 119–334). Norwood, NJ: Ablex.

Grice, H. P. (1975). Logic and conversation. In P. Cole & J. L. Morgan (Eds.), *Syntax and semantics 3: Pragmatics* (pp. 41–58). New York: Academic Press.

Grice, H. P. (1978). Further notes on logic and conversation. In P. Cole (Ed.), *Syntax and semantics 9: Pragmatics* (pp. 113–127). New York: Academic Press.

Grimes, J. (1972). Outlines and overlays. *Language, 48,* 513–524.

Grimes, J. E. (1974). *The thread of discourse.* The Hague: Mouton.

Guthrie, G. P. (1985). *A school divided: An ethnography of bilingual education in a Chinese community.* Hillsdale, NJ: Lawrence Erlbaum.

Guthrie, G. P., & Hall, W. S. (1981). Introduction. In H. Trueba, G. P. Guthrie, & K. H. Au (Eds.), *Culture and the bi-lingual classroom* (pp. 1–13). Rowley, MA: Newbury House.

Gutwinski, W. (1976). *Cohesion in literary texts.* The Hague: Mouton.

Hall, E. T. (1969). *The hidden dimension.* Garden City, NY: Anchor Books.

Halliday, M. A. (1967). Notes on transitivity and theme in English, Part 2. *Journal of Linguistics, 3,* 199–244.

Halliday, M. A. (1978). *Language as social semiotic.* London: Longman.

Halliday, M.A., & Hasan, R. (1976). *Cohesion in English.* London: Longman.

Hardison, O. B. (1966). *Practical rhetoric.* New York: Appleton Century Crofts.

Heath, S. B. (1983). *Ways with words: Language, life, and work in communities and classrooms.* Cambridge: Cambridge University Press.

Helm, J. (Ed.). (1967). *Essays on the verbal and visual arts.* Seattle: University of Washington Press.

Herrington, A. J. (1985). Writing in academic settings: A study of the contexts for writing in two college chemical engineering courses. *Research in the Teaching of English, 19,* 331–361.

Hinds, J. (1980). Japanese expository prose. *Papers in Linguistics, 13,* 117–158.

Hinds, J. (1983). Contrastive rhetoric: Japanese and English, *TEXT, 3,* 183–195.

Hinds, J. (1984). Retention of information using a Japanese style of organization. *Studies in Language, 8,* 45–69.

Hofstadter, D. R. (1980). *Godel, Esher, Bach: An eternal golden braid.* New York: Vintage Books.

Horowitz, D. M. (1986). What professors actually require: Academic tasks for the ESL classroom. *TESOL Quarterly, 20,* 445–462.

Huckin, T. (1987). *Surprise value in scientific discourse.* Paper presented at the Conference on College Composition and Communication, Atlanta, GA.

Huckin, T. & Olsen, L. (1983). *English for science and technology: A handbook for nonnative speakers.* New York: McGraw-Hill.

Huddleston, R. (1971). *The sentence in written English: Syntactic study based on an analysis of scientific texts.* Cambridge: Cambridge University Press.

Hymes, D. H. (1980). What is ethnography? *Language in Education: Ethnolinguistic Essay, Language and Ethnography,* Series 1. Washington, DC: Center for Applied Linguistics.

Ingram, E. (1985). Rapport fra kurset: Ny skrivemetodikk. *Trondheim Papers in Applied Linguistics (TRANS), 1,* 82–97.

Innes, M. (1972). *The open house.* Hammondsworth, England: Penguin.

Irmscher, W. F. (1979). *Teaching expository writing.* New York: Holt, Rinehart and Winston.

Jackendoff, R. (1972). *Semantic Interpretation in generative grammar* Cambridge, MA: MIT Press.

Jacobs, S. E. (1981). Rhetorical information as prediction, *TESOL Quarterly, 15,* 237–249.

Jacobs, S. E. (1982). *Composing and coherence: The writing of eleven premedical students.* Washington, DC: Center for Applied Linguistics.

Jenkins, S., & Hinds, J. (1987). Business letter writing: English, French and Japanese. *TESOL Quarterly, 21,* 327–349.

Johns, A. M. (1980). Cohesion in business discourse, *The ESP Journal, 1,* 35–44.

Johns, A. M. (1981). Necessary English: An academic survey. *TESOL Quarterly, 15,* 35–44.

Johns, A. M. (1986a). *Writing tasks and demands in academic classrooms.* Unpublished manuscript, Academic Skills Center, San Diego State University, CA.

Johns, A. M. (1986b). Journalogs: Tools for acquainting students with history and the task demands of an advanced history class. *The History and Social Science Teacher, 21*(3), 180–183.

Johns, A. M. (1986c). Coherence and academic writing: Some definitions and suggestions for teaching. *TESOL Quarterly, 20,* 247–265.

Johns, A. M. (1985). Summary protocols of "underprepared" and "adept" university students: Replications and distortions of the original, *Language Learning, 35,* 495–517.

Johnson, K. (1986, July). A Visit to Sagamore Hill. *Gourmet,* pp. 42–47, 99–103.

Joos, M. (1967). *The five clocks.* New York: Harcourt, Brace & World.

Joos, M. (1972). Semantic axiom number one. *Language, 48,* 257–265.

Källgren, G. (1981). Ämnesinledare/ämnesväxlare i talad och skriven svenska. *Nordic Linguistic Bulletin, 5,* 20–23.

Kantor, K. J. (1984). Classroom contexts and the development of writing institutions: An ethonographic case study. In R. Beach & L. S. Bridwell (Eds.), *New directions in composition research* (pp. 72–94). New York: Guilford Press.

Kaplan, R. B. (1966). Cultural thought patterns in inter-cultural education. *Language Learning, 16,* 1–20.

Kaplan, R. B. (1972). *The anatomy of rhetoric: Prolegomena to a functional theory of rhetoric.* Philadelphia: Center for Curriculum Development. (Distributed by Heinle and Heinle)

Kaplan, R. B. (1987). Cultural thought patterns revisited. In U. Connor & R. B. Kaplan (Eds.), *Writing across languages: Analysis of L2 texts* (pp. 9–22). Reading, MA: Addison-Wesley.

Keenan, E. O., & Schieffelin, B. B. (1976). Topic as a discourse notion. In C. Li (Ed.), *Subject and topic* (pp. 335–384). New York: Academic Press.

Kempson, R. (1975). *Presupposition and the delimitation of semantics.* Cambridge: Cambridge University Press.

Kenan, L. R. (1979). *Fact and fancy.* New York: Harcourt Brace Jovanovich.

Kennedy, C. (1985). Formative evaluation as an indicator of students' wants and attitudes. *The ESP Journal, 4,* 93–100.

Kintsch, W. (1974). *The representation of meaning in memory*. Hillsdale, NJ: Lawrence Erlbaum.

Kintsch, W., & van Dijk, T. (1978). Toward a model of text comprehension and production. *Psychological Review, 85*, 363–394.

Kobayashi, H. (1984). *Rhetoric patterns in English and Japanese*. Unpublished doctoral dissertation, Teachers College, Columbia University, New York.

Koen, F., Becker, A., & Young, R. (1969). The psychological reality of the paragraph. *Journal of Verbal Learning and Verbal Behavior, 8*, 49–53.

Koons, K. (1986). *Korean rhetorical styles*. Unpublished manuscript, The Pennsylvania State University, State College, PA.

Kuno, S. (1972). Functional sentence perspective: A case study from Japanese and English. *Linguistic Inquiry, 3*, 269–320.

Kurzon, D. (1984). Themes, hyperthemes and the discourse structure of English legal texts. *TEXT, 4*, 31–55.

Kurzon, D. (1985). Signposts for the reader: A corpus-based study of text deixis. *TEXT, 5*, 187–200.

Labov, W. (1972). *Language in the inner city: Studies in the black English vernacular*. Philadelphia: University of Pennsylvania Press.

Labov, W., & Waletzky, J. (1967). Narrative analysis: Oral versions of personal experience. In J. Helm (Ed.), *Essays on the verbal and visual arts* (pp. 12–44). Seattle: University of Washington Press.

Lackstrom, J., Selinker, L., & Trimble, L. (1973). Technical rhetorical principles and grammatical choice. *TESOL Quarterly, 7*, 127–136.

Lagerqvist, M. (1980). *Timeconnectors in native and non-native narrative texts*. Unpublished manuscript, Department of English, University of Lund, Sweden.

Langer, J. (1984). The effects of available information on responses to school writing tasks. *Research in the Teaching of English, 18*, 27–44.

Langer, J. (1986). What eight-year-olds know about expository writing. *Educational Perspectives, 23*, 27–32.

Latour, B., & Woolgar, S. (1979). *Laboratory life: The social construction of scientific facts*. Beverly Hills, CA: Sage.

Lauer, J. M., Montague, G., Lunsford, A., & Emig, J. (1985). *Four worlds of writing* (2nd ed.). New York: Harper and Row.

Lautamatti, L. (1987). Observations on the development of the topic in simplified discourse. In U. Connor & R. B. Kaplan (Eds.), *Writing across languages: Analysis of L2 text* (pp. 92–126). Reading, MA: Addison-Wesley.

Leech, G. (1983). *Principles of pragmatics*. London: Longman.

Lemke, J. L. (1985). Ideology, intertextuality and the notion of register. In J. D. Bensen & W. S. Greaves (Eds.), *Systemic perspectives on discourse* (Vol. 1, pp. 275–294). Norwood, NJ: Ablex.

Lesgold, A. M., & Perfetti, C. A. (1978). Interactive processes in reading comprehension. *Discourse Processes, 1*, 323–336.

Levinson, S. C. (1983). *Pragmatics.* Cambridge: Cambridge University Press.

Lieber, P. (1980). *Cohesion in ESL students' expository writing: A descriptive study.* Unpublished doctoral dissertation, New York University, New York, NY.

Lindeberg, A. (1985a). Cohesion, coherence patterns, and EFL essay evaluation. In N. E. Enkvist (Ed.), *Coherence and composition: A Symposium* (pp. 67–92). Åbo, Finland: Åbo Akademi Foundation.

Lindeberg, A. C. (1985b). Functional role analysis applied to narrative and non-narrative student essays in EFL. *Trondheim Papers in Applied Linguistics (TRANS), 2*, 26–45.

Lindell, E., Lundquist, B., Martinsson, A., Nordlund, B., & Petterson, I. L. (Eds.). (1978). *Om fri skrivning i skolan* (Utbildningsforskning: FoU Rapport 32). Stockholm: Liber/Utbildningsförlaget.

Linnarud, M. (1986). Lexis in composition: A performance analysis of Swedish learners' written English. *Lund Studies in English 74.* Lund, Sweden: Department of English, University of Lund.

Longacre, R. (1979). The paragraph as a grammatical unit. In T. Givón (Ed.), *Syntax and semantics 12: Discourse and syntax* (pp. 115–134). New York: Academic Press.

Lunsford, A. (1980). The content of basic writers' essays. *College Composition and Communication, 31*, 278–290.

Mann, W. C., & Thompson, S. A. (1986). Relational propositions in discourse. *Discourse Processes, 9*, 37–55.

Markee, N. (1986). The relevance of social-political factors to communicative course design. *The ESP Journal, 5*, 3–16.

Markels, R. B. (1984). *A new perspective on cohesion in expository paragraphs.* Carbondale: Southern Illinois University Press.

McCagg, P. (1984). *An investigation of inferencing in second language reading comprehension.* Unpublished doctoral dissertation, Georgetown University, Washington, DC.

McCawley, J. D. (1981). *Everything that linguists have always wanted to know about logic but were ashamed to ask.* Chicago: University of Chicago Press.

McCutchen, D., & Perfetti, C. A. (1982). Coherence and connectedness in the development of discourse production. *TEXT, 2*, 113–139.

McKenna, E. (1987). Preparing foreign students to enter discourse communities in the U.S. *English for Specific Purposes, 6*, 187–202.

McMurtry, L. (1985). *Lonesome dove.* New York: Simon and Schuster.

Mehan, H. (1980). The competent student. *Anthropology and Education Quarterly, 11*(3), 131–151.

Meyer, B. J. (1975). *The organization of prose and its effects on memory.* Amsterdam: North Holland.

Meyer, B. J. (1980). Use of top-level structure in text: Key for reading comprehension of ninth-grade students. *Reading Research Quarterly, 16,* 72–103.

Miller, C. R. (1984). Genre as social action. *Quarterly Journal of Speech, 70,* 151–167.

Mo, J. C. (1982). A study of English reading comprehension from the point of view of discourse function. *English Teaching and Learning, 6,* 39–48. (In Chinese)

Mohan, B. A., & Lo, W. A. (1985). Academic writing and Chinese students: Transfer and developmental factors. *TESOL Quarterly, 19,* 515–534.

Munby, J. (1978). *Communicative syllabus design.* Cambridge: Cambridge University Press.

Myers, G. (1986). Writing research and the sociology of scientific knowledge: A review of three new books. *College English, 48,* 595–610.

Nelson, K. (1983). The conceptual basis for language. In T. B. Seiler & W. Wannenmacher (Eds.), *Concept development and the development of word meaning* (pp. 173–188). Berlin: Springer Verlag.

NORDWRITE reports II: Exploratory studies. Report to NOS-H on grant Dnr 32/86 (1987). Trondheim, Norway: Department of Applied Linguistics, University of Trondheim.

Nower, J. (1986, May). The journalog: A versatile tool in the ESL classroom. *TECFORS,* pp. 1–3.

Olsen, L., & Huckin, T. (1983). *Principles of communication for science and technology.* New York: McGraw-Hill.

Olson, C. B. (Ed.). (1986). *Practical ideas for teaching writing as a process.* Irvine, CA: California State Department of Education.

Olson, D. R. (1977). From utterance to text: The bias of language in speech and writing. *Harvard Educational Review, 47,* 257–281.

Ong, W. J. (1982). *Orality and literacy: The technologizing of the word.* New York: Methuen.

Östman, J. O. (1978). *Cohesion and semantics.* Publications of the Research Institute of the Åbo Akademi Foundation 41. Åbo, Finland: Åbo Akademi.

Ounvichit, T. (1988). *Contrastive expository writing: Thai and English.* Unpublished master's thesis, Mahidol University, Thailand.

Pearson, S. (1983). The challenge of Mai Chung: Teaching technical writing to the foreign-born professional in industry. *TESOL Quarterly, 17,* 383–399.

Perelman, L. (1986). The context of classroom writing. *College English, 48,* 471–479.

Peterson, C., & McCabe, A. (1983). *Developmental psycholinguistics: Three ways of looking at a child's narrative.* New York: Plenum Press.

Phelps, L. W. (1985). Dialectics of coherence: Toward an integrated theory. *College English, 47,* 12–19.

Piper, D. (1985). Syllogistic reasoning in varied narrative contexts: Aspects of logical and linguistic developments. *Journal of Psycholinguistic Research, 14*, 19–43.

Prince, E. (1978). A comparison of WH-clefts and It-clefts in discourse. *Language, 54*, 883–906.

Prince, E. (1981). Toward a taxonomy of given-new information. In P. Cole (Ed.), *Radical pragmatics* (pp. 223–255). New York: Academic Press.

Quirk, R., Greenbaum, S., Leech, G., & Svartvik, J. (1972). *A grammar of contemporary English*. New York: Seminar Press.

Reinhart, T. (1981). Pragmatics and linguistics: An analysis of sentence topics. *Philosophica, 27*, 53–93.

Rodgers, P. C. (1965). Alexander Bain and the rise of the organic paragraph. *Quarterly Journal of Speech, 51*, 399–408.

Rodgers, P. C. (1966). A discourse-centered rhetoric of the paragraph. *College Composition and Communication, 17*, 2–11.

Rosenberg, S. (Ed.). (1987). *Advances in applied psycholinguistics. Vol. II. Reading, writing and language learning*. Cambridge: Cambridge University Press.

Ross, J., & Doty, G. (1985). *To write English: A step by step approach for ESL* (3rd ed.). New York: Harper and Row.

Russell, B. (1951). *Autobiography* (Vol. 1). Boston: Little, Brown.

Rutherford, W. (1983). Language typology and language transfer. In S. Gass & L. Selinker (Eds.), *Language transfer in language learning* (pp. 358–370). Rowley, MA: Newbury House.

Rygh, I. L. (1986). Connector density—an indicator of essay quality? In L. S. Evensen (Ed.), *Nordic research in text linguistics and discourse analysis* (pp. 203–213). Trondheim, Norway: Tapir.

Scarcella, R. (1984). How writers orient their readers in expository essays: A comparative study of native and non-native English writers. *TESOL Quarterly, 18*, 671–688.

Scardamalia, M., & Bereiter, C. (1987). Knowledge telling and knowledge transforming in written composition. In S. Rosenberg (Ed.), *Advances in applied psycholinguistics* (pp. 142–175). Cambridge: Cambridge University Press.

Schachter, P. (1985). Parts-of-speech systems. In T. Shopen (Ed.), *Language typology and syntactic description* (pp. 3–61). Cambridge: Cambridge University Press.

Schank, R. (1975). *Conceptual information processing*. New York: American Elsevier.

Scinto, L. F. (1984). The architectonics of texts produced by children and the development of higher cognitive functions. *Discourse Processes, 7*, 371–418.

Scollon, R., & Scollon, S. (1981). *Narrative, literacy and face in interethnic communication*. Norwood, NJ: Ablex.

Scribner, S., & Cole, M. (1973). Cognitive consequences of formal and informal education. *Science, 182*(1), 553–559.

Selfe, C. L. (1986). *Computer-assisted instruction in composition.* Houghton: Michigan Technological University.

Selinker, L., Trimble, L., & Trimble, H. T. (1978). Rhetorical function shifts in EST discourse. *TESOL Quarterly, 12,* 311–320.

Simmons, J. M. (Ed.). (1983). *The shortest distance to learning: A guidebook to writing across the curriculum.* Los Angeles: Regents of the University of California.

Sperber, D., & Wilson, D. (1986). *Communication and cognition.* Oxford: Basil Blackwell.

St. John, M. J. (1987). Writing processes of Spanish scientists publishing in English. *English for Specific Purposes,*6, 113–120.

Staton, J., Shuy, R., Kreeft, J., & Reed, L. (1982). *The analysis of journal writing as a communicative event* (No. NIE-G-80-0122). Washington, DC: National Institute of Education.

Stern, A. A. (1976). When is a paragraph? *College Composition and Communication, 27,* 253–257.

Strevens, P. (1977). *New orientations in the teaching of English.* Oxford: Oxford University Press.

Svartvik, J., & Quirk, R. (1980). *A corpus of English conversation.* Lund, Sweden: Liber Läromedel Lund.

Swales, J. (1981). *Aspects of article introductions.* Birmingham, England: Language Studies Unit, The University of Aston.

Swales, J. (1984). Research into the structure of introductions to journal articles and its application to the teaching of academic writing. In R. Williams, J. Swales, & J. Kirkman (Eds.), *Common ground: Shared interests in ESP and communication studies* (pp. 77–86). Oxford: Pergamon Press.

Swales, J. (1985). ESP—The heart of the matter or the end of the affair? In R. Quirk & H. G. Widdowson (Eds.), *English in the world* (pp. 212–223). Cambridge: Cambridge University Press.

Swales, J. (1987a). *Operationalizing the concept of discourse community.* Paper presented at the Conference on College Composition and Communication, Atlanta, GA.

Swales, J. (1987b). Utilizing the literatures in teaching the research paper. *TESOL Quarterly, 21,* 41–68.

Symposium on the Paragraph (1966). *College Composition and Communication, 17.*

Tadros, A. A. (1984). Prediction as an aspect of structuring of didactic text and its implications for the teaching of reading and writing. In J. Swales & H. Mustafa (Eds.), *English for specific purposes in the Arab world* (pp. 52–67). Birmingham, England: English Language Research Unit, University of Birmingham.

Tadros, A. A. (1985). *Prediction in text*. Birmingham, England: English Language Research Unit, University of Birmingham.

Takemata, K. (1976). *Introduction to writing newspaper manuscripts*. Tokyo: Natsumesha. (In Japanese)

Tannen, D. (1979). What's in a frame? Surface evidence for underlying expectations. In R. O. Freedle (Ed.), *Advances in discourse processing: Vol. 20. New directions in discourse processing* (pp. 137–141). Norwood, NJ: Ablex.

Tannen, D. (Ed.). (1982). *Analyzing discourse: Text and talk*. Washington, DC: Georgetown University Press.

Tannen, D. (1984). *Conversational style*. Norwood, NJ: Ablex.

Tannen, D. (1986). *That's not what I meant!* New York: Morrow.

Tarone, E., Dwyer, S., Gilette, S., & Icke, V. (1981). On the use of the passive in two astrophysics papers. *The ESP Journal, 1*(2), 123–140.

Tate, G., & Corbett, E. P. (Eds.). (1981). *The writing teacher's sourcebook*. Oxford: Oxford University Press.

Thompson, S. (1974). *One hundred favorite folktales*. Bloomington: Indiana University Press.

Thorndyke, P. (1976). The role of inferences in discourse comprehension. *Journal of Verbal Learning and Verbal Behavior, 15*, 437–446.

Tirkkonen-Condit, S. (Ed.). (1985). Argumentative text structure and translation. *Studia Philologica Jyväskyläensia, 18*(18). Jyväskylä, Finland: Kirjapaino OY, Sisä-Suomi.

Tommola, J. (1982). English connectors and non-native performance. In J. Tommola & R. Ruusuvuori (Eds.), *AFINLAN vuosikirja 1982* (pp. 69–87). Turku, Finland: AFINLA.

Tommola, J., & Ruusuvuori, R. (Eds.). (1982). *AFINLAN vuosikirja 1982*. Turku, Finland: AFINLA.

Tsao, F. F. (1983). Linguistic and written discourse in particular languages: English and Chinese (Mandarin). In R. B. Kaplan (Ed.), *Annual Review of Applied Linguistics, 3*, (pp. 99–117). Rowley, MA: Newbury House.

Urzua, C. (1984, July). *Using journal writing to enhance essay revision*. Paper presented at the Summer TESOL Meeting, Corvallis, OR.

van Dijk, T. A. (1972). *Some aspects of text grammar*. The Hague: Mouton.

van Dijk, T. A. (1977a). *Text and context: Explorations in the semantics and pragmatics of discourse*. London: Longman.

van Dijk, T. A. (1977b). *Text and cohesion*. The Hague: Mouton.

van Dijk, T. A. (1980). *Macrostructures: An interdisciplinary study of global structures in discourse, interaction and cognition*. Hillsdale, NJ: Erlbaum.

van Dijk, T. A. (1981). *Studies in the pragmatics of discourse*. Berlin/New York: Mouton.

van Dijk, T. A. (1982). Episodes as units of discourse analysis. In D. Tannen

(Ed.), *Georgetown University round table on languages and linguistics 1981* (pp. 177–195). Washington, DC: Georgetown University Press.

van Dijk, T. A. (1985a). Semantic discourse analysis. In T. A. van Dijk (Ed.), *Handbook of discourse analysis* (Vol. 2, pp. 103–136). London: Academic Press.

van Dijk, T. A. (1985b). *Handbook of discourse analysis: Vol. 2. Dimensions in discourse*. London: Academic Press.

Vygotsky, L. (1978). *Mind in society*. Cambridge, MA: Harvard University Press.

Vygotsky, L. S. (1962). *Thought and language*. Cambridge, MA: MIT Press.

Weisberg, R. C. (1984). Given and new: Paragraph development models for scientific English. *TESOL Quarterly, 18*, 485–500.

Werlich, E. (1976). *A text grammar of English*. Heidelberg: Quelle & Meyer.

Widdowson, H. (1978). *Teaching language communication*. London and Edinburgh: Oxford University Press.

Widdowson, H. (1983). *Learning purpose and language use*. New York: Oxford University Press.

Widdowson, H. (1986). Foreword. In S. Salimbene (Ed.), *Interactive reading* (pp. v–vi). Rowley, MA: Newbury House.

Widdowson, H. G. (1975). *Stylistics and the teaching of literature*. London: Longman.

Widdowson, H. G. (1979). *Explorations in applied linguistics*. Oxford: Oxford University Press.

Wikborg, E. (1985a). Types of coherence breaks in university student writing. In N. E. Enkvist (Ed.), *Coherence and composition: A symposium* (pp. 93–133). Åbo, Finland: Research Institute of the Åbo Akademi Foundation.

Wikborg, E. (1985b). Unspecified topic in university student essays. *TEXT, 5*, 359–370.

Wikborg, E. (1987). Uncertain ties in university student writing. In M. Ljung & I. Lindblad (Eds.), *Proceedings from the third Nordic conference for English studies* (pp. 453–467). Stockholm: Stockholm Studies in English.

Williams, J. D. (1985). Coherence and cognitive style. *Written Communication, 2*, 473–491.

Wilson, D. (1975). *Presuppositions and non-truth-conditional semantics*. London: Academic Press.

Winter, E. O. (1977). A clause-relational approach to English texts: A study of some predictive lexical items in written discourse. *Instructional Science, 6*, 1–92.

Witte, S. P. (1983). Topical structure and writing quality: Some possible text-based explanations of readers' judgments of students' writing. *Visible Language, 17*, 177–205.

Yutani, Y. (1977). Current English: Translation of news articles and "non-sequence" of tenses. *Academic Bulletin of Kyoto University of Foreign Studies, 18,* 52–63.

Zamel, V. (1984). The author responds . . . . *TESOL Quarterly, 18,* 154–157.

Zwicky, A. (1982). *Om tekstbinding i gode og dårlige skolestiler.* Unpublished master's thesis, Department of Nordic Language and Literature, University of Oslo, Norway.

Contributors

Kathleen Bardovi-Harlig, PhD. Assistant Professor of Linguistics, Indiana University, Bloomington, received her doctorate from the Department of Linguistics, University of Chicago. Her research interests include discourse pragmatics, the development of syntax in second language acquisition, and the application of linguistics to second language pedagogy. She has published in *Language Learning* and other second language journals.

Constance S. Cerniglia, MA. Lecturer, Indiana University in Indianapolis, has taught ESL reading and writing, freshman composition, technical writing, and business writing at the University of Louisville, the University of South Carolina, the University of Kentucky, Purdue School of Engineering at Indianapolis, and Indiana University at Indianapolis. She has presented papers on the teaching of writing with computers at national and regional conferences.

Ulla Connor, PhD. Associate Professor of English, Indiana University in Indianapolis, has taught ESL at the University of Wisconsin–Madison and in the Madison public schools, directed ESL programs at Purdue University and at the Indiana University in Indianapolis, and participated in ESL teacher training at Georgetown University. She is co-editor of *Writing across Languages: Analysis of L2 Text*. Her research on second language reading and writing has been published in *Applied Linguistics, Language Learning, TESOL Quarterly, TEXT,* and *Research in the Teaching of English*. She was principal investigator in an Exxon Foundation grant (1985–1987) to develop a comprehensive linguistic description and evaluation of student writing across cultures.

Nils Erik Enkvist, PhD. Distinguished Professor of Stylistics and Text Research and Director of the Research Institute of Åbo Akademi, Turku, Finland, has published widely on style, text, and discourse; his books include *Linguistics Stylistics*, (1973), *Stilforskning och Stilteori* (1973) and *Tekstilingvistiikan Peruskäsitteita* (1975), as well as editions of symposium volumes on *Impromptu Speech* (1982) and *Coherence and Composition* (1985). His honors include doctorates from University of Stockholm, Purdue University, and University of Poznan, and honorary memberships of the Finnish Association for Applied Linguistics and the Modern Language Association of America.

Lars Sigfred Evensen, PhD. is Researcher in the Department of Applied Linguistics, University of Trondheim, Norway. His dissertation presented a problem-oriented approach to applied linguistics. His present research interests include discourse analysis/text linguistics and student writing. He is the leader of the Scandinavian NORDWRITE project, the editor of *TRANS* (Trondheim Papers in Applied Linguistics) and the coordinating chairman of NORDTEXT (the Nordic research group on theoretical and applied text linguistics). He has published in *IRAL, Text,* and *Papers and Studies in Constrastive Linguistics.*

David P. Harris, PhD. Professor of Linguistics at Georgetown University, obtained his doctorate in linguistics from the University of Michigan. From 1963–1965 he served as the first Program Director of TOEFL, and he was president of TESOL in 1969–1970. After directing the American Language Institute at Georgetown for 19 years, he returned to full-time teaching in 1980. He has published primarily in the areas of ESL teaching and testing.

John Hinds, PhD. Professor of Linguistics, Thammasat University, Thailand, is interested in contrastive text structure and has written widely, particularly on contrastive elements in the text structures of English and Japanese. More recently he has extended his linguistic analyses to Thai and Chinese. He has published widely, including several books and articles in such journals as *Language Learning, TESOL Quarterly, TEXT,* and *Discourse Processes.*

Suzanne E. Jacobs, PhD. Associate Professor of English, the University of Hawaii, Honolulu, and Codirector of the University's Writing Workshop, has published extensively in the area of teaching writing in journals such as the *TESOL Quarterly, College English, English Journal, Language Arts,* and *Written Communication.* She is the author of *Composing and Coherence: The Writing of Eleven Pre-medical Students.* She is now studying the language and learning of sixth graders in Honolulu as well as the language of response groups in a fifth-grade class in Monterey, California.

Ann M. Johns, PhD. Professor of Academic Skills and Linguistics, San Diego State University, has published numerous articles on coherence and its relationship to reading and writing in ESL in journals such as *Language Learning, TESOL Quarterly,* and *Reading in a Foreign Language.* She is Co-editor of *English for Specific Purposes: An International Journal.*

Liisa Lautamatti, PhD. Associate Professor of English, the University of Jyväskylä, Finland, and former Director of the Language Center for Finnish Universities (1974–1977), teaches courses on spoken and written discourse analysis of English and trains EFL teachers. Her extensive publications range from the analysis of cohesion in student essays to interactional analysis of TV interviews with presidential candidates in Finland to stylistic analyses of English literature. Her work on the identification and development of topic in English discourse was pioneering and provides inspiration to applied linguists around the world.

Peter McCagg, PhD. Professor of English and Director of the English Language Program, the International Christian University in Tokyo, received his doctorate from the Department of Linguistics at Georgetown University. His research interests lie in the areas of discourse comprehension and production, and the acquisition of competence in these areas among nonnative speakers. He has authored or coauthored articles in *Applied Linguistics* and *Descriptive and Applied Linguistics* and has presented numerous research papers at international conferences.

Karen L. Medsker, PhD. Associate Professor, Human Resource Development, Marymount University, was previously Director of Instructional Development at Indiana University in Indianapolis. She is the author of several articles on instructional design. She has taught in high school, college, and corporate settings.

John Swales, Director, English Language Institute, and Professor of Linguistics, University of Michigan, has published more than 50 articles and a number of books, including the recent *Episodes in ESP*, and is Co-editor of *English for Specific Purposes: An International Journal.*

Eleanor Wikborg, PhD. Associate Professor of English, University of Stockholm, has a BA from Bryn Mawr College, an MA from Stanford University, and a PhD from the University of Göteborg (Sweden). Her publications include *Carson McCullers' The Member of the Wedding: Aspects of Structure and Style* (1975), *Typer av sammanhangsbrister i studenttexter (Types of Coherence Breaks in (Swedish) Student Writing)* (forthcoming), and the textbooks *A Guide to Essay Writing* (1981), coauthored with Lennart Björk, and *The Writing Process: Composition Writing for University Students* (1985), coauthored with Lennart Björk and Michael Knight. She is at present engaged in a project on how nonprofessional writers use the word processor at work for the various stages in the writing of proposals and reports.

PE 1128 .A2 C657 1990
Coherence in writing